– Air Travel Claims –

In Australia and New Zealand

A Guide to Rights and Responsibilities

ABRIDGED EDITION

Gary N Heilbronn

Copyright © 2016 HPEditions
All rights reserved. No part of this book may be reproduced, stored in a retrieval system, transmitted in any form or by any means without the prior written permission of the publishers, except by a reviewer who may quote brief passages in a review to be printed in a newspaper, magazine, journal or website.
Enquiries should be addressed to the publisher.
www.hpeditions.com.au

ABRIDGED EDITION

Available as an e_book on Kindle and other devices from various online bookstores including Amazon and GooglePlay
Paperback version printed by IngramSpark 2016
Available from HPEditions, Amazon and other book stores

ISBN 13: 978-0-9943240-5-4
ISBN 10: 0-9943240-5-7
Consumers – Travel – Law – Australia – New Zealand

Heilbronn, Gary N

Length: 82,750 words approx.

Published by **HPEDITIONS**

Australia

About the Author

Dr Gary Heilbronn has been researching, teaching, writing about and consulting on aviation and travel law for over three decades in Australia, Asia and Europe. He has been a practising lawyer, law professor and consultant in aviation law. He has also written Australia's leading text book on aviation law and its seminal work on travel and tourism law.

For something different. Check out the author's epic historical novel "Beginnings – Where A Life Begins", published in 2014 in paperback and available from all international on-line bookstores.

Preface

This book is designed to be read by ordinary people seeking answers to questions about how their rights are affected by air travel, especially the consumers of air travel services. It covers the situation in Australia and also in New Zealand. It is an abridged edition with no notes included.

The aim of this book is to help consumers make sense of a complicated set of legal principles and procedures that affect ordinary people who may want to make claims against airlines and other organisations or entities if they suffer some loss when dealing with those carrying out air travel-related activities or if they are injured while involved in air travel.

More details are provided in the *unabridged edition* of this book. For a deeper understanding of the issues and the law affecting any of the matters discussed here, professionals can look to "Aviation", Vol 34 of the *Laws of Australia* which is also written by this author. .....G.H.

Acknowledgements

The author wishes to express his gratitude to many people who have assisted in developing and refining his knowledge and understanding of this complicated area, in particular, Leighton Morris and Trevor Pyman, then of the Law Faculty at Monash University who stimulated the author's education in aviation law in the late 1970's and early 1980's. Since then the author has written a number of books on this and associated topics and a number of people, too numerous to mention, have provided feedback and assistance. This book makes many references to "Aviation", Vol 34 of the *Laws of Australia* which this author also wrote and naturally many persons assisted with that publication and the author wishes to acknowledge all assistance, direct and indirect, given in completing the three editions of that publication that has been given by research assistants, editors, consultants and the publishers of that series.

IMPORTANT DISCLAIMER

No version of this book is intended to offer anything other than **guidance to consumers and students. It does not offer or provide legal advice**. It is not the definitive statement on any aspect of the law. Also, with the passage of time it will necessarily lose some currency. **No person should rely on anything in the contents of this publication without first obtaining advice from a qualified professional**.

This publication is sold on the terms and understanding that (a) the author, consultants, editors and publishers are not responsible for the results or consequences of any actions taken on the basis of information contained in this publication, nor for any misleading statement, error in or omission in this publication; (b) neither the author nor anyone else participating in the preparation or publication of this book is engaged in rendering legal, professional or other services or advice of any kind at all.

The publisher, editors, consultants and author expressly disclaim all and any responsibility to any person whatsoever, whether a purchaser or reader of this publication or not, for or in respect of anything and/or any consequences of anything done or omitted to be done by any such person in reliance, whether wholly or partially, upon all or any part of the contents of this publication. Without limiting the generality of the above, the author, editors, consultants and publishers have no liability of any kind for any act or omission of any author, consultant or editor.

By reading past this point, you expressly agree to the above terms.

TABLE OF CONTENTS

About the Author i

Preface ii

Acknowledgements ii

Important Disclaimer iii

TABLE OF CONTENTS iv

Abbreviations ix

Lexique of Conventions and Protocols xi

1. Introduction 1

   What Are We Talking About? 1

       When Not To Bother Making a Claim? 2

       What You Should Be Insured For? 2

       Why Contracts And Consumer Laws Are So Important? 3

   Some Practical Considerations 4

       Perseverance, Proof, and Get Good Travel Insurance 6

       So You Want To Make a Claim? 7

2. Working Out Who Is Responsible 8

   Who Is Legally Responsible? 8

2.1 Did Injury or Loss occur during Air Carriage? 13

    When Air Carriage is Involved, Does it Matter If It Is Commercial or Private?...15

    How the Context of the Liability Rules Affects Their Scope? 20

    When is Air Carriage "International" or "Domestic"? 22

    Which IACLR Version Will Apply To A Particular Flight?.....................................23

    Air Carrier Insurance Requirements 26

2.2 Does Your Claim Concern Border Controls? 28

2.3 Does Your Claim Concern Security Controls? 32

    What Are The Powers and Duties of Security Officers? 33

    How Does Security Screening Work? 40

    What If Weapons, Prohibited Items And LAGs Are Found?...............................44

    What Pre-flight And On-Board Security Measures Are Required?.....................49

    What Specific Powers Do Aircraft Commanders Have? 52

    What Special Rules Apply to Air Carriage of Prisoners? 56

3. Consumer Protection and Airline Obligations... **59**

3.1 Small Claims Tribunals and Consumer Courts 63

    In Australia, Can Air Travel Claims Be Made in Small Claims Tribunals and Courts? 63

    In NZ, Can Airline Claims Be Made in Small Claims Courts? 66

3.2 Consumer Protections: Guarantees, Deceptive Conduct....................................68

    What Consumer Guarantees Apply To Air Carriage Contracts? 68

    When Can Claims Be Made For Misleading Or Deceptive Conduct?.................76

Courts/Tribunals for Claims: Australia 82

Courts/Tribunals etc for Claims: NZ 83

4. Airline Claims and Air Carriage Contracts **84**

What Kinds Of Contract Claims Can Be Made?...84

4.1 Passenger Air Carriage Contracts 87
    What Standard Terms Are In Air Passenger Carriage Contracts? 88
    What Other Powers Do Airlines Have Under Contracts? 93

Who Can Claim Against Airlines? 96
    Should passengers be told about ticket conditions? 100

Which Airlines Can Claims Be Made Against? 100
    What Rules Apply to Claims Against Employees etc? 106
    In Which Courts Can Claims Be Made Against Airlines? 107

4.2 Air Freight Carriage Contracts 110
    Do Differences Exist Between Passenger and Freight Carriage Rules? 110
    What Are Air Waybills And Their Legal Significance? 112

Terms and Conditions in Air Freight Carriage Contracts 114
    Which Documents Make Up The Air Freight Contract? 115
    What Are The Main Features Of Freight Carriage Contracts? 115
    What Are The Main Terms On Which Airlines Carry Freight? 119
    Do IACLRs Affect Airlines' Conditions of Carriage For Cargo? 124

5. Passengers: Injury or Death Claims 127
    What Claims Are Covered by the IACLRs? 127
    When Is Air Carriage "International" So That IACLRs Apply? 128
    Which Rules Apply to Non-International (Domestic) Carriage? 129
    When Are Airlines Liable for Passenger Injury or Death? 130
    What Are Compensation Limits For Injury Or Death? 136
    What Airline Defences Exist In Death and Injury Claims? 138
    What Formalities And Time Limits Apply to Claims? 142

6. Baggage & Freight: Loss or Damage Claims 143
    6.1 Cabin Baggage 144

    Are Airlines Liable For Damage To Cabin Baggage? 144

  6.2 Checked Baggage and Freight 150

    Is There Presumed Airline Liability For Checked Baggage & Freight? 150

    What Formalities Apply to International Baggage and Freight Claims? 153

    What Formalities Exist For Domestic Baggage and Freight Claims? 155

    What Defences Do Airlines Have To Baggage and Freight Claims? 156

    What Are Compensation Limits for Baggage and Freight Claims? 159

7. Delay: Passenger, Baggage & Freight Claims **163**

    When is Refusal to Carry Allowed and a Refund Available? 163

  7.1 Pre-Carriage Delay of Passengers and Baggage 166

    Can Air Contracts Exclude Liability For Pre-Flight Delays? 167

    How Does The EU Delay Compensation Scheme Work? 170

  7.2 Delay in Carriage: Passengers, Baggage & Freight 180

8. Surface Damage or Injury Claims **188**

    What Laws Apply? 188

  8.1 Are Airlines Liable For Surface Damage? 190

    What Is The Effect Of The Australian Legislation? 190

    What Is The Scope And Effect Of The NZ Legislation? 193

  8.2 What Common Law Remedies Exist? 195

    Can Claims Arise From Emissions, Noise or Vibrations? 199

    What Rules Govern Surface Damage Claims in Foreign Places? 201

9. Aircraft, Airport Noise & Vibrations **205**

  9.1-What noise controls apply to aircraft? 206

  9.2-What noise controls apply to airports? 208

    What is the effect of airport curfews? 208

    Can Airport Master Plans & Environmental Strategies Justify Claims?............ 209

    Which airports are affected by Environment Strategies?................................. 211

    Are duties owed by those performing activities at airports?.......................... 213

10. Airport Liabilities: Personal Claims 215

    What Are The Liabilities of Ordinary Businesses At Airports? 215

    What Are The Liabilities Of Air Transport-Related Businesses?...................... 216

    Which Air Transport Activities Result In Civil Liabilities? 220

11. Public Authorities: Duties & Immunities 226

    When Do Immunities From Compensation Claims Exist? 228

    When Do Public Authorities Owe A Duty of Care?... 230

12. Air Traffic Services Liabilities 237

    What ATS Activities May Incur Liabilities? 237

13. Manufacturer and Maintenance Liabilities 242

14. Certification and Accreditation Liabilities 246

15. Conclusions.. 249

ABBREVIATIONS

AA	AirServices Australia
AA	Airports Act 1996 (Cth)
AAT	Administrative Appeals Tribunal
ACL	Australian Consumer Law (Sch 2, Competition and Consumer Act 2010 (Cth))
ACLR	air carrier liability rules (see also IACLR)
AEPR	*Airports (Environment Protection) Regulations 1997* (Cth)
AFP	Australian Federal Police
ANANR	*Air Navigation (Aircraft Noise) Regulations 1984* (Cth)
AOC	Air Operator's Certificate (needed to operate commercial air services)
ASA	*Air Services Act 1995* (Cth)
ASIC	Aviation Security Identity Card (see also VIC)
ATC	Air traffic control and related services (sometimes ATS)
ATSA	Aviation Transport Security Act 2004 (Cth)
ATSR	Aviation Transport Security Regulations 2005 (Cth)
CAA	*Civil Aviation Act 1988* (Cth)
CAANZ	Civil Aviation Authority of New Zealand
CACLA	Civil Aviation (Carriers' Liability) Act 1959 (Cth)
CARNZ	*Civil Aviation Rules* (NZ)
CACLR	Civil Aviation (Carriers' Liability) Regulations 1991 (Cth)
CASA	Civil Aviation Safety Authority (Australia)
CASR	*Civil Aviation Safety Regulations 1998* (Cth)
CCA	*Competition and Consumer Act 2010* (Cth)
DBAA	*Damage by Aircraft Act 1999* (Cth)

DBAA	Damage by Aircraft Act 1999 (Cth)
EU	European Union (28 countries at the time of writing)
FAA	Federal Aviation Administration (USA)
IACLR	international air carrier liability rules
IATA	International Air Transport Association
ICAO	International Civil Aviation Organization
IMF	International Monetary Fund
MAP1	Montreal Additional Protocol No 1 (see Lexique)
MAP2	Montreal Additional Protocol No 3 (see Lexique)
MAP3	Montreal Additional Protocol No 3 (see Lexique)
MAP4	Montreal Additional Protocol No 4 (see Lexique)
NZ	New Zealand
NZCAA	Civil Aviation Act 1990 (NZ)
NZACA	Accidents Compensation Act 2001 (NZ)
NZCGA	Consumer Guarantees Act 1993 (NZ)
NZCaGoA	Carriage of Goods Act 1979 (NZ)
NZFTA	Fair Trading Act 1986 (NZ)
PGF	Poincaré Gold Franc: outdated monetary unit based on price of gold
PNG	Papua New Guinea
RPT	Regular Public Transport
SDR	Special Drawing Right: monetary unit of the IMF (see above)
TSP	Transport Security Program
VIC	Visitor Identification Card (See also ASIC)

LEXIQUE OF CONVENTIONS AND PROTOCOLS

Chicago Convention   Convention on International Civil Aviation (Chicago Convention) (1944) 15 UNTS 295; 23 ILM 705; [1957] ATS 5

Guadalajara Convention   Convention, Supplementary to the Warsaw Convention, for the Unification of Certain Rules Relating to International Carriage by Air Performed by a Person Other than the Contracting Carrier (Guadalajara Convention) (1961) 500 UNTS 31;[1964] ATS 4

Guatemala City Protocol   Protocol to Amend the Convention for the Unification of Certain Rules Relating to International Carriage by Air (Guatemala City Protocol) (1971) 10 ILM 613

Hague Protocol   The 1955 Protocol to Amend the Convention for the Unification of Certain Rules Relating to International Carriage by Air (Hague Protocol) (1955) 478 UNTS 371; 10 ILM 613

Montreal Convention 1999   Convention for the Unification of Certain Rules for International Carriage by Air (1999) 2242 UNTS 309; [2009] ATS 3C

Montreal Additional Protocol No 1   Additional Protocol No 1 to Amend the Convention for the Unification of Certain Rules Relating to International Carriage by Air (Montreal Protocol No 1) (1975) 2097 UNTS 28

Montreal Additional Protocol No 2   Additional Protocol No 2 to Amend the Convention for the Unification of Certain Rules Relating to International Carriage by Air (Montreal Protocol No 2) (1975) 2097 UNTS 69

Montreal Additional Protocol No 3   Additional Protocol No 3 to amend the Warsaw Convention of 1929 as amended by the Hague Protocol of 1955 and Guatemala City Convention of 1971 (1975) ICAO Doc 9147 (not in force)

Montreal Additional Protocol No 4 — Additional Protocol No 4 to Amend the Convention for the Unification of Certain Rules Relating to International Carriage by Air (Montreal Protocol No 4) (1975) 2145 UNTS 36; [1998] ATS 10

Rome Convention — Convention on Damage Caused by Foreign Aircraft to Third Parties on the Surface (Rome Convention 1952) (1952) 310 UNTS 181; [1959] ATS 1

Warsaw Convention 1929 — Convention for the Unification of Certain Rules Relating to International Carriage by Air (1929) 137 LNTS 11; [1963] ATS 18

Warsaw-Hague Convention — The Warsaw Convention as amended by the Protocol to Amend the Convention for the Unification of Certain Rules Relating to International Carriage by Air (Hague Protocol) (1955) 478 UNTS 371; 10 ILM 613; [1963] ATS 18

Warsaw-Hague-Montreal MAP4 Convention — Additional Protocol No 4 to Amend the Convention for the Unification of Certain Rules Relating to International Carriage by Air at Warsaw on 12 October 1929 as Amended by the Protocol done at the Hague, on 28 September 1955

1. Introduction

WHAT ARE WE TALKING ABOUT?

We are concerned here with compensation for various injuries and losses that can be suffered in relation to air travel. Perhaps you've suffered loss or been injured or inconvenienced by something that's happened when travelling by air? Or maybe it wasn't exactly during air travel, but it was something that an airline did, or an employee of an airline, airport or security firm, or even your travel agent did (or didn't do) – perhaps they gave misleading information that caused you to miss a flight or they didn't help you at all when you think they should have!

Maybe someone's cabin baggage fell on your head as they were rushing to exit an aircraft. Maybe you tripped while leaving an airplane or your baggage was torn open. Maybe you were a passenger on a helicopter tourist flight and were injured on a bumpy landing. Or maybe, and it's rare but it does happen, something dropped from an aircraft and landed on you or your property; or maybe you live near an airport and aircraft noise has become unbearable, or low-flying aircraft have frightened your animals and they've injured themselves. Or maybe you've been injured yourself by low-flying aircraft, or even been spied on by someone operating a drone? It happens!

Or perhaps, while you were travelling, you were badly inconvenienced and lost money or were disappointed as a result of something that happened or was supposed to happen, but didn't, and you're not really sure whose fault it was: perhaps your flight reservation was somehow "lost in the works" or you wanted to change flight dates but were told you could not do it or you could do it only if you paid an excessive administration fee. Maybe you sent some luggage or overseas purchases separately by airfreight and it never arrived or it was delayed or it was partly damaged when it did arrive. Lots of things can happen during air travel to cause you loss.

But often, it's not at all easy to know if you have any rights to compensation nor is it easy to work out who is responsible ... and maybe it's more than just one person to blame – it's several: airlines, travel agents or tour operators or even someone else, like airport staff or baggage handlers.

This book will help answer these questions and hopefully help you to get compensation, if it's at all possible.

When Not To Bother Making a Claim?

Sometimes, you should just forget it. Some injuries may be annoying but too trifling to claim for. Some claims are not worth pursuing for more practical reasons.

The law doesn't usually compensate you unless you've lost a quantifiable sum of money or a monetary value can be put on your "injury". You can get damages for a spoiled holiday or inconvenience, but it may well depend on the contract.

Also, there must be someone who is actually to blame. And that someone has to be able to be sued – within the jurisdiction – and, they must have enough funds to pay your compensation.

What You Should Be Insured For?

Some complaints are not discussed here. We are mainly concerned with air travel and are not looking at problems related to accommodation or foreign tour operators in foreign countries; nor with tour guides or companies overseas who take you on tours of tourist sites. The laws governing these matters in foreign countries are just too diverse to consider here.

Unless you paid a travel agent or tour operator in your home town for those services, you might as well forget about claims you think you have against such persons overseas, especially if they are in "third world" countries: in Asia, Africa, South America or Eastern Europe. Claims against foreign airlines are easier; especially if they have local offices. Likewise, claims against local airlines, local travel agents and local accommodation suppliers are also easier. In such cases, contracts and consumer protection laws are critical. (These are dealt with below.)

For most such overseas claims, think "insurance"! Look to your travel insurance before you make a claim against anyone else. In fact, when you buy insurance before your departure, make sure you have the most appropriate and best possible travel insurance cover. Look closely at what situations and losses are covered AND what is excluded – it's likely that many potential losses and some activities, for example dangerous sports: ski-ing, rock climbing, paragliding, are excluded and you undertake them at your own risk or need to pay extra for insurance cover.

So read the 'fine print' in your travel insurance contract, especially what's excluded – preferably before it is too late.

Why Contracts And Consumer Laws Are So Important?

Contracts are the basis for most claims although civil claims may be made for negligence or misrepresentation. If there's a contract involved – and there usually is, whether it's written or not – most of the time, that contract will determine what travellers' rights are and who they can claim from.

Another factor is that most complaints will be "consumer" matters, and some consumer protection agencies can assist. Consumer and small claims or disputes tribunals are also available to help you obtain compensation, but only in some cases – rarely in matters that actually involve "air carriage".

If your claim is specifically an "air carriage" matter, then often consumer protection laws don't apply. And for such air carriage problems, consumer information is not always that readily available. Apart from one of this author's websites, there is, in Australia, an 'Airline Customer Advocate' website set up by Qantas, Jetstar, Rex, TigerAir,

Virgin Australia that may assist customers with complaints about those airlines, **but only** if the customers have already attempted to resolve the dispute directly with the airline in accordance with each airline's 'Customer Charter'. Good luck with that!

Consumer tribunal options and some of the consumer protections available are considered in detail at the beginning of the Chapter 3.

SOME PRACTICAL CONSIDERATIONS

Sometimes getting compensation is just too difficult. It may not be an airline you are complaining about – perhaps you bought a "package" or a "flight" from a tour operator – then it can be even more complicated; and time-consuming as well.

There are some occasions when a tour operator that you have contracted with has promised to provide X and Y, and you have paid for these services, but you didn't get them. So you should be able to claim some compensation from your local tour operator, based on breach of contract or breach of consumer protection law. But did you get those promises in writing? Did you ask to be given a copy of the full contact between you and the tour operator or travel agent? Sometimes, he contract might not all be in written form, so make notes at the time. Try to avoid surprises! Avoid: "he said – she said" disputes – you have to prove what was in the contract before proving it was breached.

Remember that apart from claims based on a contract and consumer protection laws, you may have quite some difficulty making a successful claim. So here are some general suggestions:-

1. Forget disappointment, aggravation, minor annoyance you have with tourist activities in foreign countries, *unless* the service you are complaining about is part of a tour or air carriage contract, and written into your tour contract with a tour operator or airline near your home. Even if the problem occurred in the USA, UK or Europe or someplace where local law sets standards and allows for recovery of damages for losses, **unless** there is a lot of money involved and you have time on your hands and plenty of energy, the costs of proving your case and recovering damages will always outweigh the amount you'll get, especially in the UK or USA. So, forget it! **Most countries laws don't**

really care about consumers. There is one important exception: this is as regards delays and cancellation of flights in Europe – we'll talk about that later.

2. If you are going to make a claim against (or sue) someone, **it's a lot easier to do it in your own country** and especially in your own state and your own city (think of the costs of going to the other side of the country two or three times to sue someone); and even then, think of the time and energy it is going to take. Unfortunately, despite all the talk about consumer rights, the reality is that it takes an enormous amount of time, some money and lots of energy and aggravation even to pursue your consumer claim. (Going to small claims tribunals or consumer courts can also be a disappointment: see below). Consumer protection "talks the talk" but the assistance it provides is limited – at least for most individuals; even in Australia, where it is better than most other countries! If you are unhappy about that, talk to your MP - but he or she will almost certainly tell you there are already consumer protection laws. Yes, some laws are there, but they are complex and it's either expensive or difficult to get anyone to enforce them, even in the consumer courts and tribunals.

3. Often, relatively "small" amounts of money are involved – sometimes only hundreds of dollars and usually less than a few thousand dollars – so if you want to make a claim and you are eligible to do so, it's more sensible to rely on making claims in the supposedly "free" small claims tribunal (or whatever it is called where you live). But for some claims, there will be a reason why this tribunal does not have "jurisdiction" (legislative authority) to deal with your case; they will just say "sorry, it's not my job: go to a court". It's not their fault, it is the fault of the government that set up the tribunals with inadequate or limited powers.

So don't imagine that you should necessarily start to sue in a "small claims" tribunal (even if it is a "court"), despite the fact that your claim is based on consumer law: notably, **in Australia**, the *Australian Consumer Law* (ACL) found in Sch 2 of the *Competition and Consumer Act 2010* (Cth) (CCA) (and State or Territory *Fair Trading* laws); and, **in NZ**, the equivalent enactments: the *Consumer Guarantees Act 1993* (NZ) (NZCGA) and the *Fair Trading Act 1986* (NZ) (NZFTA). If your case isn't one that consumer courts or tribunals are entitled to deal with, they will eventually say: "No" and you will have wasted your time and energy.

And even if the consumer tribunal does have jurisdiction, you may find that proving your claim to the adjudicator is much harder than you might have hoped. Proof is critical.

Perseverance, Proof, and Get Good Travel Insurance

Making a claim needs preparation and takes time. Sorry to be a bit negative, but for small civil claims or consumer claims, it's often better first to try to negotiate compensation from an airline or tour operator or similar entity, perhaps making the threat of legal action. You still need to know what you are talking about because they will certainly try to obstruct or delay until you are "fed up". So, you still need documentary proof, including a copy of the contract(s) between you and them; and you need to have read the "fine print" carefully. It may well exclude the claim you want to make! Only if the exclusion is "unfair" or "unconscionable" will a court sometimes ignore it. But we'll look at that later.

What if you do try to negotiate compensation? Airlines, tour operators and insurers will doubtless try to make you "just go away" – they'll ignore letters, give you "the run around" and it's only by keeping evidence e.g. photos of what happened, names of witnesses, sending registered letters that say "the right thing" and keeping copies with delivery receipts and then threatening to go to court, that you might negotiate some compensation. If you're too busy or can't be bothered, then forget it!

One thing that may be in the complainant's favour is that it may be cheaper for the airline or travel agent etc to pay you some compensation, rather than to spend the time in court, which is expensive for everyone. Even a small claims tribunal – which you can go to relatively cheaply, is expensive as the airline etc will have to send an employee and witnesses. It will cost them something ... but sometimes they don't care or they want to avoid others making such claims; so they would rather fight every claim even in court.

So You Want To Make a Claim?

Leaving all that aside, what are the rights of travellers and others affected by airline activities and what are the obligations of air carriage operators? We'll look at that from Chapter 3 onwards.

2. Working Out Who Is Responsible

WHO IS LEGALLY RESPONSIBLE?

It is often not easy to know who is legally responsible for a loss. Who is really to blame? Perhaps the real question is: who the law will find to be *legally* responsible? That is the person or entity you should make your claim against. It is worth asking this question at a very early stage. Some activities which give rise to a claim may clearly be the responsibility of one entity or another: a travel agent, an airport, or an airline (or employee), but they may be liable only in restricted circumstances e.g. airlines are only liable for accidental injuries that occur during air carriage; but in such cases their liability is actually presumed, so you usually don't have to prove it – which is discussed below in 2.1.

Otherwise, the injury or damage may perhaps have been caused by "border control" activities which are carried out by government agencies or public authorities who have some immunities from civil claims (discussed below in 2.2) or even contributed to by several entities, some public and some private. Their involvement may make claiming compensation more complicated, such as when aviation security is involved (discussed below in 2.3), where airport operators, screening authorities, private security firms, police services, airline operators and even other passengers may share responsibility.

So, when rights to claim against an entity responsible are quite limited, you may be better off claiming against someone else, for example, such as an airport, air traffic control or maintenance organisation – whose actions might also affect injuries or losses suffered during air carriage – or more rarely, an individual employee of such an entity (later chapters look at claims against such entities and their employees).

Either way, claimants must identify at least one entity that has done something wrong if they want to make a claim for a loss.

Can claims be restricted if industry entities are to blame?

Some technical questions must also be considered before making a claim. Technical problems may stop you succeeding, with serious consequences.

First, even if you are injured or suffer a loss, your claim may fail and you may have to pay the other party's legal costs:-

(a) if the airline or entity you make a claim against didn't legally "cause" the damage, because what they did was not sufficiently closely connected to the loss; or

(b) if for one reason or another, the defendant isn't held responsible for the damage, either because:

- your claim doesn't comply with some legal principles; or

- you made the wrong kind of claim; or

- you claim in the wrong "court" or the wrong place.

Second, even when your injury or loss occurred on an airline during flight, and the law says that an airline is presumed responsible for injuries, what you are actually claiming for must have occurred exactly as required and be the kind of injury or loss that is provided for in the applicable **rules governing airline liability**.

In Australia, these **special rules** are set out in the *Civil Aviation (Carriers' Liability) Act 1959* (Cth) (from now on referred to as CACLA). **In NZ**, the special rules are in Pts 9A and 9B of the *Civil Aviation Act 1990* (NZ) (the NZCAA).

These enactments establish *international air carriage liability rules* (IACLR) for Australia and NZ. However, they don't cover every kind of claim or every loss or injury suffered during air carriage. For example, there has to be some kind of accidental event that causes the injury.

These enactments also set out many rules for most claims concerning *domestic air carriage liability* (DACLR) by airlines in Australia, although these rules cover a more limited range of claims relating to domestic air carriage by liability in NZ – there, the situation is even more complicated (especially as regards delay: see Chapter 7).

In Australia, CACLA covers personal injury and baggage loss or damage claims on *domestic* flights, but does **not** cover *in-flight delay* claims (nor air freight claims at all).

In NZ, no claims at all, except airline passenger "in-flight delay" claims on *domestic* flights can be made under NZCAA Pt 9B. This is because almost all *domestic* personal injury accident claims must be made under the "no-fault" accident compensation scheme in the *Accident Compensation Act 2001* (NZ) (NZACA) (only briefly mentioned here); and most *domestic* baggage or freight carriage claims must be made under the *Carriage of Goods Act 1979* (NZ) (NZCaGoA).

Third, other laws may restrict claims against particular defendants in specific circumstances – especially if several entities have contributed to the injury or loss – and the rules relating to their separate liabilities may differ, making claims easier or harder to prove or enforce. That is, recovering compensation may be easier or harder depending on who is claimed against or what was done wrong: for example, are you relying on the common law or consumer protection law (discussed in detail in Chapter 3); does the claim involve the special air carriage liability rules applying to airlines (see Chapters 4 to 7); or were public or government authorities involved, as sometimes they have immunity (see Chapter 11).

So even if an airline is responsible for some of your loss or injury because you were their responsibility when the injury occurred, it may be that one of their employees, subcontractors, or even an independent entity – someone in the aviation industry, such as an airport operator, maintenance organizations, equipment manufacturers – or perhaps, another third party, did something that caused or contributed to the injury. It might even have been an another passenger, an on-board air marshal, airport security or security screener or someone else who did something that you can identify as being 'wrongful' (be it negligent or intentional) and which justifies you claiming compensation from them (some of their liabilities are discussed in Chapters 10-14).

Can travel agents or tour operators be claimed against?

Travel agents can make mistakes and may cause losses especially when they are deregulated. If something goes wrong when you travel, one entity likely to be responsible is a travel agent or tour operator, but again, you have to be able to identify precisely what they did that was 'wrongful' and also show that what they did was the actual cause the loss or injury being complained of.

Australia previously had an advanced scheme for travel agent and tour operator licensing and travel compensation in force for some thirty years (and similar scheme were set up in other countries, such as the United Kingdom and Hong Kong) but it has been abolished in Australia since 2014 and travellers complaining about travel agents and tour operators (even after they have gone into liquidation) or suffering loss from their wrongful acts, no longer benefit of what had been an important part of the consumer protection system.

Worse still, the growth of travel agency conglomerates and franchising has meant that a major percentage of travel agents are no longer required to meet any criteria for training, competence, financial responsibility and integrity. Of course, very few meet the alternative criteria which IATA imposes on their *accredited travel agents* in Australia and New Zealand.

For example, in 2012, Flight Centre had 968 registered travel sales outlets dealing with 41% of the total market in Australia, but only 61 of them were IATA accredited (and had to comply with IATA quality control). Over 900 were not subject to either government nor IATA regulation or supervision.

Consumers in Australia and many other countries, now have to rely on weak or non-existent "industry self-regulation", bolstered by the old-fashioned common law, contract law, tort law and whatever consumer protection laws that can be applied to claims made in small claims or disputes tribunals and courts. Of some possible assistance in establishing standards to be met by travel agents if a claim is being made, is the AFTA Travel Accreditation Scheme (ATAS) Code of Conduct which is agreed to by those travel agents who have become ATAS accredited. In reality, this is almost a return to rules that existed in the past under "buyer beware" principles, even taking into account the limited consumer benefits provided by the consumer protection laws, notably the ACL in Australia; or in NZ, by the NZCGA and NZFTA.

2.1 Did Injury or Loss occur during Air Carriage?

Special rules make airlines liable for accidents during air carriage. Air carriers – major airlines such as Qantas, Jetstar, Virgin Australia and Air New Zealand – and indeed all aircraft operators (including many smaller ones) are presumed liable to passengers and other persons who are injured or suffer loss *in the course of air carriage*. But, for the most part, this presumed liability is subject to detailed provisions in local laws that incorporate special liability rules set out in international conventions. These local laws sometimes expand upon principles and procedures in international conventions.

The special rules apply not just to airlines (big and small). Even airline subcontractors e.g. and baggage handlers may be subject to some of those rules, notably compensation limits (provided what they are during is part of the "air carriage") – and details are discussed in subsequent chapters. Incidentally, these laws also require airlines to be adequately insured in respect of their liabilities, especially to passengers.

When is "air carriage" not involved?

Special airline liability rules only apply to injury or loss occasioned during air carriage. Airline responsibilities for their actions – when the injury or loss caused does *not* occur during air carriage – may be based solely on local law, notably consumer protection legislation: **in Australia**, the ACL (and CCA or equivalent state or territory laws, such as when on intrastate flights); or **in NZ**, the NZGCA, NZFTA or the NZACA and NZCaGoA. When such injuries or losses occur overseas, other countries' consumer protection laws may be applicable – such as equivalent European Union (EU) regulations.

Such consumer protection laws are often very important: for example, in respect of:

- misleading advertising,
- dubious booking practices,
- denied boarding,
- flight delays and cancellations etc.

Later, we'll look at those kinds of wrongful activities and see what protections and rights to make claims for compensation, may be available.

Thus, when injury and loss does not occur "during air carriage" that is, it is outside the special rules (IACLRs and DACLRs), the liabilities of airlines are basically the same as the liabilities of other aviation industry participants e.g. airport operators, airport transit bus operators, air traffic controllers (but not certifying and licensing authorities etc. whose relationship with travellers is less often subject to consumer protection laws), and is governed by general law principles, notably the torts of negligence or nuisance (although sometimes specific immunities or other legislative limits exist. These are discussed in later chapters.)

Something falling from aircraft: Less common examples of liabilities outside the special rules exist, notably those of aircraft or airport operator's for injury to persons or property on the surface of the ground, if, for example, an airplane, helicopter or hot-air balloon crash-lands or offloads cargo or fuel during a flight. Related claims are not directly about air carriage, even though something "falls" from an aircraft and injures someone during air carriage. (This is discussed in Chapter 8.)

Noise and vibrations: Another liability situation outside the special rules occurs when noise and vibrations from aircraft and airport operations cause damage, usually to someone on the ground – this particularly relates to operations at airports. Liabilities of airlines and airports for noise, vibrations and other airport activities are discussed in Chapters 9 and 10.

Commercial practices: Finally, some potential liabilities of airlines and other aviation industry participants arise out of their commercial activities, such as breaches of unfair competition laws or other commercial disputes that have very little to do with flight; the actual operation of aircraft; dealings with consumers or the carriage of persons, baggage and freight by air. Examples include, issues arising out of commercial relations either between airlines, such as in codeshare agreements or between airlines and their agents, freight forwarders, catering or baggage handling services, etc.. These arrangement may have an incidental impact on consumers and passengers, but the issues arising usually involve specialised obligations or contracts (sometimes standardised throughout the industry), and they are governed by the usual principles of competition, commercial, contract and tort law. Some of these matters may be mentioned in some contexts, but are not discussed in detail here.

When Air Carriage is Involved, Does it Matter If It Is Commercial or Private?

Special liability rules only apply to commercial flights. If some loss or damage is occasioned during air operations, the first thing to ask is if the air operator – usually the entity or person actually operating the aircraft – is a commercial entity: an airline, helicopter service, small charter airplane or business jet operator? Or, is it private? That is, is someone just taking you on their airplane as their guest? This makes a big difference – at least as far as the law is concerned. (Some businesses operate aircraft for their own use, such as for carrying employees or goods for their own purposes and not as an air transport business. This is not "commercial" air carriage.) For the special liability rules to apply, the issue is: *is the carriage commercial? Carriage is commercial if it was paid for or provided as part of an air transport operation.*

We need to answer this question. It tells us which aviation enactments govern the air carriage liabilities in question. Only commercial carriage is subject to the special air carriage liability rules based on the international conventions.

How do private and commercial air carriage laws differ?

Private air carriers' liabilities are found in the general law (including consumer protection laws, discussed in Chapter 3). Otherwise there are very few expressly applicable legislative provisions: none in **Australia**; and in **NZ**, the most important is the NZACA (which applies to all claims in respect of personal injuries, even on private flights).

Commercial air carriers' liabilities are always subject to special air carriage laws and a limited amount of general law. Some aspects of "commercial" (paid for) air carriage are subject to consumer protection laws (discussed in Chapter 3) and general law e.g. contract law, but such commercial flights are also governed by special liability laws: **in Australia**, CACLA; and, **in NZ**, NZCAA Pts 9A-9B (supplemented, for domestic commercial air carriage, by NZCaGoA and NZACA).

To put it differently:

- **private** aircraft owners/operators' liabilities are determined mainly by the general law, especially the contract of carriage (if there is one), common law e.g. the law of negligence and by relevant legislation e.g. accident compensation law, like other forms of transport;

- **commercial** airline/air service operators' liabilities are determined by the general law and the contract of carriage, but over-riding the general law are the special air carriage liability rules, **in Australia** (under CACLA) and **in NZ** (under NZCAA), and:

- **for international air carriage**, both adopt detailed rules found in several international conventions;
- **for domestic air carriage**, similar rules apply, but there are differences. **In Australia**, CACLA applies a version of the international rules to passenger and baggage claims only (but not to delay or cargo claims). **In NZ**, the NZCAA applies only to domestic passenger delay; NZACA applies to domestic personal injuries; and NZCaGoA applies to domestic air carriage of baggage and freight, loss or damage but not delay).

How do commercial air carriage laws differ for international and domestic flights?

Commercial air carriage is subject to liability principles and to certain other laws. Special liability rules don't apply to all aspects of air carriage. Also applicable are relevant state, territory and national legislation, which include air safety and technical regulations.

In Australia, liabilities in commercial international and commercial domestic air carriage are governed by CACLA, which legislation is divided into different parts. Most of those parts implement the various international conventions applicable to international air carriage, but Pt

IV applies somewhat similar rules to domestic air carriage (except for all delay claims and cargo claims – which are governed by the general law).

In NZ, liabilities in all commercial international air carriage are governed by the NZCAA, Pt 9A (which implements the relevant international conventions). But different aspects of liabilities in commercial domestic air carriage are governed by different laws: NZCAA, Pt 9B applies *only* to domestic passenger delay claims, (but not to personal injury or any cargo matters); NZACA covers domestic air accident personal injury claims (both commercial and private); and NZCaGoA covers domestic goods carriage liabilities e.g. baggage loss and damage claims – but not goods delay, which, like any other claims, is governed by the general law e.g. contract and consumer protection law.

Do criteria for what is "commercial" carriage differ?

Most air carriage is commercial; in one way or another. However, there are differences between the criteria for what is "commercial" in international flights and for what is "commercial" in domestic flights;

For international airlines or air operators, in both Australia and in NZ, the same conventions (and thus the same rules in CACLA and NZCAA Pt 9A) apply when the airlines carry passengers or goods "for reward" (payment), or even if not for reward, if they carry passengers or goods as part of their operations as an "air transport undertaking". Then, it doesn't matter if the carriage is actually gratuitous (free or not paid for). (Incidentally, this does not apply to airline employees carried as part of their employment; They are not covered by the conventions because they are not "passengers".)

For Australian domestic airline carriage liabilities, what is "commercial" is determined by different and much more inclusive words in CACLA, Pt IV. (Incidentally, Part IV governs most domestic air carriage, but it also covers the rare case of international air carriage not otherwise within any version of the IACLRs: that is, CACLA, Pts IA, I, II and III). So some domestic (and non-IACLR) passenger and baggage air carriage that is not "for reward" e.g. perhaps some aerial photography operations, would nonetheless be subject to the liability rules in CACLA, Pt IV (which Part applies to various kinds of passenger injury and baggage loss and damage in air carriage (but not delay and not freight).

To complicate matters further, the wording in CACLA, Pt IV is broader than in the conventions, and it extends to almost all domestic (non-international) air carriage; even though it appears to be limited by the rather complicated terminology in s 27(1) of CACLA to:

> "... the carriage of a passenger where the passenger is or is to be carried in an aircraft being operated by the holder of an airline licence or a charter licence in the course of commercial transport operations ..."

What does this mean? First, the term "passenger" is not defined (although it does not include crewmembers), but passenger carriage does include passengers and their baggage if lost or damaged, as s 29 creates a liability for baggage loss or damage (but not for any delay claims or any cargo claims at all). Second, by its terms, Part IV applies only to carriage by aircraft operators holding an "airline licence" or "charter licence": Both are defined in CACLA, s 26 to include any commercial operators with licences (scheduled flights) or permissions (charter flights) **and** all operators with an Australian (or recognized NZ) Air Operator's Certificate (AOC). AOCs are needed by any aircraft operator carrying out any sort of commercial activity including aerial work; such as crop dusting, surveying, aerial photography, advertising, balloon flying training, ambulance services etc. Therefore, any "passenger" on board any such an aircraft would be covered by Part IV of CACLA, even if they had **not** paid for their carriage; or even if they were **not** carried pursuant to an carriage contract.

For NZ domestic air carriage liabilities, the situation is different again for passengers, goods and delay. Claims for *passenger death or personal injury* on both commercial and private domestic flights are governed by the NZACA (unless outside its scope, which would be rare and then subject to the general law). Otherwise, the liabilities of NZ domestic air carriers to passengers is based on the contract (although the NZFTA also applies to consumer law complaints). As regards, air carrier liability for **passenger delay** – which is the only liability that is created by the NZCAA, Pt 9B, (unlike in Australia) – by s 91V(1),(2) –

> "applies to any carriage by air (other than international carriage)" [even if] "without consideration" [i.e. payment of any kind] "in which, according the contract"

... when carriage is between places inside New Zealand, as stated in the contract of carriage. As a contract of carriage is required, delay in private carriage is not within the application of Pt 9B (and military air transport is also excluded).

Similarly, all claims in NZ domestic air carriage for **baggage and freight loss or damage** are governed by the NZCaGoA which again applies only to contract claims. **Baggage and freight delay** claims are subject to the general law and liability is not determined by whether the carriage is commercial or not.

The extent of these liabilities is discussed in Chapters 5, 6 and 7.

Are police, customs and government aircraft different?

Flights by government aircraft are rarely commercial but are still subject to the special liability rules. In theory, under the IACLRs, gratuitous international air carriage by "state" aircraft, which includes police, customs and military aircraft, is considered to be commercial carriage for the purposes of the application of the IACLRs. Thus, state or government aircraft and civil aircraft appear to be subject to the same provisions of relevant liability conventions and to equivalent municipal legislation, when undertaking international air carriage.

In Australia, this area of law is even less clear although this won't concern most travellers. The various Parts of CACLA relating to international air carriage are not expressly extended to gratuitous carriage performed by the state or by government bodies, unless those bodies are also considered to be "air transport undertakings" (that is, "commercial", which would be very rare). Thus it appears they are not covered by these rules. However, CACLA, s 7 says that this Act binds the Commonwealth and all relevant State and Territory governments – and thus their aircraft operations – seemingly extending both international rules (Pts IA, II,III and IIIC) and the non-international (domestic) rules in Pt IV, to such operations. Nonetheless, it is unclear if this applies only to any such commercial operations and in practice their application to actual government carriage is quite restricted. Often, for military aircraft, military personnel would be employees of the aircraft operator and in a similar position to airline employees and not covered by these rules.

In NZ, only those aircraft used solely for military carriage are excluded from the NZCAA. Thus, in principle, all other operations are likely subject to this legislation.

How the Context of the Liability Rules Affects Their Scope?

Air transport laws and air carriage liability rules are similar for international and for domestic flights in most countries. As regards civil aviation generally, laws and regulations are similar in most countries, including Australia and NZ but more extensive and more complicated laws apply in Australia (see below). Quite similar rules apply to international and to domestic air carriage liability **in Australia** (under CACLA). However, more differences exist between international and domestic air carriage liability rules **in NZ** (under NZCAA and NZACA).

How NZ domestic air carrier liability rules differ from international rules?

In NZ, civil aviation laws are relatively simple but international and domestic air carriage liability laws are complicated. The NZCAA and NZCAR regulate most civil aviation in NZ. NZCAA, Pt 9A governs international air carriage liabilities and apply the IACLRs to passenger death, injury, delay; baggage and cargo loss damage, delay. NZCAA Pt 9B governs liability for domestic air carriage passenger delay (only). The general law, notably the NZACA governs domestic air passenger death and injury compensation claims. The NZCaGoA governs all domestic baggage and freight loss and damage claims, while delay of air passenger baggage and freight is governed by the common law.

Why liability rules in Australia are quite similar but quite complicated?

In Australia, air transport laws are complicated but the international and domestic air carrier liability rules are quite similar. As discussed above the domestic and international air carrier liability rules are quite similar in Australia, although the aviation regulation system is more complex because it is a federation.

In Australia, a complex mix of Commonwealth and State law governs domestic and international air transport. In brief, the division of powers is as follows. Technical and safety laws, including certifying aircraft, granting operational licences and crime and air security matters, are governed almost exclusively by Commonwealth laws. Commercial licensing legislation and economic regulation are shared between States and Commonwealth. For domestic commercial air services:

(a) *intrastate* air services (within a State or Territory), is largely a matter for laws in the relevant State and Territory (and there is not much); whereas

(b) *interstate* air services are now deregulated: the Commonwealth previously licensed etc. interstate air services but now there is no such licensing.

However, the Commonwealth has full control over licensing etc. of international commercial air services, as it has constitutional powers over interstate and overseas trade and commerce, international treaties and corporations. Of course, competition and consumer protection laws of the Commonwealth and (a few) States or Territories apply to both domestic and international aviation and air carriage activities.

Air carrier liability rules in Australia are found in both federal and state laws. CACLA, Pts I (preliminary) and IVA (insurance) apply to all air carriage. Otherwise, CACLA, Pt IA (and less often Pts II; III or IIIC each of which incorporates a different version of the IACLR as set out in the relevant conventions), governs most **international** air carriage liabilities for death or injury, and loss, damage or delay of passengers, baggage and freight while Pt IV and state laws govern **domestic** air carriage.

In international air carriage, the applicable version of the IACLRs governs both air passengers and baggage (cabin and registered luggage) as well as air freight (cargo), whether accompanied or not. The IACLR version most often applicable is the 1999 Montreal Convention (CACLA, Pt IA and Sch 1A). However, readers should take care when reading CACLA, as the Parts are numbered differently to the Schedules.

Although only one version will apply to each carriage contract, the four main IACLR versions contained in CACLA are:

- Pts IA and Sch 1A i.e. Montreal Convention 1999,

- Pt II and Sch 2 i.e. Warsaw-Hague Convention,

- Pt III (with or without IIIA) and Sch 1 i.e. Warsaw Convention (with or without Sch 3 i.e. the Guadalajara Convention); or

- Pt IIIC and Sch 5 i.e. Warsaw-Hague-Montreal Additional Protocol No 4.

By Art 1 of all the conventions and/or protocols establishing each IACLR version, only "international" air carriage is subject to that convention. What is "international" is discussed below.

Non-international or domestic air passenger carriage is governed by CACLA, Pt IV, but some things are excluded. Liabilities for domestic passenger death or injury and for baggage loss or damage (but **not delay**) are governed by CACLA, Pt IV. But CACLA is federal law and it does not apply to flights which are purely within a single state or territory. It only does this through complementary reciprocal legislation in each State (applying CACLA Pt IV to any air carriage within that State — as for constitutional reasons, Pt IV of the commonwealth Act does not otherwise apply there).

Otherwise, the general law applies when CACLA, Pt IV does not. So it should be noted that CACLA, Pt IV does not include:

(a) Non-international or **domestic** *passenger and baggage* **delay** claims are **not** subject to CACLA — so they are governed by ordinary contract, consumer and tort law and legislation; and

(b) Non-international or **domestic** air *freight* carriage loss, damage and delay claims are **not** subject to CACLA — so they are all governed by ordinary contract, consumer and tort law and other legislation.

When is Air Carriage "International" or "Domestic"?

Carriage is "international" for the liability rules when it falls within the definition of "international" set out in the IACLRs. This is usually not complicated. First, note that the nationality or state of registration of the aircraft and an airline's place or incorporation do not determine whether or not the carriage is international. Indeed, international (and foreign registered) airlines fly some domestic routes.

Simply put, domestic air carriage is any air carriage within one particular country not involving a stop in any foreign country. Whereas international air carriage involves flights between any particular country and a foreign country. However, as might be expected, the distinction is not always so clear.

More specifically, by IACLR, Art 1, "international" air carriage occurs when:

- **departure and destination are in two different countries (states)**, which many regional, low-cost flights now tend to be as they sell one-way tickets. Note that, irrespective of stopovers, the "destination" is the passenger's place of "ultimate destination" on the air carriage contract (as set out on the ticket).

- **departure and destination are in the same country (states), but there is an agreed stopping place in another country.** In the case of a "return" air passenger ticket, the place of destination is also almost always the place of departure. However, there must be an agreed stop in another country A flight is not "international" because the aircraft flies over another country's territory or because it passes over the High Seas (areas of ocean or sea not within the territorial limits of any State). Of course, there may be an argument as to whether a technical stop is an "agreed stopping place". It will depend on what the contract says.

- **domestic flights (sectors) that are part of an international air carriage contract**; then, those domestic flights are treated as "international" and governed by the applicable version of the IACLRs.

References to "departure" and "destination" are in the singular form in the conventions indicating that each contract of carriage has only one place of departure and one place of destination: the **ultimate destination,** and it does not matter how many airlines, tickets, stopovers of even carriage contracts there are. What is important is that the parties to the flights regarded the air carriage as a "single operation". This will usually be fairly clear, but if not, it will be a question of interpretation of the air carriage contract to see what the parties to the contract intended.

Which IACLR Version Will Apply To A Particular Flight?

The most recent version in force will apply to any flight. The IACLR version that applies to the flight on which the injury occurred is the most recent version agreed to by the country or the two countries concerned.

This is important as liability rules can differ slightly from one IACLR version to the next, especially as to (i) the places where legal claims can be made against the airlines, and (ii) the maximum compensation that airlines are liable for (as is usually reflected in a contract of air carriage).

The air carriage contract itself usually states that different versions of the rules might apply (or that a particular version will likely apply to certain flights e.g. within the European Union: see Qantas Airlines Conditions of Carriage, Clause 20).

Indeed, the Qantas Airways Conditions of Carriage – Passenger and Baggage, Clause 16.4(b), provides (viewed 12 December 2014):

****

b) International Carriage

Where your travel is International Carriage and a Convention applies, our liability for damage to Checked Baggage is limited by the Convention except where you prove that the damage resulted from an act or failure to act either done with the intention to cause damage or recklessly and with knowledge that damage would probably result.

Our liability for loss of, damage to, or delay in the carriage of, your Baggage is limited by the applicable Convention as follows:

Montreal Convention 1999 - 1,131 SDRs (about AU$1,735) cumulative for both Checked Baggage and Cabin Baggage. In the case of Checked Baggage, we will not be liable if the Baggage was defective, unless Article 22.5 of the Montreal 1999 Convention applies in which case these limits do not apply. We will only be liable for Cabin Baggage if we were at fault

Conventions other than the Montreal Convention 1999 - 250 francs (about AU$30) for each kilo of your Checked Baggage affected or 5,000 francs (about AU$600) for your Cabin Baggage, unless Article 25 of the Warsaw Convention applies, in which case these limits do not apply.

However, if the law which applies to the contract provides for different limits of liability, those different limits will apply.

For the purpose of determining our liability (if any), we will presume the weight of your Checked Baggage is not more than the applicable Baggage Allowance for the relevant class of carriage, unless you have a receipt from us or our Authorised Agent showing otherwise.

****

Thus, the particular IACLR version (e.g. either 1999 Montreal, Warsaw, Warsaw-Hague, Warsaw-Hague-Montreal Additional Protocol No 4 (MAP4) or any of the other minor versions) that applies to a particular contract of air carriage, depends essentially on where the carriage is from and where it is going to, as it is set out in the contract of air carriage (ticket).

How do you decide which version of the IACLRs applies?

The IACLR version that applies to a flight depends on departure and destination. Assuming the carriage is "international" (as discussed above), look at the place of departure and destination to see which IACLR version applies.

By identifying the places of "departure" and "ultimate destination" (indicated on that contract if carriage), we can determine which version of the IACLRs applies to that carriage contract. For example, a return flight from Brisbane to Beijing and back to Brisbane (or Sydney, or Melbourne for that matter) means that the latest version of the IACLRs that applies is the one in force in Australia (that is, the 1999 Montreal Convention). This is because Australia is both the place of departure and the place of ultimate destination.

For a one-way fare from Sydney to Hong Kong, the latest version of the IACLR that is in force in **both** places will apply, that is, the most recent version both places have in common; even if one of the places has a more recent version which has been given effect in the law in that place. Remember, as not every state quickly adopts the latest version of the IACLRs, states need to keep in force concurrently, all versions of the IACLRs that they have signed up to (though this may be unclear in some countries e.g. **in NZ**).

So how do you find this out? You look to see which countries have ratified each convention. For NZ, for the purpose of court proceedings, the Governor-General certifies by Order-in-Council the identities of the parties to the various conventions and protocols. Otherwise, for a good indication of which states have ratified which conventions, look to ICAO' website. Except where both countries have adopted the newest version (1999 Montreal Convention), ascertaining with certainty which is the latest version both countries have in force, can sometimes be a little difficult. Fortunately, many countries have adopted the 1999 Montreal Convention.

Air Carrier Insurance Requirements

Legislation demands only minimal air carriage insurance. Although this is not a critical issue to most air travellers, airlines and aircraft owners or operators take out various forms of insurance, from 'hull insurance' for each aircraft to indemnify themselves in respect of its loss or damage, to passenger injury insurance that is more significant in the context of air carrier liability, where potential liability for passenger injury and death could be substantial or even unlimited for each passenger in an aircraft in the event of an air crash.

No legal requirements exist for private aircraft owners and operators to take out insurance, but many do. However, for commercial aircraft operators, some legal requirements to be insured do exist.

Passengers: Based on Art 50 of the 1999 Montreal Convention, there is a requirement that commercial air carriers at least be insured for passenger injury and death liabilities. **In Australia**, this is done pursuant to ss 41A and 41B, Pt IVA of the *Civil Aviation (Carriers' Liability) Act 1959* (Cth). Failure to do so is an offence under s 41E. However, the obligation is only to insure to the lower limits set out in the international conventions (260,000SDRs) or AUD725,000 for the Pt IV (e.g. domestic) carriage (s 41C(3)).

In NZ, similar but more generalised obligations exists, as a condition of air operator licensing under NZCAA, s 87ZA.

Incidentally, legislation such as the *Terrorism Insurance Act* 2003 (Cth) precludes insurance companies excluding terrorism risks from airline insurance policies. The Australian Reinsurance Pool Corporation was established by s 9 of the *Terrorism Insurance Act 2003* (Cth) as a response to the withdrawal of terrorism insurance by insurance companies throughout the world following the terrorist attacks on the United States of September 2001. It provides insurance cover for any "eligible terrorism loss" and any other functions prescribed by the regulations.

Baggage or cargo damage and delay: No statutory requirement exists for insurance in respect of baggage and cargo loss and damage, nor in respect of delay of passengers, baggage or cargo, as liability limits for those claims are quite low under the four main versions of the IACLRs, and minimal in the liability rules for non-international or domestic air carriage under CACLA, Pt IV and NZCAA, Pt 9B. However, in practice there are potentially many thousands more baggage claims annually than passenger injury or death claims. Airlines will usually have contracts of insurance that indemnify them against liabilities apart from death or personal injury of passengers (CACLA, s 45C(5)).

Under the Australian legislative provisions, the airlines' own insurers are permitted to exclude their liability in respect of employees of the airline who is travelling in the course of their duties as employees, but there are restrictions on other exclusions that insurers can include in policies indemnifying air carriers in respect of their liabilities under CACLA. Nor can the insurers, by contractual terms in the policies, make foreign law the "proper law" of the contract so as to affect their obligations. In the event of non-compliance with relevant provisions by insurers, certain penalty provisions and grounds for injunctive relief exist.

2.2 Does Your Claim Concern Border Controls?

Border controls for travellers include quarantine, custom and immigration. They are primarily the responsibility of government agencies or public authorities, and making claims against them is often difficult. Government departments, public authorities and agencies involved in customs and biosecurity (quarantine and health) control, or more generally in immigration matters have wide-ranging powers. They are mentioned here briefly only to highlight how claims for compensation may be made if some of these activities cause injuries or damage, e.g. as a result of how they are performed – one example is the spraying of aircraft cabins with insecticide before flight arrival. (Also, there are immunities and limits on actionable duties of public authority: Chapter 11).

Border control functions are usually exercised at airports that are government nominated "landing places" for aircraft and other vessels arriving in the country. These functions affect passengers as well as aircraft, and involve the rights of various authorised persons not only to enter into 'prohibited areas' at an airport and to search aircraft, but also to exercise other policing and security-related powers (see 2.3 below). While customs and immigration controls and procedures do not change often, quarantine and biosecurity controls may change substantially over time, in recognition of health risks and epidemics such as "bird flu" and "ebola" in foreign countries.

Government or other authorities who cause injury, loss or damage by the negligent or abusive performance of these functions, may sometimes be claimed against for compensation. However, if they exercise powers in accordance with regulations and guidelines, their liabilities in this regard are often quite limited as there is statutory authority for their activities, (or sometimes, actual immunities from legal claims exist, as are discussed in Chapter 11).

What quarantine controls are enforced?

Activities of quarantine officers at airports may be the subject of compensation claims. In Australia, one function of the Department of Agriculture is responsibility for health, quarantine and biosecurity controls over international travellers, but from mid-2015, relevant officers have worked closely with the combined Australia Border Force which has various air passenger customs and immigration responsibilities.

Some border control duties are also imposed on airlines.

Aside from offences that can be committed, travellers are subject to the exercise of various powers of screening, search and refusal of entry and exit, as well as the quarantining of individuals and animals and the destruction or quarantining of property under the *Quarantine Act 1908* (Cth). However, the exercise of any of these powers in a manner inconsistent with that which is authorized by regulations or by approved guidelines may give rise to compensation claims, e.g. relating to illegal detention of persons or destruction of property.

In NZ, equivalent quarantine and biosecurity powers and procedures are administered by the Ministry of Primary Industries (MPI) Biosecurity Officers under the auspices of the NZ Customs Service.

In all such cases, the circumstances in which such statutory powers or discretions are exercised will usually give rise to a duty of care not to unreasonably cause injury or loss to persons affected by the exercise of those powers (subject to statutory immunities and limits on claims discussed in Chapter 11).

What activities do customs agencies perform?

Customs officers have considerable powers that will affect travellers. Customs control is the subject of a vast body of legislation and regulation, but negligence in performing their functions may cause loss which is compensable. As with health controls, aircraft from outside the country must land at an appointed airport with a 'customs boarding station' where customs officers may exercise substantial policing powers, including the boarding and searching of aircraft.

In Australia, customs boarding stations are appointed by the Comptroller General of Customs under the *Customs Act 1901* (Cth) (s 15), and officers may board and search aircraft at those places (ss 186-189). Since mid-2015, these powers are exercised by the Australian Border Force, formed by the merger of the Customs and Border Protection with parts of the Immigration service (see *Australian Border*

Force Act 2015 (Cth)). **In NZ**, the Customs Service also oversees a significant array of regulatory measures under the *Customs and Excise Act 1996* (NZ). Customs officers exercise wide-ranging powers to screen and search person and confiscate goods somewhat similar to police officers.

As with quarantine officers, injuries or damage caused by the improper, unauthorised or negligent exercise of powers by customs officers may give rise to claims for compensation, but as discussed in Chapter 11, these are always subject express common law or statutory immunities from any such civil claims that many public authorities benefit from.

What immigration control activities are performed?

Entry into and exit from countries are subject to detailed legislative provisions, but normally, citizens must be allowed entry. Border crossing in some parts of the world, especially in Europe, is quite unregulated except on first arrival in the EU or departure from a non-EU country. However, this is not the case in Australia and NZ, where stricter entry and exit controls apply. Also, visas (and passports) are needed by Australian and NZ citizens to enter most other foreign countries, even as tourists or for any other purposes (unless they also hold citizenship of those countries). Visa rules change regularly; they are not uniform and vary from country to country. Failure to comply with passport and immigration requirements of each country visited means entry will be legitimately refused or the person deported, or both. There are rarely grounds for claims in such cases, but reviews of decisions are possible.

In Australia, the entry of persons into and the exit of persons from the country are governed primarily by the *Migration Act 1958* (Cth), and a non-citizen must have been issued a visa to travel to and enter Australia prior to arrival (s 42(1)) – subject to a few exceptions, e.g. New Zealand citizens – and all non-citizens must normally enter through a proclaimed airport or port. Various kinds of visas are issued to non-citizens for travel to and entry into Australia, as well as to remain in Australia; either permanently or temporarily (e.g. to be able to remain for a specified period) (ss 29–38).

No permits are required by any persons wishing to leave and not re-enter Australia, although information is required and identities are verified (s 175(1)). Another entry visa, a return visa (ss 29(3) and 79) or a re-entry permit, is required for the re-entry of non-citizens, even if they are legally resident (s 166(1)(a)). Provision may be made for re-entry into Australia by the issue of resident return visas. Failure to return within any prescribed period stated in a re-entry permit or return visa means that new visas are required.

Australian citizens cannot, in theory, be refused re-entry to Australia (and they certainly cannot be deported once in the country), provided they can prove their national status by e.g. production of a valid Australian passport, (otherwise, the person must show that that they fall within another class of entrant exempt from obtaining an entry permit, e.g. foreign diplomatic and consular staff). In rare cases, citizenship can be lost or removed, but review and appeals will be available.

In NZ, essentially the same system of visa entry exists as in Australia for Australian citizens, NZ resident visa holders, diplomatic staff and commercial international aircraft crew members (but only for a period of seven days). Rules and procedures for visas are governed by the *Immigration Act 2009* (NZ), Pt 3, and s 46 expressly provides that possession of a visa does not guarantee permission to enter the country. Naturally, customs and police officers may exercise various powers given to immigration officers (ss 465-466).

Complaints may be made about immigration functions, but the availability of review and appeal of immigration decisions – the existence of a statutory remedy – would mean that there is less possibility of claiming compensation for negligence or breach of statutory powers, other than in exceptional circumstances (see immunities and other restrictions on claims against public authorities, discussed in Chapter 11).

2.3 Does Your Claim Concern Security Controls?

Compensation claims relating to aviation security controls may be made against some entities if they act carelessly or abuse their powers. Security controls, especially screening of passengers, baggage and airfreight (as well as of certain other persons, goods and vehicles) at airports or in security controlled areas, is a large and diverse topic, and what is focused on here are those aspects that may injure and give rise to claims by air travellers. Security controls may be imposed by several different entities or persons; including government and policing authorities as well as private security operators. Security measures are primarily preventative and designed to discover weapons, explosives and other prohibited items; but some possibilities exist for passenger claims to be made for loss or injury (even perhaps embarrassment or humiliation) suffered as a result of the failure to carry out screening and security control activities, or, performing controls improperly.

First, we need to understand what screening and security checking actions are required of each of the aviation industry participants, and what powers various security and screening officers have under applicable laws (see below). ICAO standards and practices are required to be implemented in almost all countries. Claims could not normally be made if such standards and practices are followed closely.

In Australia, most such aviation security controls are founded on the *Aviation Transport Security Act 2004* (Cth) (ATSA) and the *Aviation Transport Security Regulations 2005* (Cth) (ATSR), but other enactments such as the *Crimes (Aviation) Act 1991* (Cth), are important. Various security services may implement aviation security controls in Australia.

In NZ, similar rules apply although they are dispersed through different pieces of legislation: namely, *Civil Aviation Act 1990* (NZ) (NZCAA), Pt 8; *Aviation Crimes Act 1972* (NZ); *Civil Aviation (Offences) Regulations 2006* (NZ) and various Parts in the *Civil Aviation Rules* (NZ), especially Pts 108 and 140, as well as general enactments concerning e.g. crimes, trespass and airports etc. However, security controls are mainly implemented by a public authority: the NZ Aviation Security Service.

Rules and obligations are similar in both Australia and New Zealand, and although more of the Australian legislative and regulatory provisions are referred to in detail in the following pages, important differences between the systems in Australia and NZ are mentioned.

What Are The Powers and Duties of Security Officers?

Security officers have specific powers but some officers are also authorised to exercise policing powers by other legislation. Persons who may exercise specific powers under the aviation legislation include law enforcement officers (and eligible customs officers), aviation security officers and screening officers etc., although their powers are all somewhat different. Airport security guards (some private) also have a role and limited powers, but are quite separate. Additionally, "authorised persons" may be appointed for various security-related purposes.

Law enforcement officers, eligible customs officers – and (**in Australia**) protective service officers; (**in NZ**) aviation security officers, some of whom are screening officers – are given substantial and fairly similar powers of stop, search and seizure, detention and removal, which can be exercised in addition to any pre-existing policing etc. powers they may have under other enactments. **In Australia**, screening officers are not normally law enforcement officers and they have specific and more limited powers, primarily to conduct screening, frisk searches and detain suspects in appropriate cases (see below). Also **in Australia**, where **airport security guards** operate, they must satisfy training requirements, but they have very limited authority to stop, restrain or detain persons; exercisable only if an offence is likely and only in order to hand over a person to a law enforcement officer.

Additionally, **in Australia** – although not that relevant in the present context but playing a role in the overall security system – are **aviation security inspectors** who have wide powers to search premises (but no powers to search persons and no powers of arrest, detention or seizure), as well as to give 'compliance control directions' to aircraft operators, pilots in command of aircraft on the ground, to airport operators, to accredited air cargo agents, to screening authorities and officers. Of course, relevant Government Ministers and the Director of CASA (**in Australia**) or the Civil Aviation Authority (**in NZ**) can also give compulsory 'security directions' to airlines and other aviation industry participants.

Compensation claims based on a failure to properly perform any of the above functions are often rather restricted as they may be subject to the usual limits on the duties and immunities of public and statutory authorities (discussed in Chapter 11).

Who are aviation security officers, air security officers?

Law enforcement officers and other authorised persons have certain powers that apply in airports and on airplanes. In the aviation context, law enforcement officers are, in Australia, members of the Australian Federal Police, the police force of a State or Territory or eligible customs officers; and in NZ, they are members of the New Zealand Police Force who are also given all the powers of aviation security officers (NZCAA, s 87). Additionally, in Australia, protective service officers or special protective service officers, who have the same powers as under the *Australian Federal Police Act 1979* (Cth), are specially trained and known as air security officers or "sky marshals". They travel on commercial domestic flights and selected international air services to provide security against terrorist acts and aircraft hijacking.

Aviation legislation thus gives law enforcement officers a number of specific, additional powers to stop, detain and search persons and vehicles, even in an airside area (or "sterile area" and "security enhanced area": in NZ) of an airport. A law enforcement officer may enter and remain in any part of a security controlled airport at any time, and if such an officer reasonably believes that it is necessary to do so for the purposes of safeguarding against unlawful interference with aviation, law enforcement officers in such an airside (security) area may, but only after identifying themselves as a law enforcement officer and stating reasons for doing so, exercise the following powers (under ATSA, ss 84-89; NZCAA, ss 80-80H):

- stop a person and obtain their name, address;

- conduct an ordinary search or a frisk search of that person – if practicable, the search being conducted by a person of the same sex; or

- require the driver of a vehicle to stop the vehicle, and conduct a search of the vehicle

- request a person to leave such an area and remove them from the area, if necessary, without exercising unnecessary force.

In NZ, aviation security officers also have powers to arrest without warrant and seize of property (NZCAA, s 85).

In Australia, it is also an offence for a person to engage in conduct hindering or obstructing a law enforcement officer in the exercise of these stop and search powers (this offence is punishable by two years' imprisonment: ATSA, s 85(4)).

Customs officers, **in Australia**, if they have satisfied the training and qualifications prescribed and if on duty at a security controlled airport, may – in addition to the powers already exercisable under other enactments, notably the powers of boarding, searching aircraft, questioning and arresting without warrant passengers on board (under the *Customs Act 1901* (Cth)) – exercise the same powers as a law enforcement officer to stop and search persons and vehicles airside, remove vehicles and request a person to leave (but not the power to remove persons who refuse to leave). However, instead of the power to remove such persons, the eligible customs officer may only physically restrain and detain them until the persons can be dealt with by a law enforcement officer – but importantly, they cannot use more force or subject the person to greater indignity than is necessary and reasonable – if the persons are in an area or zone of a security controlled airport, and the customs officer reasonably suspects they are committing or have committed an offence (ATSA, ss 89C-89H).

Who are screening officers?

Screening officers are not necessarily law enforcement officers. However, they have some have powers under aviation legislation. Screening can be seen as an invasion of privacy or even assault, and issues may arise as to who should do the screening.

In Australia, the qualifications and powers of screening officers are slightly more specialised that those of security guards, and are much more limited than those of law enforcement officers. Certain functions are performed by screening officers pursuant to ATSA,s 94. In accordance with ATSR, Div 5.3, they are required to be trained and qualified in (ATSR, reg 5.06):

- maintaining the integrity of a sterile area; and

- using screening equipment; and

- methods and techniques to be used for screening persons, baggage and other goods; and

- dealing with weapons and prohibited items that are detected or surrendered.

Screening officers must be supervised by a "qualified screener" and strict obligations exist in relation to dealing with items surrendered to them.

In NZ, screening is carried out by Aviation Security Officers, who have wide powers similar to law enforcement officers (see above). Screening is conducted, under NZCAA, s 80B.

How much power do screening officers really have?

Screening officers exercise specific, but sometimes ambiguous powers. This is especially the case in relation to screening of passengers and baggage, and this can give rise to complaints. Obviously, officers performing screening have the powers to require persons and goods to pass through X-ray machines and to examine goods as required. Refusal of persons to undergo screening or failure to obtain clearance will result in denial of permission to enter a sterile or cleared area at the airport (and not catching their flights).

Screening officers also have the power to physically restrain and to detain any person at a security controlled airport, until the person can be dealt with by a law enforcement officer, but only if the screening officer:

- reasonably suspects [the person] is committing or has committed an offence, and

- reasonably believes that it is necessary to do so in order to ensure that a person who is not cleared, is not present in a cleared area or secure zone, or, to maintain the integrity of a landside or airside security or event zone.

Removal of clothing can also be required as part of screening. More controversially, screening officers may not only request the removal of clothing but perform a "frisk search", **in Australia** (under ATSA, ss 95,95B); or a "pat down" search, **in NZ** (under NZCAA, ss 80C(1), 80G). These powers are complicated; abuses may occur and claims may be made in respect of the manner in which they are exercised.

In Australia, a "request" that a person being screened remove "any item" of clothing, can be made by a screening officer who "considers it necessary" in order to screen a person properly. In theory, removal of all clothing could be sought. However, it is a strict liability offence for the officer to require any clothing removal, remove or cause the item of clothing to be removed, without reasonable excuse (and it is punishable by 50 penalty units: ASTA, s 95). Few formal and public guidelines assist the officer in the exercise of this power, whether as to what items of clothing may be the subject of the request or as to how to come to a decision to make the request. At least, the screening officer must not use more force or subject a person to greater indignity than is "necessary and reasonable" (ASTA, s 97). For example, in *Forest v Sydney Airport Corp Ltd* [2014] FCCA 208, the Federal Circuit Court found that it was not discriminatory under the *Disability Discrimination Act 1992* (Cth), to require a psychologically disabled person with an assistance dog to be screened other than through the usual machines, as the evidence showed that dogs going through the machines caused technical problems.

Importantly, a person who refuses a request to remove items of clothing may opt to be screened in a private room by an officer of same sex or to remove the item of clothing only during that screening. But if all options are rejected by the person, this is taken to mean that it is not possible to screen the person properly and the screening officer must refuse to allow the person to pass through the screening point (ASTA, s 95(5)). Issues can arise as to how the officer makes of any of these decisions, or as to the information or choices offered to the person being screened and whether consent is given and if it is voluntary, but these issues also arise in respect of the "frisk search" and are discussed in that context below.

In NZ, the law on removal of clothing items is stricter (more directive), but limited as it cannot be required if no underclothing is worn, although the wording is not clear. A person, must, if directed to do so by an aviation security officer carrying out a screening under NZCAA, s 80C(1):

(i) remove, raise, lower, or open any outer clothing, including (but not limited to) any coat, jacket, jumper, cardigan, or similar article that the person is wearing to enable the search to be carried out, except where the person has no other clothing, or only underclothing, under the outer clothing:

(ii) remove any gloves, footwear (including socks or stockings), head coverings, belts, jewellery, or other accessories (NZCAA s 80G).

No provision is made for allowing the person who refuses such a direction, or for offering the option for this to occur in a private room, but it is provided that such activities must be carried out in accordance with the search provisions in the *Aviation Security Act 1972* (NZ) s 12(2)-(8), although these provisions add little.

"Frisk" searches *or* **"pat down" searches** can also be carried out. A "frisk search" (**in Australia**) means a search of a person conducted by quickly running the hands over the person's outer garments; and an examination of anything worn or carried by the person that is conveniently and voluntarily removed by the person. A "pat-down search" (**in NZ**) seems to be more specific and apparently more thorough. By NZCAA, s 80C(2), a "pat down search"

(a) means a search of a clothed person in which the person conducting the search may do all or any of the following:

(i) run or pat his or her hand over the body of the person being searched, whether outside or inside the clothing (other than any underclothing) of that person:

(ii) insert his or her hand inside any pocket or pouch in the clothing (other than any underclothing) of the person being searched:

(iii) for the purpose of permitting a visual inspection, require the person being searched to do all or any of the following, namely:

(A) open his or her mouth:

(B) display the palms of his or her hands:

(C) display the soles of his or her feet:

(D) lift or rub his or her hair; and

(b) includes the authority to search—

(i) any item or substance carried by, or in the possession of, the person; and

(ii) any outer clothing removed, raised, lowered, or opened for the purposes of the search; and

(iii) any head covering, gloves, or footwear (including socks or stockings) removed for the purposes of the search.

In Australia, screening officers have a general power to request a person to undergo a "frisk search", if

"a screening officer considers it necessary in order to screen the person properly" (ATSA, s 95C(1)),

Undergoing a 'frisk search' is an option for persons who do not wish to pass through backscatter X-ray or other electronic surveillance procedures, but again only to the extent necessary to screen the person properly and "as an alternative to another procedure". However, the airport operator or screening authority is apparently not required to inform passengers of the availability of this alternative.

The screening officer also has a more specific power to request a 'frisk search' if a person has already undergone a screening procedure and

"the results ... indicate that additional screening procedures are necessary to screen the person properly" (ATSA, s 95B(1))

Whether the frisk search is carried out as an option, or if it is required, the screening officer "may conduct the search only to the extent necessary to complete the proper screening of the person", although the only test of the extent of the frisk search is: what is "necessary". So both the decision to carry out the search and the extent of the search is based on the subjective opinion of the screening officer, as there has been no requirement of "reasonableness". However, there are some limits, as the screening officer

"must not use more force or subject a person to greater indignity than is "necessary and reasonable" (ATSA, s 97).

The officer must not require a person to undergo a 'frisk search' or conduct a 'frisk search' without the person's consent, although consent may not be fully "informed" and completely freely given, as passengers rushing for a flight might feel considerable pressure to consent. A person who does refuse a 'frisk search' request by a screening officer, has the option (assuming they are informed of it) to undergo a 'frisk search' in a private room by a screening officer of the same sex (ATSA, ss 95B(6), 95C(6)). Refusing to consent to both options, means the officer must refuse to allow the person to pass through the screening point (ss 95B(6), 95C(6)).

How Does Security Screening Work?

What's the purpose of screening and what is required?

Screening is used to "clear" both persons and goods to permit them to enter sterile areas of an airport. Persons and baggage (and other goods and vehicles) must undergo screening in order to safeguard aviation against "unlawful interference" (terrorism and crime). Only "screened" persons and "examined" goods and vehicles are said to be "cleared" either for movement from the landside area to the airside area (or other secure areas and zones) of any "security controlled airport" or to be taken aboard a "cleared" aircraft. Almost all commercial public air transport and aircraft are subject to these screening requirements, but some minor tourist or irregular flights from small local or country airports might not.

In Australia, detailed requirements are made as to screening, receiving clearance and the circumstances in which persons, goods and vehicles are cleared. These are in ATSA, s 44(1) and regulations made under ATSA, s 44(2)(a) – (l), which deal with:

1) entities authorised or required to conduct screening (called a "screening authority"), items to be detected (weapons, prohibited items, explosives and "LAGs"), for which screening authorities must establish screening points (with various offences being created); and

2) procedures to deal with items surrendered or detected; clearance requirements for persons, goods (including aircraft stores and checked baggage – unaccompanied baggage is airfreight) and vehicles are to be cleared to board aircraft or enter a secure zone;

3) where screening is to occur and notices to be displayed;

4) methods, techniques and equipment used in screening; and

5) supervision and control measures to ensure that persons and items that have received clearance remain "cleared".

Screening officers' powers, including to request clothing removal, undertake "frisk searches" searches, refuse passage through a screening point and restrain and detain, are substantial but are subject to limits (see above).

In NZ, aviation security is the joint responsibility of New Zealand Police and "any authorised provider of aviation security services" (usually the NZ Aviation Security Service) at that aerodrome or navigational installation. Indeed; the Minister and Director of Civil Aviation have wide powers to require screening, searching and seizing of persons, property and vehicles (NZCAA, ss 76-79A). The powers of the Aviation Security Service to screen, search passengers and goods etc are exercised only if consent is given (NZCAA, ss 80-80D). Special directions have been given as to the performance of screening activities. However, refusal of consent will result in the passenger being unable to take the flight.

Improper or careless exercise of such powers may give rise to complaints and civil claims for compensation, but if public authorities are exercising these powers, claims may be restricted (see Chapter 11).

When can persons and carry-on baggage avoid being screened?

Almost all persons and goods must be screened before entry into cleared or sterile areas. Exceptionally, in Australia, VIPs, such as Heads of State, may board aircraft directly from a vehicle rather than passing through screening and a sterile area; or they may enter a "cleared area" without screening if accompanied by an officer of the Australian Federal Police or Australian Border Force (ATSR, 4.12, 4.12A). Otherwise, all persons, including passengers and crewmembers (unless considered still to be "cleared"), together with their carry-on baggage, must be screened and cleared before boarding any aircraft operating what is described as a "screened air service" – indeed, all commercial public transport flights are screened air services.

"Screening" involves persons and cabin baggage passing through appropriate X-ray equipment but it may extend to a screening officer opening and examining baggage and performing a "frisk search" ("pat-down" search) or requesting that the person remove certain items of clothing, or both (but this is done under quite complicated legislative provisions: e.g. ATSR, reg 4.53(1)). Only after being screened, do persons "receive clearance" and permission to pass through a screening point. To enter into and remain in a "sterile area" – the area that air passengers usually go after being screened – a person must be "cleared" and at all times since then, have remained in a cleared area, zone or aircraft (ATSA, s 9).

There are exceptions to this screening requirement:

1) if the Secretary specifies, by written notice, that:

- the person may pass through a screening point without being screened, or

- the person may enter a cleared area through other than a screening point (ATSR, 4.54(1)(a),(b)); OR

2) if the Regulations allow entry without screening e.g. if a person enters a sterile area from airside after disembarking from a screened air service (e.g. in transit). Otherwise, certain persons are taken to be cleared and allowed to pass through a screening point without being screened (under ATSR, reg 4.09). There are four categories of such persons (ATSR reg 4.10):

- a law enforcement officer who produces an appropriate ID card;

- a screening officer engaged in the management of a screening point;

- an ambulance, rescue or fire service officer responding to an emergency; or

- a member of the Australian Defence Force responding to an event or a threat of unlawful interference with aviation.

Other persons are also 'taken to be cleared' to enter sterile areas without passing through a screening point either: if they properly display a valid Aviation Security Identification Card (ASIC), or, if they are duly authorised and properly display a valid Visitor Identification Card (VIC) and are supervised by a person properly displaying a valid ASIC. Supervising persons include five other categories (ATSR, reg 4.11):

- aviation security inspectors;

- officers of the Australian Border Force;

- employees of the airport operator;

- employees of the operator of a screened air service aircraft; and

- contractors and employees of contractors of the airport operator or screened air service operator, engaged in loading cargo, stores or checked baggage or the boarding of passengers onto cleared aircraft operating a screened air service, or operator otherwise authorised to access to aircraft.

3) on flight stopovers, screening is not needed if no passengers disembark and all passengers were screened at the place where they boarded the aircraft. Otherwise, transit passengers must disembark from the aircraft together with their carry-on baggage if they are on inbound international screened air services whose final destination is not that place of landing in Australia. Further, they must be screened and their baggage inspected before they re-board the aircraft. Exceptions are made for disabled passengers, who may remain on board and be screened with their carry-on luggage in their seats.

How is checked baggage screened?

Checked baggage is screened and examined systematically and specifically if there is a risk. In Australia, all airports handling regular jet services and required to screen passengers and carry-on baggage, are also required to screen checked baggage and to use explosive trace detection equipment and full X-ray screening.

Such checked baggage screening is required if there is any risk, (or, more generally, if the Secretary requires such screening by notice in writing). Airlines operating an outbound international flight that transits through an airport in Australia (making the flight a "screened air service") e.g. Brisbane to Hong Kong transiting Cairns, must have all checked baggage screened at the aircraft's last port of call in Australia, unless the airline can show that the checked baggage was screened at any of the aircraft's previous ports of call in Australia, and kept continuously secure since that screening. Similarly, where some of an airline's passengers transfer to a screened air service in Australia, and the airline cannot show that their checked baggage was screened at any of the aircraft's previous ports and kept continuously secure since screening, then their checked baggage must be screened before its transfer to the other screened air service.

What happens if screening obligations are not met?

Offences can be committed by screening authorities. Offence provisions apply if screening authorities fail to properly carry out screening duties (ATSR, regs 4.23- 4.39). For example, it is an offence for a screening authority, who carries out screening and clearing of baggage, to fail to have appropriate procedures in place to ensure that no item can be placed in or on any cleared baggage during the "supervision or control period" (defined as the period from when the baggage is checked in until the baggage is cleared). This is particularly important at smaller airports with limited space to undertake screening after check-in occurs.

Opening checked baggage cannot be done without consent of the person entitled to its possession, unless a reasonable attempt has first been made to find that person and the person has not been found (ATSR, reg 4.39).

Committing such an offence may be evidence of negligence, for example in a common law negligence action for damages, but breach of a regulation would normally not itself found a civil claim as the fact that offence provisions exist is one factor that may tend to negative the existence of a separate statutory duty derived from legislative provisions imposing the obligations that were breached (see Chapters 11-14).

What If Weapons, Prohibited Items And LAGs Are Found?

No claims can be made by travellers over confiscation of prohibited items. On the other hand, there are consequences – confiscation of goods, the possible commission of offences and even civil claims for damages against passengers – if they carry weapons, prohibited items or LAGs (see below) in their baggage (or send them in airfreight), although much greater restrictions apply to carry-on (hand) baggage.

What things are considered to be" weapons"?

Weapons are the primary items persons are screened for. Several offences exist in respect of the possession of weapons by passengers and others at airports, but various persons (security officers etc) are authorised to carry weapons through screening points and into sterile areas. **In Australia**, these matters are governed by the ATSA and ATSR.

Lots of things can be a "weapon". It includes a firearm of any kind, or a device which is reasonably capable of being converted into a weapon, or which, but for a defect or absence of a part, would be a weapon (ATSA, s 9). Even some worker's tools e.g. hammers and screwdrivers may be weapons. More specifically, certain things are prescribed by the ATSRs to be weapons e.g. flares, flick-knives, blackjacks, blow-pipes, biotoxins, grenades and spear guns (ATSR, reg 1.09), and even imitation or replica weapons (reg 1.90(4)). Excepted however, are things that are part of an aircraft's stores or emergency equipment (provided they are not readily accessible to passengers or the public) (reg 1.09(6)).

Who can carry weapons through screening?

Various persons may, in different circumstances, carry through screenings, things considered to be weapons. A screening officer or authorised representative of the airline may carry a weapon to or from an aircraft, if it is accepted for carriage by an airline or if it is being removed from the aircraft (ATSR, reg 4.53(1)).

The regulations may also permit weapons to be carried. Air security officers ("sky marshals") and Australian Border Force officers have authority to carry weapons that are not firearms in "secure areas" (zones subject to special security arrangements), both landside and airside.

In addition, the same persons are authorised to carry firearms in all airside areas (even airside secure areas). Others may carry firearms in airside areas if duly authorised:

- uniformed security staff, who are licensed to carry firearms, hold a valid 1A Security Guard licence and properly display a valid Aviation Security Identification Card; and

- persons who are licensed to engage in controlling wildlife or other animals at the airport.

However, **in Australia**, in an area designated as a "sterile area" at an airport, the only persons authorised to carry firearms are air security officers ("sky marshals": see below) (ATSR, reg 4.56).

Otherwise, when they are on duty, screening officers, employees or contractors of airport operators or screened aircraft operators, may carry "weapons" (which may be merely tools-of-trade) that are detected during screening or surrendered for passage through screening points, subject to certain restrictions (e.g. the weapon not being apparent to members of the public) (ATSR, regs 4.57, 4.58).

Carrying a "weapon" through screening points or possession of weapons in security zones (airside or landside), by a person who is neither a law enforcement officer authorised by the Regulations, nor a person permitted in writing by the Secretary, may be either a strict liability offence punishable by 100 penalty units, or, in more serious cases, an offence punishable by a penalty of up to seven years' imprisonment (ATSA, ss 46-47).

Who can carry weapons on board aircraft?

It is also an offence carry a "weapon" (or something that can be used as a weapon) on board a "prescribed aircraft". It is even an offence to have possession of a "weapon" in a place accessible to any person on board a prescribed aircraft (but this would not include having a weapon in a person's checked baggage in the hold of the aircraft, as it is not accessible).

Breach of this rule will also either be a strict liability offence punishable by 100 penalty units, or in more serious cases, an offence punishable by up to seven years' imprisonment (ATSA, ss 48-49). Of course, this offence does not apply to:

- a law enforcement officer; authorised by Regulations or permitted in writing by the Secretary to carry a weapon (ATSA, s 51); or

- a pilot in command of an aircraft where the weapon is carried because either it is part of the aircraft equipment; or the aircraft is carrying an animal that could endanger the safety of the aircraft or persons on board.

Authorisation or permission to carry a weapon may be subject to conditions, and failure of a person to comply with any such conditions, without any reasonable excuse, is also an offence (punishable by 50 penalty units: ATSA, s 50).

What are "prohibited items"?

Many ordinary items are nonetheless prohibited at screening points and their unauthorised possession may be an offence. As with "weapons" (discussed above), the term "prohibited item" includes any item prescribed in the regulations that could be used for unlawful interference with aviation (ATSA, s 9). A non-exhaustive list is prescribed, ranging from metal cutlery to ski poles, screwdrivers to snooker cues, cable ties to corkscrews and knitting needles (ATSR, reg 1.07(1),(2)). Replicas of such items are prohibited and anything prescribed as both a weapons and a prohibited item is taken to be a weapon (ATSR, regs 1.07(4), 1.09(5)).

Who can take prohibited items through screening or on aircraft?

Aside from air security officers etc persons with medical conditions may carry certain prohibited items. As with weapons (see above), air security officers, Australian Border Force officers and authorised representatives of the aircraft operator, may have such items in their possession both in sterile areas and on board a prescribed aircraft.

Persons suffering from a medical condition or anyone caring for such a person, if they have a medical certificate and if it is medically necessary, may also carry prohibited items through a screening point or have them carried through it by screening officers on duty when such items are detected by screening or are surrendered; and may have them in their possession on board a prescribed aircraft.

Who else can have prohibited items in "sterile areas"?

Airline employees may also carry prohibited items through screening points. Aviation industry participants and authorised persons can have prohibited items in their possession in "sterile areas". Employees, acting in the course of their employment, may be such persons if the items are tools of trade (ATSR, regs 4.61, 4.62).

Otherwise, prohibited items may be held by an air security officer ("sky marshal"), or by someone escorting a person in custody, provided it is reasonably necessary to have the item in connection with the escort.

The same offences exist for unauthorised carriage or possession of prohibited items as exist in respect of weapons (in virtually the same terms) (see above and ATSA, ss 54-58).

What are LAGs and who has responsibilities for them?

Special rules govern the possession of liquids and gels. The danger of terrorists making explosives on board aircraft from small quantities of household or cosmetic products caused airlines to prohibit all but small quantities of such items being allowed in cabin baggage. As with unauthorised weapons and prohibited items, failure of any person to follow LAGs procedures may be an offence. Being required to comply or having property confiscated will certainly not give rise to any claim for damages, unless there is some abuse of powers, but perhaps, a failure of another passenger or person to comply may give rise to a civil claims for damages in cases where it causes loss or injury to the claimant.

"LAG products" are defined as all liquids (when at room temperature), aerosols, gels, creams and pastes, except for those allowed (as specified below), when carried by a person travelling on an international air service, or when carried into a LAGs cleared area "other than through a screening point", or even if brought through a screening point for business purposes at the airport, provided they are in approved "security tamper-evident bags".

Some LAG product items may be carried. These are:

- baby products for the care of a an infant or toddler on the flight in a reasonable quantity;

- a medical product on prescription for the person;

- a therapeutic product used to treat or manage a medical condition for the person in a reasonable quantity (e.g., contact lens solution);

- contents of a bag used to manage a medical condition (e.g. a colostomy bag);

- biological tissues, blood products etc and substances for medical research or reproductive health; or

- items or classes of items, as the Secretary may determine by written notice, when carried by a particular person, class or person or on a particular flight. (ATSR, 44.22C)

Offences committed may be committed by passengers and also by airlines etc. They may either evidence of negligence in a civil action for damages or, in there may be a breach of a statutory duty, which may be itself the basis for a damages claim (this is discussed in Chapter 11).

Screening authorities commit an offence if they do not establish a LAGs screening point designed to detect LAG products (if it is technically possible to do so), display prescribed warning signs, and have procedures and facilities for handling and destroying LAG products, at every security controlled airport or area thereof from which an international air service operate (the offence is punishable by 50 units: ATSR, reg 4.22D, 4.22J).

Airlines operating inbound international air services commit an offence if they do not put in place appropriate procedures to ensure that no passengers have any LAG products in their possession, during the flight from the aircraft's last port of call before Australia and arrival in Australia (punishable by 200 penalty units: ATSR regs 4.22E, 4.22F), **other than**:

- those supplied by the aircraft operator during the flight;

- exempt LAG (e.g., duty free) items; and

- in a "LAGs container" having a capacity of 100 ml or less in a sealed "LAGS bag".

Passengers commit a strict liability offence (that is, intention to do so is irrelevant) if they pass through a LAGs screening point with a LAG product in their possession, unless it is exempt or the product is in a LAG container in a sealed LAG bag, or in a "care bag" for the use of an ill person or child accompanying the person through a screening point (punishable by 20 penalty units: ATSR, reg 4.22HA).

What Pre-flight And On-Board Security Measures Are Required?

Requirements exist for pre-flight security checks and on-board security management. Non-compliance may be negligence or evidence of negligence if any claim is made in respect of injuries caused. Airlines are responsible for pre-flight security checks of aircraft and for on-board management and control of passengers and baggage; as well as the control of passengers who are in custody (ATSA, s 64).

To safeguard against unlawful interference with aviation, the regulations impose requirements as to:

- pre-flight checks of aircraft cabins and other parts of an aircraft;
- security of unattended aircraft;
- security features of an aircraft;
- management and control of passengers including persons in custody on board; and
- procedures and measures relating to baggage to be loaded on a "prescribed aircraft" (which can be any jet service).

Who has responsibility for pre-flight security?

Airlines are responsible for pre-flight security checks. Before an aircraft undertakes a "prescribed air service", that is, a commercial public transport flight, its operator must ensure that a "pre-flight security check" of the aircraft occurs as required (see below), **if either**:

- it is the aircraft's first flight since returning to service after maintenance carried out outside the airside area of a security controlled airport, **or**
- since the aircraft's previous flight, it has not been continuously protected as set out in the aircraft operator's Transport Security Program (TSP).

Failure to keep an aircraft that is used for a "prescribed air service" under the continuous supervision of a person authorised for that purpose by the airline, or, to take reasonable measures to prevent unauthorised persons having access to the aircraft, is an offence (punishable by 50 penalty units: ATSR, reg 4.71). It may also be grounds for a civil claim for compensation against the airline concerned, whether in negligence or, in some cases, for breach of statutory duty.

What measures are required for a pre-flight security check?

Pre-flight security checks include a comprehensive inspection. Checks should involve inspection of the interior of the aircraft, before any passenger boards, including the passenger cabin, the seats, overhead baggage lockers, food preparation areas, crew rest stations, toilets; and baggage compartments, before any baggage is loaded; the cargo hold before any cargo is loaded; and any unlocked facilities anywhere in those areas, as well as an inspection of the parts of the aircraft's exterior that are accessible (ATSR, reg 4.72).

The regulations do not prescribe who should perform these checks on behalf of the operator (although often it is the pilot), nor how long should be spent performing the security check, nor how "in-depth" such checks needs to be. There are even occasions when the checks need not be performed at all. These uncertainties can give rise to controversy.

What powers exist to control passengers on board aircraft?

Aircraft operators are required to manage and control passengers on board aircraft, However, along with this power comes responsibility for wrongful acts. Commanders of aircraft (pilots) on international and domestic flights have considerable but quite specific powers over persons and property on board (discussed more fully below), as do air security officers ("sky marshals"). In Australia, sky marshals are specially trained protective service officers under Pt II Div 3 of the Australian Federal Police Act 1979 (Cth), and are present on selected domestic and international flights.

Operators of virtually all commercial air services are required to carry on their aircraft, at least two restraining devices, readily accessible to crew, but not visible or readily accessible to passengers (ATSR, reg 4.66). The operator of a "prescribed air service" must not only establish and maintain training programs for crew to ensure they are able to assess the seriousness of an occurrence, communicate and coordinate, use appropriate self-defence and non-lethal protective devices permitted by law, understand the behaviour of terrorists; but also undertake exercises simulating threatening situations, flight deck procedures for aircraft protection, aircraft searches and ensure aware of bomb locations posing least-risk for aircraft (ATSR, reg 4.70).

Physical security measures must also be taken, e.g. the door of the flight crew compartment of all aircraft operating on a "prescribed air service" must be lockable (but with a means for communication between cabin crew and flight crew) and remain closed while the aircraft is in flight; except to allow authorised and properly identified persons such as crew members, aircraft operator employees and authorised civil aviation officers to enter and leave or when otherwise necessary for safety reasons. Pilots in command of aircraft commit an offence if they allow an ineligible person to enter the cockpit while the aircraft is in flight (punishable by 50 penalty units: ATSR, reg 4.67(4). Furthermore, access of passengers or other unauthorised persons to parts of the aircraft not designed for accommodation is prohibited.

What Specific Powers Do Aircraft Commanders Have?

Aircraft commanders' powers are substantial but specific. Aircraft commander's powers are based on those detailed in Chapter III of the Tokyo Convention, and have been given the force of law in Australia and New Zealand, as in almost all other countries. **In Australia**, the *Crimes (Aviation) Act 1991* (Cth), Pt 3, especially s 29(1)(a) enacts these powers and expands on them, especially as regards arrest. **In NZ**, the *Aviation Crimes Act 1972* (NZ) ss 15-17 set out the powers of the aircraft commander in terms similar to those stated in the Tokyo Convention, Ch III.

The powers granted to the aircraft commander under the Tokyo Convention, Ch III, apply to an aircraft "in flight", but limited to international flights. Thus, flights which do not leave the airspace of the aircraft's state of registration are apparently not within the Convention's provisions. However, the implementing legislation uses terminology which extends these powers to such non-international (and domestic) flights, both **in Australia** and **in NZ**. Additionally, if an aircraft is forced to land, Tokyo Convention, Ch III powers continue to apply to offences and acts committed on board until competent authorities of a state take over responsibility for the aircraft and for persons and property on board. This is confirmed in the *Crimes (Aviation) Act 1991* (Cth) ss 5-6 and the *Aviation Crimes Act 1972* (NZ) ss 2(2) and 15(1).

When can a commander restrain and disembark passengers?

Aircraft commanders' powers include to impose reasonable restraint and to force disembarkation of passengers. A person on an aircraft who is reasonably suspected of committing an offence or being about to commit an offence on board aircraft may be restrained or disembarked (Tokyo Convention, Art 6 – in Australia, this applies to any offence against Pt 2 of the *Crimes (Aviation) Act 1991* (Cth)). However, any measures, including restraint, which are taken must be reasonable and necessary to protect the safety of the aircraft and persons and property on board, to maintain good order and discipline, or enable delivery of the person to competent authorities. Abuse of powers may be the subject of a claim for compensation.

Aircraft commanders can even require and authorise crew members to assist, and can request and authorise (but not require), the assistance of passengers. A member of the crew or a passenger may even take reasonable preventative measures without authorisation if this is considered immediately necessary to protect the aircraft and persons and property on board.

Restraint of persons is not permitted after landing, except:

- where the landing is in the territory of a non-contracting state which has refused to allow disembarkation;

- where a forced landing is made and delivery of the person to competent authorities is not possible; or

- where the person agrees to onward carriage under restraint.

Forced disembarkation is authorised, but improper disembarkation may be the subject of a claim for compensation if improperly carried out. Aircraft commanders may disembark a person suspected of committing or being about to commit, on board the aircraft, any act which may either jeopardise the safety of the aircraft or persons or property on board or merely jeopardise good order and discipline.

The same applies if a commander reasonably suspects that a person has committed an offence on board the aircraft which

> "in his [or her] opinion, is a serious offence according to the penal law of the State of registration of the aircraft" (Tokyo Convention, Art 9(1)).

Thus, passengers are subject to the criminal laws of the state of registration of the aircraft in which they fly. This may be problematic. Such laws can be draconian, e.g. if they required all women to wear a veil, although punishment would depend on the state in which the passenger is forcibly disembarked. Of course, this power wrongly assumes that aircraft commanders will have a good knowledge of the criminal law of their aircraft's' state of registration, even though they may not even be citizens of those states and sometimes they are not even a resident of the state of the aircraft's registration. Fortunately, problems do not usually arise in practice.

Aircraft commanders do have some immunity from claims. Under the Tokyo Convention, no responsibility rests with the aircraft commander, crew, passengers, owner or operator of the aircraft in any proceedings as a result of the **proper** exercise of powers in respect of a person against whom actions under the Tokyo Convention are taken (Tokyo Convention, Art 19).

When persons are disembarked, **in Australia**, "authorised persons" (e.g. protective services officers, members of the AFP and airport managers) in 22 Australian airports and outside the country in every airport serving international civil aviation, may accept delivery of such persons and take offenders into custody. (**In Australia**, *Crimes (Aviation) Act 1991* (Cth), ss 30,33. **In NZ**, police officers exercise these powers under the *Aviation Crimes Act 1972* (NZ), ss 15(5),16.)

What are a commander's powers of arrest and search etc?

Aircraft commander's powers of arrest and search are substantial and based on legislation. The Crimes (Aviation) Act 1991 (Cth) and, to a lesser extent, the Aviation Crimes Act 1972 (NZ), also establish powers of commanders or others to search, restrain, and in some cases, take into custody and arrest persons on board aircraft if they are reasonably suspected of committing any of the envisaged offences.

There is no express power of arrest given to the aircraft commander in the Tokyo Convention or **in NZ** legislation, although there is power to exercise "reasonable measures including restraint" (in Art 6(1) and s 15(1) respectively) which would seem adequate to deal with offences on board aircraft. **In Australia**, powers to restrain and to arrest without warrant, persons found or reasonably suspected of committing any of the envisaged offences are set out expressly in the *Crimes (Aviation) Act 1991* (Cth), ss 34-35; and they apply to commanders of "prescribed aircraft", which are widely defined by s 3(1) to include not only Australian aircraft anywhere, but also foreign aircraft in Australia and visiting government aircraft (and not limited to aircraft in international flights). These powers are complemented by other legislation, notably *the Aviation Transport Security Act 2004* (Cth) and *Aviation Transport Security Regulations 2005* (Cth).

Search powers are implicit in the aircraft commander's "reasonable measures" powers under the Tokyo Convention, Art 6. However, further powers to search suspects are expressly provided to the commander of the aircraft or an "authorised person" by the *Crimes (Aviation) Act 1991* (Cth), s 49 and in NZ, *Aviation Crimes Act 1972* (NZ), s 17.

In NZ, the commander or such authorised persons carrying out the search, must reasonably suspect an offence has been or is about to be committed on board or in relation to the aircraft.

In Australia, such persons must also reasonably suspect an offence has been or is about to be committed against Pt 2 Div 2 of the *Crimes (Aviation) Act 1991* (Cth) (which includes offences on board aircraft) or Pt 2 Div 3 (which includes offences against the safe operation of aircraft).

Suspicion of the latter kinds of offences may also result in search of any person who is about to board the aircraft and any luggage or freight that is about to be placed on board. Additionally, by s 49(2), an authorised person who reasonably suspects that a Pt 2 Div 5 offence (reckless acts or threats endangering the safety of aerodromes or navigational facilities)

"has been, is being or may be committed in respect of a Commonwealth aerodrome, or Commonwealth air navigation facilities"

may also search any area or any person, luggage, freight or vehicle found within the limits or in the vicinity of the aerodrome or facilities. The aircraft commander's role is supplemented by the air security officer (or sky marshal), a specially trained protective service officer under Pt II Div 3 of the *Australian Federal Police Act 1979* (Cth).

What Special Rules Apply to Air Carriage of Prisoners?

Special security requirements govern carriage of persons who are in custody. The presence of prisoners or persons in custody on board aircraft may present a security risk. Injuries could be caused by such persons and may be the subject of claims for compensation. Special rules governing their carriage on prescribed aircraft or their presence at security controlled airports (ATSA, s 65(2), prescribe:

- circumstances in which such persons may be on aircraft or at airports;

- security and escort arrangements that must be implemented;

- information that must be provided to the airport and aircraft operators;

- information to be provided to the pilot in command;

- circumstances in which the airline or pilot may refuse the person in custody to board;

- circumstances in which the security controlled airport operator may refuse to allow the person in custody to be at the airport; and

- the number of persons in custody on a prescribed aircraft or at a security controlled airport at any one time.

Airport operators and airlines may commit offences by breaching these rules. Fines incurred are up to 200 penalty units (airport operators and aircraft operators); 100 penalty units (other aviation industry participant) and 50 penalty units (any other person) (ATSA, ss 62,65), although a court may impose up to five times these penalties if a body corporate is convicted of the offence (*Crimes Act 1914* (Cth), s 4B(3)).

What responsibilities relate to escorting prisoners?

There are different levels of escort control. Some persons, whether already convicted or on remand, must be in strict police custody, for example, on transfer between penal facilities. Others may be in more or less restrictive custody of immigration officers. Both are provided for (ATSA, s 65 and ATSR, Pt 4 Div 4.5), although other legislation such as the *Migration Act 1958* (Cth) may also impose some requirements.

The ATSR provides for the arrangements which are to be made between the relevant enforcement agency, the aircraft operator and the operator of a security controlled airport, as well as providing information to the pilot and the conditions of escort of persons in custody. (The regulations are detailed and repetitive).

More specifically, different escort arrangements are made depending on the dangerousness of the prisoner:

1) Non-dangerous persons and persons in custody under the *Migration Act 1958* or otherwise, must be escorted unless the Secretary approves otherwise in writing, but no number of escorts is specified.

2) A person in custody who is considered dangerous (e.g. likely to try to escape or charged with an offence with a sentence of five years or more), must be accompanied at all times by at least two escorts (usually law enforcement officers), at least one being of the same sex as the person, and not usually responsible for any other person.

3) No more than two escorted persons in custody, where one may be dangerous, can be carried on the same flight without the Secretary's written approval (except if three or more members of the same family unit are all escorted and none are dangerous, but the enforcement agency and aircraft operator must agree on escort arrangements).

For ordinary (non-immigration) prisoners, information must be given to the airline by the relevant enforcement agency at least 48 hours before the intended flight; and the consent of the airline obtained if the person is dangerous.

Information must also be provided to the operators of all security controlled airports through which any escorted person will travel at least 12 hours before the person's arrival at the airport, although for escorted persons in custody under the *Migration Act 1958* (Cth), only if they are dangerous is notification to airport operators required.

Are requirement less strict for immigration offenders?

Other less strict arrangements exist for less dangerous persons. Notably, this applies to persons in custody under the *Migration Act 1958* (Cth); and these are provided for in detail in the ATSR. Some travel of such persons is unescorted and simpler provisions apply to "turnaround departures" (persons refused entry and who leave within 72 hours) or "monitored departures" (persons on bridging visas whose departure is monitored by the Department of Immigration); and persons who have been taken into custody at a security controlled airport or on a prescribed aircraft (not under the *Migration Act 1958*).

However, as regards persons in immigration detention who are co-operating in "supervised departure" (i.e. unescorted departure after boarding the aircraft out of Australia), the Immigration Department must provide information to the airline at least six hours before the departure of the intended flight (Part A of Form 1). For escorted domestic air travel of person in custody under the *Migration Act 1958*, information is to be provided at least 24 hours before departure (Parts A and B of Form 1) (ATSR 4.78).

In all cases, it is the responsibility of the aircraft operator to inform the pilot in command that a person in custody is being carried on the aircraft and the conditions of such carriage.

3. Consumer Protection and Airline Obligations

Consumer protection laws and consumer tribunals deal mainly with pre-travel liabilities of travel industry entities. Unless air passengers or other travellers have been killed or sustained serious injuries during carriage, the amounts being claimed by them (or by shippers of airfreight) will, in many cases, be quite small, often less than a few thousand dollars. Thus, small claims (consumer) tribunals or their equivalent would seem to be appropriate venues for hearing and deciding these claims. Tribunals have specific powers and can deal with many kinds of small claims and minor civil disputes but cannot hear claims under CACLA (**in Australia**) or NZCAA (**in NZ**), as "courts" and not tribunals must decide these claims. This is a major defect in the consumer protection system as many passenger, baggage and freight carriage claims involve small amounts of money and going to a "court" is expensive (as legal representation is usually needed), and claimants who lose their cases, also risk having to pay all the other party's fees and legal costs.

It is important to note that when CACLA (**in Australia**) or the NZACA or NZCaGoA (**in NZ**) do apply to the injury or loss suffered **in the course of air carriage**, claims made can only be based on those enactments and no claims can be made if based on other grounds e.g. tort, breach of contract, consumer protection (see below) because of the "exclusivity" principle in the special liability rules (also discussed below).

For the kinds of claims that can be made in consumer tribunals – and there are some – there must always be a breach of consumer law or contract law, or be a claim in tort, if an action for compensatory damages is to be pursued. It should also be borne in mind that most breaches of consumer law provisions will also be offences punishable by fines or by imprisonment.

How do consumer laws and contract law interact?

Consumer protection law exists to protect people who enter into consumer transactions. Consumer law is an overlay on the basic principles of contract law. Travellers enter into contracts, usually with commercial entities such as airlines, tour operators, hotels, restaurants etc, to purchase goods or services. The parties to the travel contract do not usually have equal bargaining power. Fundamentally, under contract law, the parties to a contract are bound by all the terms in the contract and can only claim damages from the other party or seek to annul the contract if there has been a breach of the terms or conditions.

However, a standard form contract may say e.g. that the consumer cannot make a claim at all or that compensation is limited to $1; then that has been what was agreed to and no further questions can be asked. Consumer law modifies this to provide protections for consumers against abusive or unfair business practices and contract terms that e.g. take away a consumer's right to claim damages for breach of the contract.

In practice, consumers may enter a contract (buy a product or service) after seeing advertising or being told about the product or service by the seller – so it is important that such information is not false or misleading – and when they sign a contract, often it is without having read all of the terms and conditions either because they have no real choice, or they trust the seller, or because it is too complicated or they might not even be shown all the terms and conditions. In brief, consumer protection laws aim to legally require

- certain pre-contractual false or misleading statements and conduct made by the commercial entity are illegal and can be a basis for annulling the contract or claiming damages from the commercial operator;

- certain terms protecting the consumer, be implied into these contract e.g. as to the quality of the goods or service (when not expressly stated) and become part of the contract;

- certain abusive selling practices, or conditions in the contract e.g. that protect the commercial entity from claims by the consumer are to have no effect or limited effect.

Not only are offences created by consumer protection laws to discourage businesses from abusive or unfair practices, but remedies are also created for the consumer to obtain compensation if losses are suffered. Usually tribunals exist for such claims to be made without great expense (see below).

What grounds for claims exist in tort law: mainly negligence?

Anyone caused loss or injury by another person's wrongful actions, omissions or statements can claim compensation under tort law. Tort law involves lots of differing principles of general law. These principles are based on the common law which has been affected by legislation in some cases. To claim in tort, there does not need to be any contractual relationship between the claimant and the wrongdoer, but if there is, the contract might try to exclude claims being made in tort although consumer law protections may nullify such contract terms.

In the air travel claims context, various torts may be relevant, notably:

- *negligence*: that breach of a duty to take care not to injure persons who you could reasonably foresee might be injured by your acts, omissions or statements, will give rise to a claim for compensation;

- *breach of statutory duty*: where the legislature intends a legislative provision to meet the criteria necessary to establish a duty to a certain class of persons enforceable by civil action for damages;

- *product liability*: where there is strict liability of a product manufacturer, distributor or seller for a defective product causing injury or loss to a user;

- *occupier's liability*: where the occupier of land or premises is liable to persons injured on the premises for compensation, because of some defect of the premises or dangerous condition e.g. slippery floor in a shop (but this is largely based on negligence law);

- *nuisance* (private): where a person occupying premises uses them in such a way as to unreasonably interfere with a neighbour' peaceful use and enjoyment of its premises; and

- *trespass to land*: where a person is liable for intentionally entering another person's land without permission;

To be compensated, claimants must prove all elements of the tort being relied upon and the wrongdoer must have no defence against the claim e.g. contributory negligence, consent or necessity.

3.1 SMALL CLAIMS TRIBUNALS AND CONSUMER COURTS

In Australia, Can Air Travel Claims Be Made in Small Claims Tribunals and Courts?

Many consumer claims can be made cheaply in tribunals. (A table of such tribunals is set out at the end of this chapter). Most States and Territories in Australia have small claims (consumer) tribunals, though their names may differ (civil and administrative tribunals or magistrates courts); and some, if they are actually "courts" and not tribunals, could also have jurisdiction to hear claims under CACLA. But there are limits on how much compensation can be claimed in those tribunals; often it is as low as AU$10,000. There are tribunal fees, sometimes several hundred dollars, and 'out of pocket' expenses for the claimant, but both can be part of the claim. No legal costs are usually awarded, even if lawyers are allowed to represent parties.

None of the following **tribunals** have jurisdiction over any CACLA-based air passenger, baggage, freight injury, damage or delay claims. However, they can deal with consumer claims under the *Australian Consumer Law* (ACL) (in most cases, but not claims for personal injuries). Time limits for making claims can also be critical and can range from 3 months to within 6 years of the breach of contract or the dispute.

In the ACT, there is the **ACT Civil and Administrative Tribunal (ACAT)** set up by the *ACT Civil and Administrative Tribunal Act 2008* (ACT) which has a civil claims jurisdiction of up to AU$10,000 and parties may be represented by other persons, including lawyers.

In Queensland, the **Civil and Administrative Tribunal (QCAT)**, was set up by the *Queensland Civil and Administrative Tribunal Act 2009* (Qld) to deal with minor consumer and other claims up to AU$25,000, and with the tribunal's prior permission, claimants can be represented by someone else including a lawyer.

In NSW, the **NSW Civil and Administrative Tribunal (NCAT)** set up under the *Civil and Administrative Tribunal Act 2013* (NSW), has a diverse jurisdiction, including over civil claims in commercial and consumer matters up to AU$40,000; and with the tribunal's prior permission, claimants can be represented by someone else including a lawyer.

In Victoria, the **Victorian Civil and Administrative Tribunal (VCAT)** likewise has diverse jurisdiction under the *Victorian Civil and Administrative Tribunal Act 1998* (Vic), including over civil claims in consumer matters to AU$10,000, but higher amounts may be claimed. Claims must usually be brought within six months of the dispute.

In Northern Territory, South Australia, Tasmania and Western Australia, it is the **Magistrates Courts** that deal with small (consumer) claims and certain other matters as a part of the civil jurisdictions they exercise. These courts potentially could deal with at least some claims under CACLA, but care is needed as specific claims may be outside the powers of the court concerned. In minor civil claims (from AU$5,000 to AU$25,000), parties can sometimes be represented by others or by lawyers if the court consents, but "party and party" legal costs are not usually awarded, no matter who wins.

In the Northern Territory, the Local Court (which exercises general civil jurisdiction for claims up to AU$100,000), also deals with small claims in respect of a debt; the performance of work (which could include air carriage); and replacement or repair of goods valued at up to AU$10,000 under the *Small Claims* Act (NT), s 5. Claims must be made within 3 years. Thus, some claims made under CACLA may well be within the definition of a small claim here. Otherwise, any claims arising from a contract, including consumer claims would fall within the Local Court's general civil jurisdiction, and be subject to the usual legal principles.

In South Australia, the Magistrates Court hears general civil claims for up to AU$100,000 and "minor claims" which are defined in *Magistrates Court Act 1991* (SA), s 3, as a monetary claim of AU$25,000 or less, including debts, unpaid wages, disputes with neighbours, damage to property or faulty work done. Lawyers are not permitted and no costs are ordered. Thus, "minor claims" would normally include claims in respect of air carriage contracts, and could also include CACLA claims, but if for some reason they did not, the claim would be taken to be a general claim in the Magistrates Court under s 10B, and subject to usual legal principles.

In Tasmania, the Magistrates Court has power under *Magistrates Court (Civil Division) Act 1992* (Tas), s 7, to hear minor civil claims, being any claim for damages of up to AU$5,000, where legal representation is not normally permitted and costs are not normally awarded. Thus, "minor civil claims" would normally include claims in respect of air carriage contracts, and should also include CACLA claims, but if for some reason they did not, the claim would be taken to be a general civil claim in the Magistrates Court and subject to usual legal principles.

In Western Australia, the Magistrates Court has power under the *Magistrates Court (Civil Proceedings) Act 2004* (WA) to hear and determine any minor claims for debt or damages for up to AU$10,000 and consumer claims, where legal representation is not normally permitted and costs are not normally awarded. Again, "minor claims" could include claims in respect of air carriage contracts, and should also include CACLA claims, but if for some reason they did not, the claims would be taken to be a general civil claim in the Magistrates Court and subject to usual legal principles.

Can airline claims be made in the Australian Federal Courts?

Consumer claims can be made in Federal Circuit Courts, but not CACLA claims. Aside from the tribunals and consumer courts with more limited jurisdictions mentioned above, a Federal Circuit Court (FCC) functions throughout Australia. It has jurisdiction over all claims for up to AU$750,000 under the ACL and a number of other pieces of Federal legislation, but CACLA is not specified as one (at the time of writing) – although it could be if government was willing to do it – and claims under human rights or equal opportunity (discrimination) laws are included. They are sometimes the basis of traveller disputes with airlines e.g. over facilities for disabled persons; and some such claims may be actionable in the FCC, except when excluded because civil aviation liability laws apply. Of course, it is not really a consumer court and there are fees and quite substantial legal costs involved in pursuing civil actions in the FCC.

In NZ, Can Airline Claims Be Made in Small Claims Courts?

Consumer claims can be brought in the Disputes Tribunal. In New Zealand, some air claims can be brought in the New Zealand Disputes Tribunal which was created by the *Disputes Tribunal Act 1988* (NZ) and is an informal 'small claims' dispute settlement service of the District Court. It has jurisdiction to hear and settle civil claims in contract, quasi-contract and tort up to NZ$15,000 (or NZ$20,000 by agreement); and under several pieces of legislation, including the NZCGA and NZFTA (the prime sources of consumer protection and implied guarantees in consumer contracts: see below), expressly confer jurisdiction on the tribunal (Sch 1, Part 2). (A table of tribunals is set out at the end of this chapter).

However, claims for loss or damage to baggage (hand or checked) and freight cannot be brought there, although "delay" claims could. The NZCaGoA (which deals only with goods loss and damage) makes many references to "court" defined in s 2 to mean "any court of competent jurisdiction" but the NZCaGoA is not (at the time of writing) included on the list of enactments in Pt 2 of Sch 1 of the *Disputes Tribunal Act* 1998 (NZ) which allows the tribunal to exercise powers given to courts in certain enactments, and until it is listed, this tribunal does not have jurisdiction to deal with NZCaGoA claims. This omission is a serious defect in consumer protection for travellers, in view of the low carrier liability claims limits.

In the Disputes Tribunal, legal representation is not permitted and costs are not normally awarded (ss 52,43).

The Disputes Tribunal would lack the jurisdiction to hear claims under NZCAA Pt 9A and Pt 9B. As it is not a "court", there is limited scope for claims under Pt 9A, which provides for international air carrier liabilities; or Pt 9B which, provides for domestic carriage liabilities, but, only for passenger carriage delay under s 91Z: see below). Any domestic passenger personal death or injury is subject to the exclusive jurisdiction accident compensation scheme of the NZACA (s 317); and baggage and freight loss and damage claims are within the exclusive jurisdiction of the NZCaGoA (s 6).

Any claims for damages that can be made must be brought in a "court", whether the District Court, whose general civil jurisdiction extends to claims for up to NZ$200,000, or the High Court which has unlimited civil jurisdiction. Principles of the general law apply, including the need for legal representation and the award of costs.

3.2 Consumer Protections: Guarantees, Deceptive Conduct

Various consumer protection laws assist travellers. Consumer protection law is a vast subject and here, we can only highlight principles which may be relied on by travellers to make claims against airlines or others involved in the air travel process. Similar consumer protections exist under the *Australian Consumer Law* (ACL) and New Zealand legislation: *Consumer Guarantees Act 1993* (NZ) (NZCGA) and the *Fair Trading Act 1986* (NZ) (NZFTA). Claims for breaches of consumer protection laws concern different kinds of wrongful behaviour than carriage claims covered by CACLA or NZCAA.

Consumer laws don't apply to some kinds of claims. Claims for injuries and losses covered by the special air carriage liability laws: **in Australia**, CACLA (all accidents or damage occasioned during air carriage), or **in NZ**, NZCAA (all accidents or damage occasioned during *international* air carriage and some domestic carriage); NZACA (dealing with all *domestic* accidents causing personal injury or death; and NZCaGoA domestic baggage and freight loss or damage) can **only** be made under those pieces of legislation. (see Chapters 4-7).

What Consumer Guarantees Apply To Air Carriage Contracts?

Several important consumer guarantees are implied into air travel contracts. In any contracts, terms and conditions, including warranties, may be either expressly stated in, or, otherwise incorporated by reference into those contracts. However, when warranties are required by legislation – as in the case of consumer guarantees – such terms are implied into standardised contracts, including those for air carriage used in both scheduled and unscheduled international and domestic air travel.

Rarely, the common law may also imply terms into contracts to clarify ambiguity. This is more likely when less formal contractual documents are used, for example in local tourist or sightseeing flights, or for occasional air carriage by light planes in remote areas.

In both Australia and New Zealand, similar legislative provisions exist to imply into consumer contracts automatically, these consumer guarantees e.g. as to performance within a reasonable time, fitness for the purpose etc, although remedies available may differ slightly.

In Australia, breach of such guarantees may invalidate a term in a contract or justify an award of compensatory damages for loss, damage or injury, provided the claim is brought within 6 years of the day on which the cause of action that relates to the conduct accrued (ACL ss 63 and 236).

In NZ, aside from the right to seek repair or replacement, damages for the loss of value of the goods or services to which the breached guarantee relates may be sought by a person suffering a loss; with two exceptions: either, where the breach was from a cause independent of human control; or, when caused by an act or default of someone other than the supplier or an employee of the supplier (NZGCA, ss 32,33).

These implied guarantees do not apply to every type of contract – the kinds of cases where these guarantees can be used to claim compensation for loss or injury, in the air travel and carriage context, are limited to events occurring outside the air carriage itself. This is because of the "exclusivity" of the special liability rules: if remedies exist under CACLA, NZACA and NZCAA, then all other remedies are prohibited (see below).

Which specific guarantees are important?

Consumer guarantees are important but imprecise. Guarantees as to 'the exercise of due care and skill'; "supply within a reasonable time" and as to "reasonable fitness for the purpose" of services rendered, are implied into consumer contracts for services, including travel and air carriage contracts (by ACL, ss 60-62 and NZCGA, ss 28-30). Obviously, the provision of air carriage is a "service". Of less significance here, are the similar guarantees for goods supplied e.g. in-flight meals and drinks (especially if special meals are requested) which have to be of "acceptable quality" and "reasonably fit for the particular purpose"; or "corresponding with a description", which are also implied by the ACL, ss 54-56 and NZCGA, ss 6-9. (These implied guarantees expressly do not apply to commercial freight transactions in Australia (ACL, s 63)).

For a service or item to be "fit for the purpose", it is enough that "the consumer makes known, expressly or by implication, to the supplier" any particular purpose for which the service or goods are required or the result that the services are to achieve. It would be obvious with an air carriage contract that the consumer wants safe, reasonably comfortable and efficient air carriage between two points. (There is an exception to the application of these legislative provisions, namely, if the consumer does not rely on, or that it is unreasonable for him or her to rely on the supplier's skill or judgment; but it would seem impossible that an air carrier could argue this.) If the air carriage provided was not fit for the purpose, e.g. a seat being broken or perhaps being seated next to an obese person whose fat overflowed onto your seat, then recovery of compensation would seem possible *unless* the consumer court or tribunal takes a ridiculously broad interpretation of the exclusivity rule in CACLA and NZCAA so as to exclude this kind of claim (see below).

Otherwise, consumer guarantees have wide application to any individual's air travel and air carriage contracts provided they are "consumer transactions" – services ordinarily acquired for personal consumption, even if a person is on a business trip (ACL, s 3(3)(b), NZCGA, s 2(1)), or, if the price paid for the service is less than AU$40,000 (ACL s 3(3)(a)). This is a threshold eligibility requirement in Australia (no NZ equivalent).

When can consumers rely on implied guarantees in air travel contracts?

Implied consumer guarantees have particular application to claims relating to pre-flight wrongdoing. The big question is when will the air travel consumer be able to rely on such guarantees? The answer is: most of the time – **usually for wrongful acts except acts of airlines that actually occur during the air carriage itself**; as CACLA and NZCAA make exclusive provision for air traveller damages claims (see below).

All international air carriage claims that are subject to the IACLRs i.e. passenger death, injury or delay and baggage or cargo loss damage or delay occurring during air carriage – and of course there can be argument over the precise scope of this concept (see Chapter 3), can only be made under and in accordance with the IACLRs (in CACLA, Pts IA, II, III or IIIC; or the NZCAA, Pt 9A). Thus, the kinds of services for international flights, which are outside CACLA and NZCAA and thus subject to consumer guarantees are those usually provided **before embarkation** (or a carrier taking charge of baggage) **and after disembarkation** (or carrier delivering baggage)

In **Australia, domestic** air carriage claims of passengers against airlines and their subcontractors for "bodily injury" or death (CACLA, ss 28,35,36), and for baggage destruction, loss or injury (CACLA, s 29(1)) can only be made under the special rules in CACLA, Pt IV (which does not cover delay). Clearly both passenger and baggage **delay** claims are subject to general law principles and implied consumer guarantees.

In **New Zealand, domestic** air carriage claims by passengers (whether ordinary residents of NZ or otherwise: NZACA, s 20) for personal injury or death can only be made under the NZACA, s 317(1). Non-residents might find it impractical to make a claim in NZ (but only rarely can they make the claim against an airline or subcontractor outside NZ). However:

(a) domestic passenger delay claims must be made under NZCAA, s 91Z-91ZF, except for a single domestic flight departing and returning to the same place e.g. a sightseeing flight (wholly military flights are also excluded). But it is not stated that this statutory cause of action for passenger delay is exclusive. Thus it seems that passenger delay claims based on general principles and implied guarantees would be available in the alternative to the statutory cause of action.

(b) domestic baggage loss, damage and delay claims are not provided for in NZCAA. Baggage and cargo loss or damage are subject to NZCaGoA, while baggage delay claims are governed by to general law principles, including implied consumer guarantees.

(NZ only) How do NZCAA Pts 9A, 9B relate to NZACA and NZCaGoA?

Most domestic NZ air carriage liability claims are not made under NZCAA, but international air carriage claims are. For *domestic* NZ air carriage, the NZ accident compensation scheme (in the NZACA) and the baggage and cargo loss and damage scheme (in the NZCaGoA) both expressly exclude claims being made on any other legal basis. (This is different from the rules establishing liability of air carriers for domestic passenger delay under NZCAA Pt 9B).

Unsurprisingly, this already complex situation is not as clear-cut as it might sound – what ever is? A few clarifications may be made:

1) claims for compensation for passenger death and personal injury on any domestic flights in NZ are **only** made under the NZACA (no provision is made for airline liability for them in NZCAA, Pt 9B).

Thus, the claims which can be made outside the NZACA are for:

(a) passenger delay: as the NZCAA Pt 9B creates a separate statutory remedy, and, the general law likely also provides a separate remedy; and

(b) baggage loss, damage or delay: as a separate and exclusive remedy exists under for baggage loss or damage under the *Carriage of Goods Act 1979* (NZ); and a separate claim for baggage delay exists only under the general law e.g. breach of contract, implied guarantees etc.

(c) air freight, a separate and exclusive remedy exists under for freight loss or damage under the *Carriage of Goods Act 1979* (NZ); and a separate claim for freight delay exists only under the general law e.g. breach of contract, implied guarantees etc.

Thus, all persons (NZ residents, non-residents and foreigners) who have a claim against an airline in NZ for personal injury or death on a domestic flight, cannot make that claim in a NZ court. (Exceptionally, and this would be rare, if they wish to claim exemplary (punitive) damages, they may make such a claim in a court: see NZACA, s 319 (see below)).

2) Claims as to international air carriage within the IACLRs must all be made under the NZCAA Pt 9A, which gives the force of law to

- the Montreal Convention 1999,

- what it describes as the "amended convention" and

- the Guadalajara Convention (which is an accessory convention, slightly modifying two earlier versions (Warsaw and Warsaw-Hague) so that they apply to all subcontracting airlines (see Chapter 4) and does not by itself, create a separate version of the IACLRs).

This wording implies that aside from the IACLR set up by the Montreal Convention 1999, there is only one other version of the IACLRs in force, but in fact, all the other versions are given effect by the operation of NZCAA Pt 9A, ss 910-91RA. Thus, any IACLR-based actions in respect of the international air carriage they apply to, can be brought in NZ courts.

3) Although NZACA, s 317(1) prohibits any claim for damages (based on grounds apart from those in the NZACA) being brought in a court in NZ for an accident covered by the NZACA (which includes most personal injuries), it expressly and exceptionally allows international air carriage claims (NZACA, s 317(5), stating:

"Subsection (1) does not prevent any person bringing proceedings in any court in New Zealand for damages for personal injury of the kinds described in subsection (1), suffered in New Zealand or elsewhere, if the cause of action is the defendant's liability for damages under the law of New Zealand under any international convention relating to the carriage of passengers."

Thus, subject to an authoritative judicial interpretation to the contrary, the words "under the law of New Zealand under any international convention relating to the carriage of passengers" seem merely to be a reference to NZCAA Pt 9A, which gives the force of law to the conventions mentioned in item 2 above and other relevant provisions in Pt 9A. (Even claims against airlines and their subcontractors for exemplary (punitive) damages may be made under NZACA, s 319.)

4) NZCaGoA, s 6 prohibits any claim for the "loss or damage" to goods (baggage or freight), except in accordance with the terms of the contract of carriage and the provisions of NZCaGoA (other than where the carrier intentionally causes the loss or damage). However, s 5(1),(2) states:

"this Act applies to every carriage of goods, not being international carriage, performed or to be performed by a carrier pursuant to a contract ... whether the carriage is or is not incidental to the carriage of passengers."

Thus, NZCaGoA does not apply to claims for intentional damage to goods, delay to goods (which could be brought in the Disputes Tribunal), nor to any international air carriage claims under the IACLRs.

Can implied guarantees justify claims for losses if flights are cancelled or delayed?

Implied consumer guarantees can also be the basis for claims for excessive delay. If the services contracted for were not supplied at all, e.g. a tour or flight was cancelled, or they were not able to be supplied within the period specified or within a reasonable time – and this could arise in the event of pre-flight delays, cancellations or denied boarding – a claim for loss suffered may sometimes be made **based on breach of the implied guarantee that services be performed within a reasonable time**: ACL, s 62 and NZCGA, s 30. But the problem is: what is "reasonable". This will depend on the circumstances; and in some places and for some journeys, a 24 hour delay may be reasonable; in others it may not. Also, there are other exclusions and uncertainties.

First, delay occurring in the course of air carriage – after the flight has begun – is within the exclusive scope of CACLA and NZCAA. So the consumer laws do not apply to claims against airlines.

Second, these guarantees don't apply if a term in the contract fixes the time for performance of the service (making it an enforceable term of the contract). Air carriage contracts usually provide a date and time when carriage is to occur, but the Conditions of Carriage specifically allow the airline to change flight times, cancel or make a significant change to the departure and make an alternative booking or give a refund. In these circumstances, it would be likely that a court or tribunal would find that the contract had set no fixed date and time for performance of the service. Thus, implied guarantees as to performance within a reasonable time would apply and in consumer transactions, the guarantee could not be contracted out of by the airline (ACL, s 64: NZCGA, s 43).

But compensation for breach of such a guarantee is still uncertain.

Aside from questions as to what is a "reasonable" time for performance, it may be that a remedy is expressly provided for in the carriage contract, such as being given a refund by the airline or an alternative booking, and this may be considered to be adequate compliance with the implied guarantee, unless other consequential losses resulted (such as non-refundable missed connections or hotel bookings). Care needs to be taken before pursuing a claim to ensure that the tribunal or court is authorised to award damages for such consequential losses and not just order a refund or its equivalent in damages (for NZ, the NZGCA envisages only this remedy). If a refund is offered before the trial and refused but the court decides that this all that is obtainable, then both parties' legal and courts costs may have to be paid by the complainant.

Third, denied boarding is different. It is a special kind of delay – it is usually caused by a deliberate commercial policy of "overbooking" flights (see below and Chapter 7) – and is another situation when this implied guarantee might apply. It may be that implied guarantees or other consumer protection provisions apply to denied boarding because e.g. there is misleading conduct in that the air ticket shows a departure time and date, but it is known that the time or date that is likely not to be adhered to. While air carriage contracts often provide specifically for these eventualities by saying times are not guaranteed, such terms cannot override or detract from consumer guarantees (except in non-consumer transactions): ACL, ss 64,64A: NZGCA, s 43. (Misleading conduct is discussed below).

Also, passengers may have accepted payments or other offers made by the airline at the time of denied boarding in accordance with the airline's contract of air carriage (see below). It is only if this acceptance does not involve the renunciation of any other claims that may be made by the passenger – and this could well be set out in the air carriage contract or in a document which is required to be signed on accepting such payments etc (although this is illegal in the EU: see Chapter 7) – that separate claims might be made against the airline for breach of this consumer protection guarantee in an appropriate tribunal or court.

When can punitive (exemplary) damages be claimed in air travel cases?

Punitive damages are rarely awarded. Merely compensating a small loss may not be enough. Some may think that airline overbooking practices – which are all about making as big a profit as possible – warrants punishment and punitive damages awards. Punitive or exemplary damages are to punish a wrongdoer – like a fine – and are only awarded in a civil claim when a defendant's conduct shows "conscious wrongdoing" or "contumelious disregard" for the plaintiff's rights. However, these criteria are quite extreme and difficult to prove.

Punitive damages are more likely to be awarded in consumer claims, than in air carriage liability claims. Note that in NZ, there seems to be a conflict between the clear words of NZACA, s 319 which very explicitly allow exemplary damages to be awarded for personal injuries claims generally, including those involving domestic air carriage within the ambit of the NZACA compensation scheme; and, for international air carriage claims under the NZCAA, as the last sentence of art 29 of the Montreal Convention 1999 states that such damages are not recoverable (although this prohibition does not exist in other older versions of the

IACLRs). Of course, the NZACA does not govern international air carriage liability claims; only domestic ones, so the two different systems can co-exist. But should this issue arise, for the sake of international uniformity, it may be that courts in NZ might find that exemplary damages should not be awarded even in domestic air carriage injury claims, and the principle set out in the international convention is to be followed. Indeed, Air New Zealand expressly states in Clause 15.9 of its Conditions of Carriage that it is "not liable for exemplary damages, indirect or consequential losses". Of course, such a contractual term may be an "unfair contract term" and void (NZFTA, ss 26A, 46I and 46M as from 17 March 2015),

When Can Claims Be Made For Misleading Or Deceptive Conduct?

Any misleading words or deceptive conduct by a seller may give rise to consumer claims. Various provisions in the ACL and the NZFTA protect the consumer (including air travel consumers – passengers and shippers) from **unfair practices**, such as misleading or deceptive statements, false advertising or other conduct by airlines, and of course, other entities involved in air carriage e.g. travel agents etc. (see below).

In the case of deceptive etc conduct, claims for compensation for resulting loss, damage or injury are possible in Australia under ACL,s 236. In NZ, compensation can be recovered for loss or damage (presumably not including personal injury) under NZFTA, ss 43,43A,43B. These remedies are available even if the statement is made or conduct occurs outside the country: (**for NZ,** NZFTA, s 3; or **for Australia,** Competition and Consumer Act 2010 (Cth), s 5(1)). In appropriate cases, refunds may also be ordered by the court or tribunal.

What kinds of unfair practices are wrongful?

Several specific unfair practices are prohibited by consumer laws. The unfair practices that can give rise to claims for compensation are very similar in Australia and in NZ.

In Australia, the ACL prohibits (if it occurs "in trade or commerce"): and

In NZ, the NZFTA, prohibits (if it occurs "in trade"),

a person making or engaging in:

- **"unconscionable conduct"** in connection with the supply of goods or services, and this unconscionability is determined by relative strengths of the parties, the reasonable necessity of conditions imposed, the customer's inability to understand any documents, the ability of one party to vary terms unilaterally etc (ACL, ss 20-22: but this grounds for a claim does not exist in NZ)

- **"unsubstantiated representations"** where the person making it does not have reasonable grounds for doing so (NZFTA, s 12A but not in Australia)

- **false or misleading representations** about goods or services as to quality, testimonials, approvals, prices, place of origin, availability, need, effect of any warranties etc, the requirement to pay for a right (ACL, s 29: NZFTA, s 13)

- **misleading or deceptive conduct**: that is, conduct likely to mislead or deceive or statements capable of misleading the public as to the nature, characteristics, suitability for purpose, quantity or any service (and similarly for goods) (ACL, ss 18,33-34; NZFTA, ss 9-11)

- **offering rebates, gifts or prizes without intending to provide them as offered** (ACL, s 32: NZFTA, s 17)

- **misleading statements or conduct** as to the nature of goods or services (ACL, 33,34: NZFTA, ss 11,13)

- **demanding or accepting payment wrongly**, that is, if at the time of the acceptance, there was an intention not to provide the goods or supply goods that are materially different, or there being reasonable grounds for believing that the goods or services sold will not be able to be supplied (ACL, s 36: NZFTA, s 21).

There are a range of other provisions in the relevant legislation giving consumers protection against various kinds of unfair conduct, unfair practices and unfair contract terms in consumer transactions. What is set out above is merely a summary of some principles potentially applicable to air travel advice and transactions. A legal practitioner should be consulted if advice is needed on these matters.

Claims for cancelled, delayed flights, denied boarding or refused carriage?

Misleading words and deceptive conduct causing delay can found claims for compensation. Airlines, travel agents and tour operators often advertise and accept bookings and payments for services that are proposed to occur in the future. An issue can arise as to whether or not such statements, representations or conduct, if wrong or misleading and causing loss, can give rise to a claim for damages for breach of any of the above-mentioned provisions of the ACL or NZFTA. Terms in the air carriage contract often specifically try to exclude liability for these matters (and this is discussed in Chapter 7 in the context of delays and cancellations). But the law overrides such terms.

Here are a couple of examples, but there may be others.

(a) When does seller accept payment for different services from that promised?

Deception can occur if a service supplied is materially different to that advertised and paid for by a traveller. Thus, it is mainly in respect of advertising and advice, especially from tour operators and travel agents, that these issues arise, though misleading information may be given by others including airline staff at another stage of travel (see below).

If a flight is cancelled, delayed or unavailable, there may have been either misleading statements or deceptive conduct as to the quality or nature of services offered (see above); or demands made for, or acceptance of, payment for, something the supplier ought reasonably be aware either is not going to be provided, or, is likely to be provided in a materially different form (see above). Both may justify compensation.

While an intention **not** to supply a service could amount to fraud, and would be quite difficult to prove, the knowledge or reasonable belief that a materially different service might be provided, is easier to establish because it is enough that the person accepting the payment ought reasonably have been aware of the facts constituting such a reasonable belief. For example, a holiday itinerary including two consecutive full days in Singapore which was later reduced to one full day and one night, but was not corrected in the brochure, was held to be something "materially different" and entailed the supply of materially different services to those advertised: see *Dawson v World Travel Headquarters Pty Ltd*. However, in that case, Fisher J noted that the issue of a "material difference" was a "question of degree"; and further, that it is not even a defence that the goods or services supplied are superior to those promised: as long as they are "materially different".

(b) When do airlines know an overbooked flight will result in denied boarding?

Even "overbooking" may be deceptive conduct. Aside from cases where a proposed tour does not go ahead when planned or at all, or a series of cheap flights turn out not to be as cheap as advertised, there could be an application of these provisions to the situation where airlines overbook flights knowing that some passengers' bookings will almost certainly not be honoured (see above). This may be "deceptive conduct".

It should be noted that some air carriage contracts do make specific provision for this to try to limit airline liability, e.g. Clause 10.3 of the Qantas Airways Conditions of Carriage.

****

10.3 Overbooked Flights - Denied Boarding Compensation

Airline flights may be overbooked. This means there is a slight chance that there may be more reservations than available seats on your flight. In these circumstances, where practicable, we will offer an incentive for volunteers not to travel on their booked flight. Volunteers will not be entitled to any further payment, refund or compensation. If there are not enough volunteers, we may need to deny boarding to one or more Passengers involuntarily.

If you are denied boarding due to an overbooking of our flight for which you have a valid Ticket and a confirmed reservation, and you have met our Check-In Deadline and complied with all applicable requirements for travel as set out in these Conditions of Carriage, we will offer you a seat on the next available flight on our services. If this is not acceptable to you, we will provide compensation and any care required by any law which may apply or in accordance with our policy if there is no applicable law. This will depend on the jurisdiction in which the denied boarding occurs.

Our denied boarding compensation policy is available on request.

****

This air carriage contract states that the airline will provide "any care required by any law which may apply or in accordance with our policy if there is no applicable law". The author was unable to find such "policy" on the Qantas website. Also, there are no laws in Australia or New Zealand requiring specific care in the event of denied board, though there are such laws in the European Union.

What does "misleading or deceptive" mean?

Misleading or deceptive is a little vague but such words or conduct must involve awareness of inaccuracy. The words "misleading" and "deceptive" are to be broadly interpreted and apply to contractual terms as well as non-contractual statements made, for example, in promotional advertising or even airline timetables – these are essentially representations as to the existence and scheduling of future air services (although confusingly, contracts of air carriage usually state that timetables are not part of the contract). The prohibition of misleading or deceptive conduct in trade or commerce applies generally to a traders' dealings with consumers in all Australian jurisdictions under especially the ACL, ss 18, 29 and 33 – 34, and in NZ, the NZFTA, ss 9-11. So claims could be brought by one consumer or a group or class of consumers.

Of course, it is not misleading or deceptive merely to break a promise, although it may be a breach of contract. There must be some awareness of inaccuracy. It is when made as to future matters that such conduct and statements are more complex. How can this "awareness" be discovered. The ACL, s 4(1) clarifies this by saying that the test is the reasonableness of the grounds upon which the person making the misrepresentation actually relies, when making the statement.

Indeed, there is actually a presumption of deception:

> If (a) a person makes a representation with respect to any future matter (including the doing of, or the refusing to do, any act) and (b) the person does not have reasonable grounds for making the representation, the representation is taken for the purposes of [the Australian Consumer Law] to be misleading.

It is important that the **burden of proof** that these reasonable grounds for belief existed and that the belief in them also existed, rests upon the person making the statement, as ACL, s 4(2) says:

> For the purposes of the application of [ACL, s 4(1)] in relation to a proceeding concerning a representation made with respect to a future matter, by (a) a party to the proceedings; or (b) any other person; the party or other person is taken not to have had reasonable grounds for making the representation, unless evidence is adduced to the contrary.

Is there liability for misleading statements by airline staff?

Even if made during air carriage, misstatements by airline staff may found a claim for compensation. Contracts of air carriage usually provide in their General Conditions of Carriage (GCC) that no employee or other person is authorised to vary the conditions of carriage. So it would be relatively rare that anything said by employees or agents will affect the airline's powers or liabilities under the contract of carriage. However, airline staff may still be liable for misstatements.

Of course, if statements by employees of airlines or other entities cause loss, the employees may be liable independently, although the airline may perhaps avoid any vicarious liability – that is under the rules which make employers liable for the acts of their employees done in the course of their employment – if (and this is unlikely) such employees can be proved to be acting outside the scope of their employment.

Indeed, there are marginal situations when wrong information is given by an airline employee, and the airline is held liable as the acts were sufficiently connected with the employment. For example, in the 2011 decision in the NSW District Court, on appeal from the NSW CTTT (now Civil and Administrative Tribunal), in *Patel v Malaysian Airways Australia Ltd*, the complainant suffered loss, damage and mental suffering (anguish) from his children being given misleading and deceptive information by inexperienced check-in staff at Mumbai airport on a return flight to Australia, to the effect that they could not check in 30kg of luggage (although that was allowed under their carriage contracts) and they had either to pay excess baggage or throw out their excess luggage which they did. The airline was held to be liable.

COURTS/TRIBUNALS FOR CLAIMS: AUSTRALIA

			AUSTRALIA		
claim	air carriage type	Court-with appropriate monetary and other jurisdiction	Civil & Administrative Tribunal (ACT & Vic: <$10K; Qld: <$25K; NSW:<$40K.	Magistrates Court (NT, SA, Tas, WA)	Federal Circuit Court (max $750K)
passenger injury or death	international	yes	no	yes	no
	domestic	yes	no	yes	no
	private (not CACLA)	yes	yes	yes	some e.g.ACL
passenger delay	international	yes	no		no
	domestic	yes	no	yes	
	private (not CACLA)	yes	yes	yes	some e.g. ACL
baggage/ freight loss or damage	international	yes	no		no
	domestic	yes	no		no
	private (not CACLA)	yes	yes	yes	some e.g. ACL
baggage/ freight delay	international	yes	no		no
	domestic		no		no
	private (not CACLA)	yes	yes	yes	some e.g. ACL
consumer complaint (if not within the scope of CACLA)	all	yes	yes	yes	yes
Human rights/ discrimination (if not w/in scope of CACLA)	all	yes	ACT yes Qld: yes Vic: yes NSW: only referrals	yes	yes

Courts/Tribunals etc for Claims: NZ

		NEW ZEALAND		
claim	air carriage type	Court (with appropriate monetary and other jurisdiction)	Disputes Tribunal <$15K (branch of District Ct <$200K)	Accident Compensation
passenger injury or death	international (only NZCAA)	yes	no	no
	domestic	(exemplary only)	no	yes
	private	(exemplary only)	no	yes
passenger delay	international (only NZCAA)	yes		no
	domestic (only NZCAA)			no
	private	yes	yes	no
baggage or freight loss or damage	international	yes	no	no
	domestic	yes	yes	no
	private			no
baggage or freight delay	international (only NZCAA)	yes		no
	domestic (not NZCaGoA)	yes	yes	no
	private (not NZCaGoA)			no
consumer complaint (not with in scope of NZCAA Pts 9A,9B; NZACA or NZCaGoA)	all	yes	yes	no
Human rights/ discrimination	all	yes	no	no

4. Airline Claims and Air Carriage Contracts

WHAT KINDS OF CONTRACT CLAIMS CAN BE MADE?

Air carriage contracts are the basis for many kinds of claims against airlines but most contract terms favour airlines. Pre-travel claims against airlines and others were discussed in Chapter 3. In this and following chapters (5 to 7), we look at other kinds of the claims that can be made against airlines. They fall into two categories:

- claims governed by the special liability rules; and
- other claims based on the air carriage contract.

The kinds of claims which are usually based on the special liability rules are for passenger death, injury or delay, and baggage or freight loss, damage or delay when **arising in the course of carriage by air** on international or domestic airlines. Baggage and airfreight claims are based on similar rules and so are discussed together with any relevant differences being mentioned as they arise. For other claims, see below.

Can buying tickets from travel agents complicate liability?

Buying tickets from travel wholesalers complicates passenger rights and airline obligations. Just one point to remember, if you buy your air ticket through a major tour or travel agent chain (wholesaler) rather from the airline, you may be distancing yourself from the airline(s) actually carrying you and complicating the legal relationship between the airline and passenger by adding layers it – these are found in:

- the terms of the contract between you and the wholesaler; and

- the terms of the contract between the wholesaler and the airline.

In such cases, your air carriage may be part of a commercial 'block booking' deal between the airline and the wholesaler, pursuant to which your ticket resembles a sort of 'charter' ticket and some of the usual passenger "rights" may be affected, especially as regards incidental matters, like changing reservation dates, flight delays etc. Airlines may require you to organize such matters through the tour or travel agent; meaning that if you are overseas, you cannot use the airline's local services, but have to make these arrangements with the wholesaler back home. Thus, the airline's own contract of air carriage with you is only part of the story.

How will injury occurring "during air carriage" affect claims?

Strict airline liability is a central principle in the special rules that govern injury occurring during air carriage. The most significant factor is that, in most cases, if a claim falls within the parameters (of time and place) that delimit "air carriage", the special domestic or the special international air carriage liability rules (DACLRs and IACLRs) apply almost exclusively, provided these are claims for:

- personal injury;
- baggage or freight damage; and
- passenger, baggage or freight delay.

These special rules make airlines "strictly" liable (that is, there is no need to prove the fault of the airline) or sometimes "absolutely" liable (no need to prove airline fault and the airline has no defences). Of course the claimant must be able to prove that injury, loss or damage was suffered.

However, in return for this advantage to the claimants, there are airline advantages: some formalities e.g. notices are required and strict time limits are to be complied with; some limits are imposed on compensation airlines are liable for; and importantly, all other legal claims against the airline in respect of the injury or loss are excluded. This exchange of advantages is the rationale, right or wrong, for the system that exists.

Detailed analysis of the IACLRs occurs in Chapter 5 to 7.

What other obligations in the carriage contract found claims?

Airline liabilities, other than their strict liability for air carriage injuries can also arise out of air carriage contracts. In the rest of this chapter, which is divided into two parts: passenger carriage contracts (4.1) and freight carriage contracts (4.2); we examine the nature and legal significance of the standard air carriage contracts and the terms and conditions in them, that establish other kinds of airline contractual obligations. These obligations are separate from the presumed airline liabilities set out in the ACLRs, and include questions such as:

- can airlines refuse carriage, and
- when are airlines liable if they cancel flights or cause delays or deny boarding. (Special contract terms relate to denied boarding resulting from overbooking; although some consumer law aspects of those issues have already been mentioned in Chapter 3).

Associated with, but not necessarily dependant on, the air carriage contract, are possible claims in respect of misleading or deceptive advertising, advice or conduct, which usually occur prior to the air carriage being performed but may be subject to the carriage contract and consumer protection law principles (as was discussed in Chapter 3).

4.1 Passenger Air Carriage Contracts

Air tickets and associated documents comprise and establish the contract for the carriage of air passengers. The basis of all claims for loss or injury occurring during air carriage is the contract of carriage between the traveller-claimant and the airline or its subcontractors, although the contract deals with various other obligations as well.

Most rights and obligations are found in the ticket and associated documents (or air waybill if sending unaccompanied baggage as airfreight: see below 4.2). These documents set out the terms of air carriage, in particular, airline liabilities and any limits on, or exemptions from, liability that an airline purports to have. However, there are areas of uncertainty.

Air carriage contracts contain some **terms that will always vary** from one passenger to the next, namely:

- passenger name, airline names and dates of travel; and

- place of departure, stopping points (if any) and place of destination.

These are important because they establish not only who can claim and who can be claimed against; but also:

(a) if the air travel is international or domestic (as some different laws apply); and

(b) which version of air carrier liability rules (IACLR) applies to international air carriage.

Otherwise, air carriage is governed by the airline's **standard contract** terms which are partly set out on the ticket (or other document provided) and partly contained in incorporated documents usually found on the airline's website; but usually the standard terms and conditions include:

- some significant provisions required by or made part of the contract by laws implementing international conventions e.g. liability limit notices,

- lots of terms and conditions purporting to protect airlines and clarifying when airlines can do certain things, like refuse carriage, and

- other terms and conditions that relate to or try to limit the effect of other local legislation, notably consumer protection laws (discussed in Chapter 3), being, **in Australia**, the *Australian Consumer Law* (ACL) or, **in NZ**, the *Fair Trading* (NZFTA) and *Consumer Guarantees* laws (NZCGA).

What Standard Terms Are In Air Passenger Carriage Contracts?

Air carriage contracts consist of several documents; some hidden. Almost all air tickets are now in electronic form, and after passengers make their bookings and pay for the flights – at which time it is assumed the contract is made, as it is too late to ask for a refund except on the terms and conditions set out in the contract – prospective passengers are emailed (sent) their "ticket" with related paperwork, which is then printed out by them (or not, as the case may be).

Then, when (or if) this paperwork is read, the 'Conditions of Contract', which are usually found on the second page, set out some of the contract's standard terms and also, significantly, incorporate various others, notably:

> (i) *the airline's 'Conditions of Carriage'*, usually obtainable from the airline's website (after a bit of searching); and

> (ii) *the applicable tariffs* (which are detailed documents reflecting **fares and related ticket conditions** e.g. date changing possibilities etc (and agency commissions) often filed by the carrier with relevant aeronautical authorities, usually the Secretary of the relevant Department of Government (whatever it is at the time), but these are pretty close to impossible to obtain by prospective passenger. Airlines and travel agents usually know the details of **ticket conditions** which may be relevant to issues like rights to cancel or change flight dates, frequent flyer points: see below.

Are "Conditions of Carriage" and" tariffs" contractual?

It is uncertain what matters form part of the contract of carriage. As the passenger does not normally even see the 'Conditions of Contract', let alone the 'Conditions of Carriage' until after the contract documents are received, it could be argued that these documents are not part of the contract at all. On the other hand, it could be replied that the standard contract terms are accessible as they are on airline websites (sometimes fare conditions as well e.g. for Air New Zealand fares) and passengers could have read them if they wanted to.

So, assuming hidden documents cannot be part of the contract, at the time when the contract is formed; it is somewhat uncertain which of these documents are actually contractual documents and which are not; and as a result, which written statements are actually contractual terms and which are not.

It is even uncertain precisely when the contract is formed. In practice, it is usually assumed that the carriage contract is formed when the air travel is paid for; that is, before the ticket document etc is handed over. (It is possible, but would only create confusion to challenge this idea because of an older Australian decision – even if it is in the High Court – that air carriage contracts are only executory, until the passenger has been seated on the aircraft. That decision should probably be confined to its own special facts.)

But if it is upon payment being made that the contract is formed, the passenger will not have seen the "Conditions of Carriage" or "tariffs" with their ticket conditions – in fact, they are very difficult to obtain. So, in theory, they cannot be part of the agreement. At this stage, such questions remain uncertain as they have not been judicially determined.

Are liability exclusion clauses effective in air carriage contracts?

Some liability exclusion clauses in the contract may not be enforceable. Airline **liabilities for air carriage** are based on international law, and local legislation cannot be excluded by terms in a contract of air carriage (see below). But other liabilities may be affected.

Of course, airline standard contracts are designed to protect the airline, and a number of contractual terms limit or try to exclude their liabilities to passengers and shippers. However, even though contractual terms appear to exclude liabilities under the contract they might not be as effective as airlines may hope. As courts have not had to consider the effect of such terms in air carriage contracts, the effectiveness of these liability exemption clauses is still open to argument.

At least sometimes, restrictive contract terms and exclusion clauses in consumer contracts can be challenged as:

- unfair and void (under the ACL, ss 23-27, Pts 2-3: unfair contract terms; or NZFTA, ss 9-11,41 and (as from 17 March 2015) ss 26A,46I,46L (unfair contract terms); or

- "unconscionable" (under ACL, s 20; no NZ equivalent).

What "unfair" means is perhaps vague, but can be explained by asking if the terms appear to cause an imbalance in the parties' rights; if they are not reasonably necessary; and if they would cause detriment if relied on (ACL, s 24 and NZFTA, s 46L). This should be fairly easy to prove.

Do laws affecting international and domestic air carriage differ?

Air carriage laws liability laws are mostly similar throughout the world. If claims for compensation for air carriage injuries or losses are properly brought in Australian or NZ courts (see Chapter 2), then the legislation and common law in that place will apply to both international and domestic air carriage claims.

Usually, no conflicts will occur between the consumer laws (**in Australia**, ACL or **in NZ**, NZFTA and NZCGA discussed in Chapter 3) and the air carriage laws which create special air carriage liabilities and exclude all other remedies (see Chapter 2). This is the case for both international or for domestic air carriage (**in Australia** CACLA, Pts 1A-III and **in NZ**, NZCAA Pts 9A), although slightly differing air carriage liability rules apply to domestic (non-international) air carriage (**in Australia**, CACLA, Pt IV; and **in NZ**, NZCAA Pt 9B, NZACA and NZCaGoA.

International air carriage is subject to the rules and limitations relating to international air carriage liability (IACLRs); slightly differing versions being established by various international conventions, whichever is applicable to the air carriage contract in question (determining which applies was also discussed in Chapter 2).

Essentially, four basic and slightly differing sets of the IACLRs exist and set out airline liabilities for air carriage: the most common Montreal Convention 1999. (The others are the 1929 Warsaw Convention; 1955 Warsaw-Hague Convention; or 1975 Warsaw-Hague-Montreal Additional Protocol No 4 Convention (MAP4).)

In Australia, all four versions of the IACLRs are made part of the law by ss 9B, 21, 11 and 25K of CACLA, respectively.

In NZ, the legislation, NZCAA Pt 9A, can be misleading as it appears to apply only two versions of the IACLRs: the Montreal Convention 1999 and what they call the "amended convention", as defined in s 91A, (that is, the Warsaw Convention as amended by every amending convention and protocol possible, though those amendments ordinarily create up to three major and another five minor alternative versions of the IACLRs).

However, some complex provisions in NZCAA, s 91RA, seem to give effect, in NZ, to all the other versions of the IACLRs.

Fortunately, only one version of the IACLR will apply to any particular air carriage contract, and in both Australia and NZ, it should be assumed that these four basic and slightly differing sets of the IACLRs exist. (The other minor versions based on the application or otherwise of certain protocols are complex and are ignored for present purposes.)

What terms must be in air carriage contracts by international law?

International air carriage liability rules (IACLR) are paramount but there are some limits. All versions of these rules also require that clear notices be given to passengers (or shippers): first, that the IACLRs apply, and second, that airline compensation for liabilities for passenger death, injury or delay and baggage or freight loss damage or delay will be limited to specified amounts. These notices are invariably given by airlines in or with the contract of air carriage (but there is now no penalty even if proper notice is not given; although this was different under older versions of the IACLRs: discussed below).

Are similar terms included in domestic air carriage contracts?

Domestic air carriage liability rules also prevail over contract terms but they don't cover all domestic air carriage claims. Similar rules to those in the IACLRs apply to most domestic (and other non-international) air carriage (DACLRs), but there are exceptions.

In Australia, domestic liability rules quite similar to the IACLR apply to domestic air travel under Pt IV of CACLA.

In NZ, the situation is more complicated, as domestic air carriage liability rules similar to the IACLR apply, but **only** to domestic passenger "delay" claims (all other delay claims are subject to the general law etc.: see below). All passenger death and injury claims in domestic carriage are exclusively governed by NZACA; and domestic baggage and freight damage and loss claims are exclusively governed by NZCaGoA.

In both countries, claims that are not within the ambit of those specific legislative enactments, are governed by general law principles: other legislation e.g. consumer protection laws and the common law e.g. contract and tort law.

Do consumer laws imply terms into air carriage contracts?

Consumer guarantees are implied into air travel contracts; except as regards air carriage claims covered by the special liability rules. Airlines try to incorporate various terms into their air carriage contract, but some consumer guarantees e.g. as to performance within a reasonable time, reasonable fitness for purpose of the services, are also implied into the air carriage contracts by virtue of the ACL, ss 60-61 and NZCGA, ss 28-30 (this was discussed in Chapter 3).

These guarantees are recognized in the airlines' (General) Conditions of Carriage (GCC) e.g. of Qantas and Air New Zealand (as at December 2014), although the contracts purport to limit remedies given by such implied guarantees "provided the relevant terms may by law be excluded" and "to the extent permitted by law" (see Qantas GCC Clause 2.4(a) and (b)). Similar, but more general provisions are made in the Air New Zealand GCC at Clauses 2.4 and 17. Other airlines may use slightly different terminology. In summary, this means that where the implied guarantees do apply – for example, not when the IACLRs apply – airlines seek to limit their effect to the extent possible.

****

2.4 Overriding Law

These Conditions of Carriage do not apply to the extent that they are inconsistent with laws that apply to your carriage.

In respect of any goods or services we may provide other than carriage, certain statutory guarantees or warranties may apply for the benefit of consumers. For example, for consumers, services may come with a non-excludable guarantee or warranty that they will be provided with due care and skill. The nature and application of these guarantees or warranties will depend on the relevant jurisdiction. Nothing in these Conditions of Carriage is intended to exclude or restrict the application of such consumer laws.

In respect of goods or services acquired for business purposes and not as a consumer:

(a) consumer guarantees and warranties, including under the Competition and Consumer Act 2010 (Cth), a Fair Trading Act or the New Zealand Consumer Guarantees

Act 1993 (NZ), will not apply where these Conditions of Carriage apply, provided that the relevant terms may by law be excluded; and

(b) if a statute or other law provides a guarantee or warranty that cannot be excluded, to the extent permitted by law our liability for a breach of the guarantee or warranty will be limited to either supplying the goods or services again or paying the cost of having them supplied again, as determined by us.

****

Incidentally, it is not necessary that air carriage contracts recognize that consumer law implied guarantees and warranties may apply – they will apply anyway – but if airlines want to limit the remedies available against them to the extent that the consumer laws permit, then this must be expressly stated in the contract. However, as far as Australia and NZ are concerned, any other purported contractual limitations of liability for goods and services, apply only to non-consumer transactions.

What Other Powers Do Airlines Have Under Contracts?

Airlines have substantial powers under their air carriage contracts. Under the contract of air carriage, passengers "agree" to the airline acting potentially to the detriment of passengers in certain situations, notably refusing carriage. Cancellations and delays may also be to the passenger's detriment, and to some extent airlines may limit liabilities for these (see Chapters 3 and 7).

Can airlines refuse carriage?

Air carriage may be refused on various grounds. "Denied boarding" is allowed for in contracts, if airlines overbook flights (see Chapter 3); and contracts may allow for flight delays and cancellation (see Chapter 7).

However, contracts also allow airlines to refuse to allow passengers to check-in or to board aircraft in several specific situations. In most respects, such refusals are usually the passenger's fault and any resulting claims for compensation rarely succeed.

1. Mostly, **safety and security** are the basis for such refusals. More specifically, airlines can refuse check-in or boarding, if passengers do not comply with requirements as to:

- arriving in good time to check in,

- having with them the proper identification documents (usually a passport or driver's licence for domestic air travel),

- submitting to search and inspections;

- carrying no prohibited items (firearms or dangerous) in baggage without permission;

- providing proper crating for animals;

- satisfying any health or vaccination controls, and

- complying with local and foreign immigration (e.g. visa) controls.

2. There are also many other (what may be called) **convenience or commercial grounds** for refusing passenger boarding set out in the air carriage contracts, ranging from:

- breaching government regulations,

- not having made arrangements for specialised medical or other assistance needed,

- being drunk, under the influence of drugs, abusive to or interfering with crew or ground staff, making threats,

- being unable to prove you are the person named in the ticket,

- not obeying the directions of ground staff, or

- having committed misconduct on another flight and there being a belief this may be repeated.

3. Furthermore, during the flight, if the airline (or crew) consider it **reasonably necessary for the comfort, safety or security of other passengers**, because of passengers conduct, obstruction, objectionable behaviour or interference with the aircraft equipment, they may restrain passengers, remove them from the flight – even making a course diversion if needed at the costs of the passengers – and hand them over to the authorities for prosecution. Prosecutions do sometimes occur.

What conduct can travellers be arrested or prosecuted for?

Careless conduct or joking remarks can be offences justifying restraint or offloading. Aircraft commanders have such powers. Only improper exercise of such policing powers may give rise to claims for compensation. Persons may commit an offence of being a threat or making false statements, even if jokes or careless remarks are made by passengers at airports and on an aircraft. These have resulted in prosecutions carrying custodial sentences, (s 28, *Crimes (Aviation) Act 1991* (Cth), which has a maximum penalty of ten years' imprisonment).

There are various examples of these offences. **In Australia,** it is an offence to make a threat to destroy, damage or endanger the safety of a Commonwealth aerodrome or any part of it, or any Commonwealth air navigation facilities or to threaten to kill or injure any person who is or may be within the limits thereof. It is also an offence to make a statement or communicate information known to be false, from which it can reasonably be inferred that there is or will be a plan, proposal, attempt, conspiracy or threat (under the *Crimes (Aviation) Act 1991* (Cth), s 28:

(a) to take or exercise control, by force, of a Commonwealth aerodrome, or part of a Commonwealth aerodrome, or any Commonwealth air navigation facilities; or

(b) to destroy, damage or endanger the safety of a Commonwealth aerodrome, or part of a Commonwealth aerodrome, or any Commonwealth air navigation facilities; or

(c) to kill or injure anyone who is, or may be, within the limits of a Commonwealth aerodrome or any Commonwealth air navigation facilities.

Finally, the commander of the aircraft or an "authorised person" (police, security or immigration personnel etc), who reasonably suspects that an offence on board aircraft or against the safe operation of aircraft has been committed, may search the aircraft, persons, luggage or freight on board almost every aircraft. Furthermore, where the offence is one concerning the safe operation of aircraft, those authorised persons may search anyone about to board the aircraft and luggage or freight that is about to be placed on board most aircraft (s 49(1) of the *Crimes (Aviation) Act 1991* (Cth)).

Also if an authorised person reasonably suspects that an offence involving a reckless acts or threats endangering the safety of aerodromes or navigational facilities has been or is about to be committed, they may search any person, luggage, freight, or vehicle found in the vicinity of the aerodrome or facilities or any area in the vicinity of the aerodrome or facilities (s 49(1), *Crimes (Aviation) Act 1991* (Cth)).

Can airlines collect passengers' personal information?

Personal data must, by law, be collected in some cases. Airlines are entitled to ask for passengers' personal information (though if for marketing reasons, giving it for is voluntary), and airlines are sometimes required by legislation to collect various personal information about passengers and transmit it to the appropriate authorities for immigration customs and security controls (e.g. in Australia, *Migration Act 1958* (Cth), s 245L). Failure to provide required information means the airline can properly refuse carriage. No compensation can be claimed.

Other times, airlines may request personal information with the intention of exploiting it commercially for their own purposes (but this may be presented as wanting to meet the passenger's needs) as is set out in Qantas Airways GCC, Clause 3.6, and its policy on privacy; and also in Air NZ's GCC Clause 5.3 which also refers to that airline's policy on privacy.)

Full disclosure of the use made of information provided, is to be given, to meet the requirements of privacy legislation. However, even if full disclosure does occur, issues might arise as to whether or not the reasons for the collection of personal information have been properly and accurately represented to passengers asked to supply it. If not, a passenger may have an action for compensation (ACL, ss 18 and 236;or NZFTA, ss 9-11 and 41,43 for misleading or deceptive conduct) or, in rare case, there may even be privacy legislation offences committed.

WHO CAN CLAIM AGAINST AIRLINES?

Carriage contracts and the special liability rules usually determine who can make claims and also who claims can be made against. In general, in the air travel context, anyone suffering injury, loss or damage as a result of the negligence or other wrongful conduct of any person or entity (other than an airline) involved e.g. baggage handling companies, airport management corporations, intermediaries such as travel agents, may commence a civil action for compensatory damages against that person or entity based on the common law e.g. negligence or breach of contract, nuisance. Such actions are usually heard in a court, but some may be heard as small civil claims in some tribunals (see Chapter 3).

There are exceptions. **In NZ**, all domestic air passenger carriage death or other personal injury claims must be made to the **Accident Compensation Commission** and not the airline. Only passenger and shipper claims in respect of international air carriage are made against airlines, as are passenger claims for domestic air carriage passenger delay under NZCAA Pt 9B. Claims are made against the airline concerned for baggage loss and damage under the NZCaGoA; and claims for baggage delay under the contract itself and the general law.

Some wrongful acts or omissions that cause injury or loss to passengers are recognized as breaches of consumer protection laws, and it may be that complaints can be made to bodies such as the **Australian Competition and Consumer Commission (ACCC)** or the **Commerce Commission in NZ** and then that organization may take action, for example for the recovery of penalties or the prosecution of offences. However, for passengers wanting compensation for loss or injury, this option is of limited benefit. Passengers suffering injury, loss or damage as a result of breaches of consumer or fair trading laws, may be able to take civil actions for damages against the person responsible (including the airline, except when the special liability rules apply) (ACL, ss 64-64A and s 236 or NZFTA, s 9-11, 41,43). As discussed in Chapter 3, these claims can be pursued in consumer, small claims or disputes tribunals, to avoid costs and lawyers' fees, but claimants must be careful that the tribunal chosen does have jurisdiction (power) to hear and decide on the claim.

Otherwise, claims for compensation for injury, loss, damage or delay **arising during air carriage**, are normally made in courts under the special liability rules e.g. applicable IACLR or DACLR, by the passenger (or shipper) concerned, against the airline responsible. (Who is responsible is discussed in Chapter 2).

Who can claim against airlines as a passenger?

Not everyone carried is a passenger. As regards claims against airlines under the IACLRs and DACLRs, it is primarily the "passenger" – the person named in the contract of carriage – who can take legal action in the courts, although there are some ambiguities, and in theory, stowaways and persons carried free or gratuitously (but not airline employees performing their functions) can claim under the rules well.

Personal representatives of deceased or dependent passengers may also sue on the passenger's behalf (or the passenger's relatives themselves may also sue: see below), not only for the injuries suffered by the passenger but also, in appropriate cases, for psychological trauma that those relatives suffer themselves. Persons wanting to make such claims should seek legal advice.

In Australia, an important somewhat technical addition to who can claim is that employers may also claim for indemnity of workers compensation payments made to employees injured in international or domestic air carriage (CACLA, ss 9F, 14, 24, 25L and 37), but these are not claims made under the IACLR and are not subject to its rules (e.g. its 2 year time limit for making the claim may not apply).

Somewhat similarly **in NZ**, the NZACA may require persons entitled to make claims, to enforce their right or assign them to the ACC and the ACC may recover any monies awarded to the person concerned (NZACA, s 320). Of course, no right to claim exists for domestic air carriage injuries under the NZCAA Pt 9B, although general law and common law rights still exist.

Which relatives may claim for persons injured in air carriage?

Passengers' relatives can also claim. In claims against international and domestic airlines, the applicable legislation gives a wide range of passenger's relatives, even illegitimate children, an adoptive or reputed father (as well as a deceased passenger's personal representatives) a right to claim from the airline responsible under all the versions of the IACLRs **in Australia and in NZ.** (The kinds of compensation available are discussed below.)

In Australia, liability under CACLA is enforceable for the benefit of all family members and personal representatives of an injured passenger. Basically the same persons can sue and be sued under the various Parts of CACLA giving effect to the various versions of the IACLRs, as under the domestic (non-international) provisions in Pt IV of CACLA. Claims by personal representatives of a deceased passenger can also be made under quite similar provisions in Pt IV (domestic) as are found in Pts IA,II III and IIIC (concerning international air carriage subject to the various versions of the IACLRs).

Psychological injury is more complicated. It is less certain when, and if, these related persons can claim for mental anguish or psychological effects arising from the passenger's death, injury or being put in peril, except where the claimant has witnessed the accident or was a close family member. This is the subject of legislative provisions (some of which are worded in different ways) in most jurisdictions of Australia. If the legislation does not apply, common law may. Even before the legislation was enacted, Beaumont J (dissenting) in *South Pacific Air Motive Pty Ltd v Magnus* (1998) 87 FCR 301; 157 ALR 443 already suggested that the provisions of Pt IV, especially s 28, might entitle persons other than the passenger to sue for nervous shock (anxiety, stress) resulting from the death or personal injury of a passenger. However, in that same case, Hill and Sackville JJ. interpreted s 28 in Pt IV to have the more restrictive meaning found in the equivalent provisions of Art 17 of the oldest Sch 1 version of the IACLR (the Warsaw Convention version) That version rarely applies now, so Beaumont J's view should be preferred.

In NZ, for international air carriage, the rights of family members and personal representative to claim also exists (NZCAA, s 91E and *Death by Accidents Compensation Act 1952* (NZ), ss 2,5 and 6).

But this is not the case in domestic air carriage claims, as:

- naturally, no equivalent provision is made as regards a deceased passenger's representatives in NZCAA Pt 9B because it does not cover personal injuries and only creates airline liability in respect of passenger *delay*;

- passenger death and injury (including some mental injury) claims come within the jurisdiction of the NZACA (which applies generally and is not discussed here in detail); and

- baggage and freight loss or damage claims come within the NZCaGoA (but baggage and freight *delay* claims are subject to the general law, especially contract).

Should passengers be told about ticket conditions?

Consumer laws may require full disclosure of travel terms and conditions. Airlines may provide in their air carriage contracts for the circumstances when passengers can change flights, departures etc, although specific types of tickets sold may have virtually hidden conditions many of which are very complex but are set out in the "tariffs" which are incorporated into contracts and sometimes filed with governments (see Chapter 2). Such hidden conditions may, for example, prohibit flight changes or allow them only in certain cases e.g. paying administrative fees; or, say that certain types of tickets carry no airline "mileage points".

When travel agent or ticketing wholesalers make bulk purchase arrangements with some airlines, they may also take over some of the airline administrative arrangements for passengers. For passengers who buy their tickets from such wholesalers, the contract between the wholesaler and passenger should make it clear how obligations owed to passenger are affected.

Whoever sells the air ticket (airline or travel agent) should make known to the consumer at the time the ticket is sold, relevant ticket conditions, but the diminished competence requirements on travel agents in Australia since licensing laws were repealed in 2014, makes it more likely that the agents will not even know that such conditions exist, what they mean, or understand the need to communicate them. Thus, it's better to buy tickets direct from airlines who should have knowledge of all ticket conditions.

Omitting to inform a consumer about such ticket conditions may itself be "misleading" and a breach of consumer protection law (discussed in Chapter 3). The airline may perhaps avoid this liability if the details of such ticket conditions are set out on the airline's website, but travel agents are unlikely to do this.

WHICH AIRLINES CAN CLAIMS BE MADE AGAINST?

Special air carriage liability rules also specify which airlines can be claimed against or sued. Under all versions of the IACLRs, claims for passenger death, bodily injury or delay, and for baggage loss and damage or delay, in the course of international air carriage, may be made against specific airlines (although there are some pre-requisites for their liabilities). Non-airline subcontractors and responsible employees can sometimes also be claimed against under the special rules.

Airlines often subcontract carriage and IACLRs expressly provide rules for claims being made against:

- **contracting carriers** – airlines named on the ticket,

- **successive carriers** (who are deemed to be contracting carriers for the carriage they perform) – even if not named on the ticket; and

- **actual carriers** – the airline performing carriage under some arrangement, when the injury or loss occurred,

as well as against their various subcontractors (including non-airlines) and employees.

Of course, there is still a limit on total compensation that can be obtained, no matter how many airlines are sued. The aggregate amount that can be recovered as damages from all air carriers or their subcontractors and employees (for liability under any version of the IACLRs), cannot "exceed the highest amount which could be awarded against either the contracting carrier or the actual carrier under this Convention" (Montreal Convention 1999, Art 44 and other IACLR versions,]) and none are liable individually for a sum over the limit in the applicable IACLR (liability limits and exceptions are discussed below).

This compensation limit is quite apart from any separate claims not based on the IACLRs, that can be made against aviation industry entities other than airlines e.g. airport management corporations, if they cause an injury. Such claims are not subject to maximum limits.

Of course, in all cases, only proved losses will be compensated and a loss that has been compensated by one defendant cannot be claimed again from another defendant (as it would no longer be a loss).

Which airlines are liable under the IACLRs as "contracting carriers"?

Contracting airlines as well as named and deemed subcontractors are liable for air carriage claims as contracting carriers. A contracting air carrier is an airline which is party to the air carriage contract, and this should be obvious from it being named in the air carriage contract. Usually also named in the contract is any alternative air carrier, e.g. an airline operating in a code-sharing agreement (essentially, party to the contract through the agency of the contracting carrier), if, as is common practice, routes are operated by two airlines jointly.

Also, **some airlines are deemed to be contracting carriers** even if not necessarily named on the contract, but if they are contemplated by it. Note that "successive" carriers when specifically defined as such in the IACLRs (see below), are deemed to be "contracting" carriers, and liable instead of the original contracting carrier for any part of the carriage they perform. So if a "successive" carrier is responsible, the claim must be made against it and **not against** the "contracting" carrier.

When are non-contracting air carriers liable?

Non-contracting actual carriers may also be liable. Occasionally, carriage is subcontracted to an airline which is neither a contracting nor a successive carrier, because it is an airline not mentioned in or contemplated by the contract of carriage. Liability of that "actual carrier" depends on which version of the IACLRs applies (discussed in detail below):

- The widely applicable Montreal Convention 1999 (which 119 countries are party to) expressly makes all such "actual" carriers liable for carriage they perform (and that liability is concurrent with the liability of the contracting carrier).

- Such "actual" carries are also liable under the Warsaw, Warsaw-Hague or Warsaw-Hague-MP4 Convention versions of the rules, BUT only when the Guadalajara Convention itself also applies to the carriage (that is, both countries concerned have also adopted it: and some 86 countries have). Thus, in most cases, "actual carriers" will also be liable under the IACLRs.

Who are "successive" carriers and when are they liable?

Successive air carriers are subcontracting airlines that are liable instead of contracting carriers. The injury or loss must occur on that airline. Provisions as to who are "successive" carriers and when a claim can be made against them are the same in all versions of the IACLRs.

More specifically, an airline is a "successive carrier" if it performs carriage which is part of a "single operation of undivided carriage" whether in the form of "single contract or a series of contracts" ("successive" carrier is described this way in Art 1(3) of all versions of the IACLRs).

Taking the example of the most common IACLR version applicable: the Montreal Convention 1999, Art 36 states:

"[Each successive] carrier which accepts passengers, baggage or cargo is subject to the rules set out in this Convention and is deemed to be one of the parties to the contract of carriage in so far as the contract deals with that part of the carriage which is performed under its supervision." [Art 36(1)]

It further provides that a passenger suffering injury or death can **only** claim against the airline performing the carriage when the accident occurred. (It will usually be clear on which airline an accident causing injury or death occurs). So:

"..the passenger or any person entitled to compensation in respect of him or her can take action only against the carrier which performed the carriage during which the accident or the delay occurred, save in the case where, by express agreement, the first carrier has assumed liability for the whole journey." [Art 36(2)]

Baggage and cargo claims have more options. The passenger whose baggage is damaged or lost is in a different position, as it won't always be clear on which carrier the damage occurred. That passenger can claim against several different airlines, notably the first and last.

"As regards baggage or cargo, the passenger or consignor will have a right of action against the first carrier, and the passenger or consignee who is entitled to delivery will have a right of action against the last carrier, and further, each may take action against the carrier which performed the carriage during which the destruction, loss, damage or delay took place. These carriers will be jointly and severally liable to the passenger or to the consignor or consignee." [Montreal Convention 1999, Art 36(3)]

Similar provision is made in the other three main versions of the IACLRs.

Who are "actual" carriers and when are they liable?

Subcontracting airlines liable under IACLRs also include actual air carriers. Airlines performing any part of the air carriage are all known as "performing" carriers; but to be liable under the IACLRs, they must either be "contracting" carriers, named in the contract; or contemplated by it (that is, carriers falling within the definition of a "successive carrier" and deemed to be "contracting" carriers: see above); or be what is called "actual carriers". This is a performing carrier (which is not also a contracting or successive carrier), when **either**:

- the most common Montreal Convention 1999 (to which 119 countries are parties) version of the IACLR applies (as it expressly provides for this category in Arts 39-48), **or,**

- the other main versions of the IACLR apply, provided the states between which the air carriage occurred are both also parties to the Guadalajara Convention (see: **in Australia**, CACLA, Sch 3 and **in NZ**, NZCAA, Sch 5).

The Guadalajara Convention 1961 (to which 86 countries are party), and the equivalent provisions in the Montreal Convention 1999 were designed to clear up any uncertainty as to the liability of such subcontracting but unnamed air carriers.

So virtually no commercial air carriage situation will involve "performing" **carriers who fall outside all these categories**. If they did, claims against such subcontracting airlines would be subject to general law principles and not the IACLRs (but if the flight involves **Australia**, some would anyway be subject to CACLA, Pt IV; and if it involves **NZ** or NZ residents, it may be within the scope of NZACA or NZCaGoA).

To be clearer about precisely who are "actual" carriers and what their liabilities are, let's look at, for example, the Montreal Convention 1999, Arts 39-48 (which closely resembles the terms used in the Guadalajara Convention). There, Art 39 states that when an airline, which is not a "successive" carrier (see above), performs part of carriage on the authority of a contracting carrier – that is, carriage is subcontracted without telling the passengers – it is an "actual carrier"; and then

"..both the contracting carrier and the actual carrier shall, except as otherwise provided ... be subject to the rules of this Convention [that is, liable for injury and loss etc], the former for the whole of the carriage contemplated in the contract, the latter solely for the carriage which it performs." [Art 40]

A contracting carrier is liable for anything its subcontracting "actual carrier" does (unlike for a "successive carrier" who is independently liable: see above), as acts and omissions of "actual" carriers (and their employees) – as regards the carriage they perform – are deemed to be those of the contracting carrier (by Art 41(1)). So contracting carriers can also be claimed against – making claiming compensation easier as such an "actual" carrier may be based in a foreign country.

Conversely, if the contracting carrier performs functions for the actual carrier e.g. ground handling, still within the scope of the overall air carriage, then such acts etc "shall, in relation to the carriage performed by the actual carrier, be deemed to be also those of the actual carrier" [Art 41(2)]. This is useful if suing the "actual carrier" and the loss occurred during e.g. groundhandling (although there may also be a separate claim made against the groundhandling entity, whoever it is).

Are contracting carriers liable when actual carriers are not?

Complications can arise if claims are made against actual air carriers. There is no contract between an "actual carrier" and the passenger (although the contracting carrier may state in the contract that the passenger has the same obligations to any actual carrier as it has to the contracting carrier).

Indeed, the actual carrier's liabilities to passengers are only as are stated in the applicable version of the IACLRs. The contracting carrier cannot e.g. agree to higher liability limits or waive defences etc on behalf of an actual carrier, unless the "actual carrier" has also agreed to this [Art 41(2)]. Passengers are unaware of the details of any agreements between contracting carriers and actual carriers. Occasionally this may make a difference, as where a contracting carrier, for example, agrees in its contract with the passenger:

- to higher compensation limits than the applicable IACLR allows (more important when versions of the IACLRs other than the Montreal Convention 1999 apply – as with older versions airlines sometimes voluntarily increase limits and waive defences in their contracts), or

- to the application of consumer protection law giving consumers protections and rights (as discussed in Chapter 3) in addition to what are in the IACLR.

So, the flight on the actual carrier may be subject to more restrictive terms (e.g. consumer protection laws may not apply) than for carriage on the contracting carrier. This would seem to be an additional reason for claiming against the contracting carrier alone, or jointly with the actual carrier, rather than claiming against the actual carrier alone.

What Rules Apply to Claims Against Employees etc?

Only some of the special liability rules apply to claims against airline employees and non-airline subcontractors. The IACLRs establish the liability of – and create a remedy against – airlines performing carriage the subject of a passenger's injury or baggage damage claim (though the wording differs for the different categories of carrier).

Also, the IACLRs do not exclude the possibility that a claim may be brought against a "servant [employee] or agent" of such a carrier (airline employees or ground-based subcontractors that are not airlines) for their acts or omissions causing loss or injury. Such persons would include those who perform incidental or related functions on behalf of the airline e.g. handling passengers, baggage or freight, cleaning aircraft etc.

Which parts of the IACLRs apply to employees etc?

All claims against employees, agents or non-airline subcontractors must be based on general law principles.: To make a claim against such persons, the injury or loss must be caused by an actionable "wrong" (for which the person claimed against is responsible under the general law), and not based on the IACLR, which is silent as to the bases for liability of "servants or agents" (as it only creates a strict liability of airlines). Thus, only remedies outside the IACLRs, such as in the tort of negligence, breach of statutory duty, breach of consumer protection laws etc can be relied on in claims against such airline employees, agents or non-airline subcontractors.

However, claims against employees etc are subject to other parts of the IACLRs. The Montreal Convention 1999, and all versions of the IACLRs allow the airline's "servant or agent" to

> "be entitled to avail themselves of the conditions and limits of liability which are applicable under this Convention to the carrier whose servant or agent they are."

These "conditions and limits" extend, at least, to matters like the two-year time limit for commencing legal proceedings and the compensation limits (probably the two most important conditions and limits), but there seems little application of any other IACLR requirements such as notices of losses etc.

In Which Courts Can Claims Be Made Against Airlines?

All air carriage claims under special rules must be made in courts situated in specified jurisdictions (places). It is easier to sue an airline in a "court" (Art 33) (not a tribunal: see Chapter 3) where the claimant lives – it is often also where the travel was contracted for.

Claims for airline liabilities under the IACLRs that are made against a carrier for passenger death, injury or delay, baggage (or even freight) loss, damage or delay, occurring during carriage must be made in courts at the "places" (jurisdictions or countries) specified in each version of the applicable rules.

For the Montreal Convention 1999 version, there is an extra option for making passenger injury or death claims: namely, in the territory of a state in which the passengers have their principal and permanent residence at the time of the accident, **but only provided** it is also a place:

- to or from which the carrier operates services for the carriage of passengers by air (either on its own aircraft or on another carrier's aircraft pursuant to a commercial agreement); and

- in which that carrier conducts its business of carriage of passengers by air from premises leased or owned by the carrier itself or by another carrier with which it has a commercial agreement (e.g. a code-share partner or agent)

Often, these two additional requirements are easily satisfied but when disputed, they may be quite difficult for a traveller to prove. If so, it is preferable to use traditional options (below).

For all IACLR versions, claims can be brought in a court:

1. at the place where the air carrier (being claimed against):

- has a place of business through which the carriage contract was made; or

- has its principal place of business; or

- is "domiciled " (for Montreal Convention 1999) or is "ordinarily resident" (for air carriage under all other versions of the IACLRs)

and:

2. at the place of destination of the carriage in question (for return carriage this would also be the place of departure).

This last option is easier for the traveller to determine, as it is the place of "ultimate destination" mentioned in the contract of carriage (as evidenced by the e-ticket or air waybill).

When "actual" carriers (unnamed subcontracting airlines: see above) are claimed against, any actual carrier may be sued either (a) in a court having jurisdiction at the place where the carrier has its domicile or principal place of business, or (b) place where the contracting carrier can be sued, (that is, at the places set out above).

Can claims be made in State or Territory courts in Australia?

Other laws allow claims under the special liability rules to be made in State and Territory courts. Finally, Australia is a federation (unlike NZ) and this raises an issue in respect of claims relating to international air carriage. Article 33 of the *Montreal Convention 1999* (and Art 28 in the other IACLR versions) refer to a "place" as meaning a nation (state or country), which is the federal jurisdiction, and not a state or territory jurisdictions within a federation. No reference is made in the IACLRs to jurisdictions within federations, but federal jurisdiction may be exercised by State and Territory courts in Australia, and, other laws allow such claims under treaties to be made in State or Territory courts in Australia.

These jurisdictional problems do not arise where domestic air carriage claims concern **purely internal flights within a State or territory**. Then, reliance should be had on the State or Territory legislation applying CACLA Pt IV to such flights.

4.2 AIR FREIGHT CARRIAGE CONTRACTS

Similar rules apply to claims in respect of freight loss or damage as apply to passenger injury and baggage. Air freight carriage is mentioned as air travellers sometimes send items of baggage and other goods unaccompanied by air freight. Most of the time, they just fill out the form and hope for the best. Airfreight carriage is a large and complex topic, so here we look at only those issues in air freight liabilities that are relevant to air travellers as shippers, especially if they differ from passenger carriage. Indeed some basic rules for freight carriage are the same as for all air carriage generally; and others are the same as for checked (registered) baggage. Very few rules are quite different.

Do Differences Exist Between Passenger and Freight Carriage Rules?
Freight air carriage is less regulated than passenger carriage. Traditionally, there has been less regulatory and licensing control (both government and IATA) over commercial air freight carriage than air passenger carriage, probably because of the greater public interest in the safety of passengers. However, some consumer protection principles apply to **consumer contracts** for carriage of goods, but as with passenger carriage, if the special liability rules apply, then they prevail over them.

Airline contracts for air freight or cargo carriage do differ somewhat to air passenger carriage contracts, as regards:

- use of air waybills (which perform the function as passenger tickets, but which have different documentary requirements);

- standard contract terms (though they still protect the airlines); and

- provisions for loss, damage, delay and disposal of non-delivered goods which exist in both the IACLRs and domestic law carrier liability rules and regulations.

Freight carriage is often further complicated by the fact that it may involve more than one air waybill (contractual document) as carriage is subcontracted and agents (wholesalers) as well as several different entities may be involved: the consignor (shipper), the freight forwarder (sometimes airlines act as freight forwarders); the airline(s) and the consignee (person taking delivery). If travellers send airfreight and collect it themselves, they are both the consignor and the consignee.

Do air carriage rules differ for passengers and freight?

IACLRs contain provisions applying to freight as well as to passengers. As with passenger carriage, some significant contractual terms as to liabilities are imposed by legislation (CACLA or NZCAA) giving effect to international conventions governing claims against airlines for freight damage, loss or delay. (However, more differences exist for domestic goods carriage liability in Australia and NZ: see below).

Rules that are basically the same for both passenger and freight carriage claims include e.g. when air carriage is "international", the definitions of "contracting", "successive" and" actual" carriers; the two-year time limits for making claims (see above); and some "notice" provisions. The rules determining which airlines can be claimed against: contracting, successive and actual are also the same, except for an additional rule that for checked (registered) baggage and freight claims, there is a right of the consignee to claim against the last carrier. So, aside from being able to claim against the airline performing the carriage when the destruction, loss, damage or delay occurred,

> "... the passenger or consignor will have a right of action against the first carrier, and the passenger or consignee who is entitled to delivery will have a right of action against the last carrier..." [Montreal Convention 1999, Art 36(3)].

Differences in the applicable rules do exist mainly as to:

- documentation required (but there are very few compared to the differences under the older rules) (see below);

- presumed liabilities imposed on airlines (see Chapter 6);

- defences of airlines to claims (see Chapter 6),

- claim formalities (see Chapter 6), as well as

- compensation monetary limits (see Chapter 6).

The 1999 Montreal Convention and Warsaw-Hague-MAP4 versions incorporate simplified documentation and procedures as well as higher air carrier compensation limits. (Specific differences exist in various versions of the IACLRs but they are less relevant today and only briefly mentioned here.)

What Are Air Waybills And Their Legal Significance?

Air waybills are like tickets and establish the contract of airfreight carriage. Legally, tickets and air waybills are quite similar. Contracts for carriage of air freight (cargo) derive mainly from documents called air waybills (AWBs) (or sometimes called cargo receipts). More specifically, they:

- set out the *variable terms* (who are the consignor, consignee, the contracting carrier, what is the departure, destination, the description of the goods);
- contain 'Conditions of Contract' (standard terms of which may vary from one carrier's air waybill to the next), as well as required notices relating to carrier liability and limits;
- incorporate (either expressly, by reference or by legislative requirement, various other documents containing other detailed standard terms (including Conditions of Carriage for Cargo and airline cargo tariffs); and
- are affected by consumer laws (except for air carriage claims), such as implied guarantees in the ACL (Australia) and NZCGA (NZ). Consumer laws usually don't assist businesses.

Which laws govern freight claims?

Most freight claims in respect of air carriage are based on the same laws as passenger claims. Freight claims are made for losses (including presumed thefts), damage or delays to goods arising in the course of air carriage and are governed:

- if on international flights, by a version of the IACLRs; or

- if on domestic flights: **in Australia**, by general law principles (as CACLA does not apply); and, **in NZ,** by NZCaGoA; (for those shippers who are consumers, supplemented by NZCGA and NZFTA: see below).

What is the legal status of an air waybill?

Documentary formalities for AWBs have recently been reduced, but the AWB's legal significance remains. Essentially, an air waybill (AWB) is the contractual document between the shipper and the air carrier. All four versions of IACLRs provide that the AWB (or cargo receipt or shipment record), is:

"... prima facie evidence of the conclusion of the contract, of the acceptance of the cargo and of the conditions of carriage mentioned therein".

Also, all four versions of the IACLRs provide (again almost identically) that:

"... any statements in the air waybill or the cargo receipt relating to the weight, dimensions, and packing of the cargo, as well as those relating to the number of packages, are prima facie evidence of the facts stated" [Montreal Convention 1999, Art 11(2)].

This is significant, as it means that:

- it is difficult to prove that anything written on the AWB is incorrect; and

- compensation for loss or injury to registered (checked) baggage and airfreight is based on its weight, under all versions of the IACLRs.

Do all air waybills have the same legal significance?

Domestic and international air waybills have similar legal significance. Although legal provisions differ, the rules and legal significance are similar.

In Australia, no legislative provisions specify the nature and legal effect of the AWB or cargo receipt – Pt IV of CACLA applies to non-international (domestic) air passenger carriage, but does not apply to domestic air freight carriage. So general law principles, including the common law apply to the terms in the contract, subject to consumer protection laws.

In NZ, the domestic carriage of cargo (and baggage) by air (and other transport modes) is governed exclusively by the NZCaGoA (discussed below), s 8 of which prescribes the various possible kinds of contracts of carriage e.g. "owner's risk", "limited carrier's risk"; "declared value risk" or on "declared terms" – which involve slightly different obligations.

What are electronic air waybills and when are they used?

Electronic air waybills are now common. Electronic air waybills (e-AWB) and use of electronic data interchange (EDI) – based on bilateral or multilateral agreements between airlines, freight forwarders and handling agents – is becoming pervasive and usually, a Cargo Receipt (or Shipment Record) is the only hard copy document in use.

The two main versions of the IACLRs that apply to most cases of international carriage of air freight and cargo, are the Montreal Convention 1999 (which came into force in Australia in 2009) and Warsaw-Hague-MAP4 (which came into force in 1998). Both recognize e-AWBs and allow for electronic (paperless) air carriage documentation to be used (with the consent of the shipper). This eliminates the need for documents to be handed over with any freight. Earlier versions of the IACLRs pre-date e-AWBs and EDI and don't mention them.

What AWB document requirements, liability notices exist?

Few documentary requirements exist for modern AWBs. As mentioned, the Montreal Convention 1999 and Warsaw-Hague-MAP4 are the two main versions of IACLRs applying to carriage of air freight and its documentation. Both simplify the details of cargo documentation and require little more than the delivery of an AWB (cargo receipt or shipment record) with an indication of places of departure and destination and the weight of the consignment (Arts 5-8), though there are slight differences between the rules that each establishes. (Requirements were stricter under earlier IACLR versions.)

Failure to meet documentary requirements for freight carriage has no consequences at all under these two most recent and common versions of the IACLRs (unlike older IACLR versions where omitting a detail was a ground for excluding compensation limits meaning that claimants could obtain unlimited compensation: see below).

The Montreal Convention 1999 and the Warsaw-Hague-MAP4 versions of the IACLRs no longer require that AWBs and cargo receipts display a statement or **notice** that the air carriage is subject to the IACLRs and compensation limits. (Failure to include this notice was another ground for claimants being able to avoid compensation limits when the older versions of the IACLRs applied to the carriage).

TERMS AND CONDITIONS IN AIR FREIGHT CARRIAGE CONTRACTS

Terms in air freight and air passenger contracts are similar. As with air tickets, there are **variable terms** in air freight contracts that describe the individual shipper, the freight, the airline(s) doing the carrying, and the departure and destination places for the freight carriage. As with air tickets, these variable terms help determine who can claim, who is claimed against, and if the carriage is international or domestic.

Standard terms and conditions are also incorporated in and apply to shippers and freight (see below), but there are specific differences between air freight and air passenger contracts relating to liabilities, compensation limits and notices for claims under the IACLRs.

Which Documents Make Up The Air Freight Contract?

Air freight contracts consist of several documents. Aside from when only electronic air waybills (e-AWB) and electronic data exchange (EDI) are used, the initial document signed by the shipper or its agent when the shipment is accepted by the air carrier or freight forwarder is an air waybill (AWB), (Cargo Receipt or Shipment Record) or Shippers Instructions. It contains the variable terms relating to the shipment (often given online by registered users) (see above).

The AWB documents also contain a standard liability limitation **notice** and applicable "Conditions of Contract" (see below). Like the air ticket, references in the AWB incorporate various other documents into the contract, notably the air carrier's "General Conditions of Carriage" (GCC) for Cargo (freight). All such documents should be read together to try to understand the contract, despite possible inconsistencies.

There are several other documents (some virtually unobtainable e.g. the airline's tariffs) that are also purportedly incorporated into the contract, but, they are usually less relevant to individual contracts of air freight carriage.

Documents used and precise terms change from time to time and may differ from one airline to another.

What Are The Main Features Of Freight Carriage Contracts?

Standard terms and conditions are contained in air freight carriage contracts. Detailed General Conditions of Carriage (GCC) for cargo are incorporated into the freight carriage contract by express reference in the Shippers Instructions (Cargo Receipt, Shipment Record or air waybill itself), which is usually signed by the shipper (consignor) at the time freight is "accepted" (often physically, but also electronically) by the air carrier or its forwarding agent.

The GCC set out most of the airline's standard terms for the air carriage (which prevail over the "Conditions of Contract" set out on the Shippers Instructions (Shipment Record, Cargo Receipt or AWB). For example, the Qantas GCC for Cargo International, states that the carriage is subject to:

- the carrier's rules, regulations and tariffs (clause 2.7) as well as the applicable laws including the relevant conventions and/or protocols and the terms and conditions of any e-freight agreement entered into as regards electronic data interchange (EDI) (clause 2.2.3);

- the limitation of carrier liability to 19 SDRs per kilogram, unless otherwise expressly stated, for example in cargo carriage under a charter contract which will take precedence over the Qantas GCC cargo (clause 2.5, which applies to cargo carriage not governed by any IACLRs based on those conventions and/or protocols in clauses 2.2 – 2.3; but the terminology is ambiguous); and

- the statement that no servant or agent of the carrier has the authority to waive any of the conditions of carriage (clause 2.8).

Which law applies to the air freight contract?

Air freight carriage contracts can specify the law that applies to some claims. The first issue for any contract is: which law applies? Usually it is the law of the place where the claim is made, but the contract may specify otherwise. A typical example is the Qantas Airways GCC for Cargo International. It applies to all international and to domestic cargo carriage (clause 2.1), but only international carriage is subject to the applicable IACLRs contained in CACLA; while domestic air freight carriage is stated to be governed by Australian federal and state laws (CACLA does not apply to domestic freight carriage). However, the GCC conditions are expressly:

"to be interpreted in accordance with the law of New South Wales" (clause 16).

It is also stated in the Qantas GCC for Cargo (although probably unnecessarily as it merely declares the situation under the general law) that:

- the conditions of carriage apply to the extent that they are not overridden by laws or regulations (clause 14) and

- the contract and GCC is subject to the *Competition and Consumer Act 2010* (Cth) including the ACL, "to the extent that the Act implies a warranty in this contract and prevents the exclusion, restriction or modification of any such warranty" (otherwise most liabilities may be and are excluded by terms in the contact) (clause 17) (see below); and

- the conditions of carriage apply except as provided in the "applicable Convention" which is the conventions and protocols establishing the various IACLRs (defined in clause 1.3).

More controversially, there is a "catch-all" liability exclusion clause, although it is unclear how much effect this has: Qantas GCC, clause 2.9 maintains the "full force and effect" of

"[a]ll the rights, immunities and exemptions from liability in these conditions ... in all circumstances and notwithstanding any breach ... by [the] carrier or any other person entitled to benefit from such provisions and irrespective of whether such may constitute a fundamental breach of contract or a breach of a fundamental term".

The intent of this clause is to seek to rely on all liability exemption clauses, whether or not there has been a fundamental breach of contract (a total failure to perform the contract) although it may also set up some form of estoppel. Again it is probably unnecessary to include this clause, as of course, the airline will rely on whatever immunities and exclusions of liability that exist under the law. On the other hand, the clause minimizes any application of legislation governing unfair contract terms and misleading and deceptive statements to the extent possible, as regards consumer transactions and business contracts.

What is the effect of liability exclusion clauses in air freight contracts?

Liability exclusion clauses can have some effect. Aside from the specific exemption of airline liability for loss or damage of freight or baggage, which is proved to have **inherent defects** (provided for in both CACLA and NZCaGoA: see below), there are numerous liability exclusion clauses in air carriage contracts, (including that mentioned in the paragraph above).

However, the effect of such liability exclusion clauses in contracts has been reduced by legislation and court decisions.

First, the IACLRs nullify terms in international air carriage contracts purporting to exclude or limit the airline liabilities expressly provided for in the IACLRs (see below). However, some liability exclusion or limitation clauses in the air freight carriage contract will apply to obligations or liabilities that are outside the scope of the airline liabilities for international air carriage imposed by the IACLRs. Furthermore, the IACLRs and the nullifying provision do not apply to domestic air freight carriage **within Australia**, which is governed by the general law and common law; and **within NZ**, domestic air freight carriage is governed by the NZCaGoA in NZ: see above).

Second, general law and common law principles minimize the effect of all such contractual terms that purport to limit or exclude air carrier liability in contracts of air cargo carriage in the airline's GCC. In Australia, the High Court has consistently adopted a practical attitude to liability exclusion clauses, saying that their application is a matter of construction having regard to the particular circumstances of the case. Courts generally restrict the application of liability exclusion clauses, interpreting them against the interests of the entity relying on the exclusion. The main exceptions are ordinary commercial contracts where parties are of equal bargaining power, or perhaps when consumers are otherwise protected from liability exemption clauses by e.g. consumer protection legislation.

Third, a quite theoretical argument could be raised, at least in consumer transactions, that given the complex nature of air carriage documentation and the fact that the document signed is described as a shipping record (or something else: see above), the document signed by the shipper-consumer was not a contractual document but a receipt, and the shipper did not see, was not aware of and did not accept the liability exemption clauses in other documents, such as the airline's GCC.

Fourth, and this may be quite unusual, if persons have been induced to enter a contract by a misrepresentation, especially if the nature or effect of a liability exclusion clause has been misrepresented, they are not necessarily bound by that contract, and any liability exclusion clauses it contains.

Do implied consumer guarantees affect freight contracts?

Implied consumer guarantees apply only to consumer transactions. As previously discussed (in Chapter 3), **in Australia**, the ACL and **in NZ**, the NZCGA imply consumer protection guarantees into air cargo carriage contracts involving consumers (but not commercial shipping contracts: see e.g. ACL, s 63). Included are guarantees to exercise due care, to supply services within a reasonable time, and that are reasonably fit for purpose. Also, air carriage consumers (e.g. shippers) are protected from improper business practices such as misleading or deceptive statements or conduct, unfair contract terms etc by the ACL and NZFTA.

Those guarantees and other statutory protections cannot be contracted out of by any liability exclusion or limitation clauses in the air carriage contract. Indeed, it is prohibited to exclude implied guarantees in consumer contracts for the sale of goods or services (if acquired for personal, domestic or household use), at least to the extent to which such guarantees operate to protect affected persons and consumers contracting with air cargo carriers (e.g. sometimes they only require that a refund be given).

What Are The Main Terms On Which Airlines Carry Freight?

Rights and obligations of airlines and shippers are specified in the carriage contract. An airline's General Conditions of Carriage for cargo (freight) prescribe the terms upon which cargo is accepted and carried, as well as certain other obligations of the carrier, consignor (shipper), consignee. The Qantas Airways (QF), "Conditions of Carriage for Cargo – International" (GCC) which are available on the airline's website, is again used as a typical example.

Does the airline have an obligation to carry?

Air freight carriage contracts minimize airline obligations. The extent of their obligations is as follows:

(a) Airlines may refuse to carry of freight at their discretion. The QF GCC states that the airline has a right

"to refuse carriage of cargo in its own absolute discretion ... without assuming any liability" (clause 3.2).

The airline "reserves the right to inspect the packaging and contents" (clause 3.11). It is also authorised to advance the payment of any duties, taxes or charges and to make any disbursements with respect to any cargo and the shipper and consignee are stated to be jointly and severally liable for these (clause 6.2). Special requirements exist if airlines accept to carry perishables and dangerous goods (clause 3.7, 3.9).

(b) Freight is carried only in accordance with regulations and if space is available. Airlines only agree to transport the described freight

"subject to the availability of suitable equipment and space ... [and] unless otherwise excluded by carrier's regulations"

which "regulations" are not defined in the GCC but would include the airline's dangerous goods regulations – and air carriage will only occur if goods are suitably packed and documented as required (clause 3.1, 3.3).

(c) Air carriage may be subcontracted. It is stated that airlines and even any subcontractor are also

"entitled to subcontract on any carriage or part thereof"

and all liability exclusion and limitation clauses extend to such persons, their subcontractors and employees (for liability exclusion discussion, see above) (clause 10.1, 10.2).

What are the shipper's obligations and rights?

Shippers have several important obligations and few rights under air carriage contracts. Non-compliance with these shipper obligations may mean airline liabilities are nullified and may even make shippers liable to the airlines.

(a) Shippers agree to comply with applicable laws, including those relating to customs, packing, carriage or delivery of cargo; and in this context, the shipper must "indemnify carrier against any damage occasioned by the failure of the shipper to comply with this provision" (clause 6.1.1),

and a carrier

"shall not be liable for refusing to carry any shipment if carrier reasonably determines in good faith that such refusal is required by any applicable law, government regulation, demand, order or requirement" (clause 6.1.2).

(b) Standard documentary practices are required, as set out in the Qantas Airways GCC for:

- the proper preparation and completion of an air waybill (AWB) or a "shipment record", which is to be delivered "simultaneously with the acceptance of cargo" (clause 4.1), and

- the responsibilities of the shippers for the correctness of details provided (clause 4.5).

Shippers should make note on the AWB, of any defects, but if this is not done and there is a defect in condition or packing of the goods, the air carrier may insert a statement to that effect on the AWB or shipment record (para 4.3). Otherwise, no agent, servant or representative of the airline has authority to alter, modify or waive any provision of the contract or of the conditions (clause 14).

(c) Shippers do maintain some control over the freight they send, and the shipper or its agent has the right

- to alter, in writing, delivery instructions in respect of the whole of the cargo under any single air waybill at any time until the consignee takes possession or requests delivery or otherwise shows acceptance of the cargo (clause 7.1, 7.4), provided it does not prejudice the carrier or other shippers; and

- at its own expense, [to] dispose of the cargo by withdrawing it at the airport of departure or destination; stopping it in the course of the journey; having it delivered to a person other than the named consignee; or by requiring it to be returned to the airport of departure (clause 7.2).

(d) Shippers also guarantee payment of all unpaid rates and charges, advances and disbursements made by the airline, who has a lien on cargo and any documents, as well as a right to sell them, by public auction, to obtain compensation for any amounts unpaid. (clause 5.1-5.5). More controversial is the provision affecting the **rights of the consignee**, who has not signed the contract and is not a party to it, which states:

> "[b]y taking delivery or exercising any other right arising from the contract of carriage, the consignee agrees to pay such amounts." (clause 5.5).

What happens if problems prevent delivery of the carriage?

The airline also has wide powers to deal with the freight, but has minimal liabilities to the shipper or consignee under the contract. An airline, may (by clause 6.3.2, 6.3.3)

- "without notice substitute alternate carriers or any other means of carriage"; and

- "reserves the right without notice, to cancel, terminate, divert, postpone, delay or advance any flight, or the further carriage of any cargo, or to proceed with any flight without all or any part of cargo, in its own absolute discretion".

Airlines limit their liabilities to anyone if problems arise from cancellation, diversion or delay: for example, if an airline substitutes slower or non-refrigerated carriage for perishable goods (subject to any express contractual terms).

(a) The airline "undertakes to carry the cargo with reasonable dispatch", but this duty is much qualified by other contract terms limiting the airline's obligations and liabilities (see above for effect of liability exemption clauses):

- the airline assumes no obligation to carry cargo by any specified aircraft or over any particular route or routes, or to make connections at any point according to any particular schedule"

- the "[t]imes shown in carrier's timetables or elsewhere are approximate and not guaranteed and form no part of the contract of carriage", and

- the airline is expressly authorised to deviate from routes of the shipment stated on the face of the air waybill (and no employee, agent or representative of the carrier is authorised to bind the carrier as to dates or times of departure or arrival)."

(b) The airline is usually not liable "in the event the carriage of any shipment is so cancelled, diverted, postponed, delayed, advanced or terminated",

- shall "not be under any liability with respect thereto" and

- has a right to prioritise cargo carriage and delivery, and in exercising its right, the airline "may decide to remove any articles from a shipment, at any time or place whatsoever, and to proceed with the flight without them ... [and] will not be liable to shipper or consignee or to any other party for any consequences".

(c) If the air carriage is terminated, delivery of freight is deemed to be completed by delivery to a transfer agent (for transfer or delivery), or by placing it in storage. The airline has no liability except to give proper notice to the shipper or the consignee. If a carrier forwards the shipment for onward carriage, the costs of doing so attaches to the cargo (clause 6.3.4 - 6.3.5) and must be paid.

(d) The airline may, if necessary, suspend and hold the shipment at any place for any purpose at any time. Airlines may, provided they give notice to the shipper at the address stated in the air waybill or shipment record, store the shipment for and at the expense of the shipper in any warehouse or other available place, with the customs authorities, or another transportation service for onward carriage to the consignee. Furthermore, the shipper

"shall indemnify [the] carrier against any expense or risk so incurred" (clause 6.4).

What delivery obligations are owed by airlines and consignees?

Airlines owe few obligations in respect of freight delivery, but consignees do owe obligations to the airline.

(a) The airline is obliged to notify, by ordinary methods, the consignee and any other person whom the carrier has agreed to notify "as evidenced in the air waybill or shipment record" (but has no liability for non-receipt or delay of the notice) (clause 8.1)

(b) Delivery may only be made to the consignee or other person producing the shipper's authority for delivery (but the airline is under no obligation to inquire into the validity of the authority) (clause 8.2).

Actual, physical delivery of the cargo to the consignee is not required. By the Qantas Airways GCC, clause 8.2.1 - 8.2.3, delivery is deemed to occur when

- the consignee or agent is given the carrier's authorisation to obtain release of the shipment;

- the shipment has been delivered to customs or other government authorities as required by law; or

- when the consignee or its agent takes delivery of the shipment.

(c) A consignee must accept delivery of and collect the freight at the destination airport (clause 8.3). Receipt of freight without complaint is *prima facie* evidence that the shipment has been delivered in good condition and in accordance with the contract of carriage (clause 8.4).

(d) By accepting delivery of the air waybill and/or shipment, the consignee becomes liable, jointly and severally with the shipper, to pay all costs and charges in connection with the carriage and the carrier may make delivery conditional upon the payment of the costs and charges (clause 8.7).

(e) Consignees are penalised for refusal or failure to take delivery of freight, for example, if perishable goods were delayed and lost, there are various consequences:

- if the shipper has given any instructions on the face of the air waybill or shipment record, then the carrier is to "endeavour to comply" with them (clause 8.5.1); or

- the carrier must notify the shipper and seek its instructions and if none are received within 30 days (immediately in the case of perishables), the shipment may be sold, destroyed or abandoned by the carrier and the shipper will be liable for all charges and related expenses (clause 8.5.2 – 8.5.3).

Perishable freight shipments which are delayed, unclaimed or refused at the place of delivery, may be dealt with immediately at the sole discretion of the carrier (clause 8.6.1), for example by sale. In the event of a sale (in any circumstances), the carrier may pay all its expenses, charges and advances out of its proceeds and merely account to the shipper for any balance (clause 8.6.2).

Do IACLRs Affect Airlines' Conditions of Carriage For Cargo?

When IACLRs apply, they override some contractual terms. For international air freight carriage, an airline's Conditions of Carriage (GCC) – as discussed above – are subject to the applicable version of the IACLRs. However, the IACLRs only concern airline liability for loss, damage or delay **"taking place during the carriage by air"** (Art 18). So claims for other loss or damage, or losses caused in other ways, are not within the application of the IACLRs. They are subject to the other terms and conditions in the contract of carriage and the general law.

Carriage contracts state that the IACLRs prevail, if there is a conflict. It is expressly stated in the Qantas Airways GCC for Cargo International, which are typical of most airlines' conditions of carriage for cargo, that they are subject to six possibly "applicable Conventions" (clause 1.3), each of which establishes a version of the IACLRs (although two versions, marked # are of no effect in Australia).

Any applicable IACLRs take precedence over any inconsistent provisions in the GCCs and any airline rights or liability exclusion clauses set out there, by virtue of:

- Arts 23 and 32 of the Warsaw Convention (and where, unlike subsequent liability regimes, there is no exception in respect of "inherent defect, quality or vice of the cargo carried", so airlines cannot exclude liability for this);

- Art 23(1) of the Warsaw-Hague Convention (but this "shall not apply to provisions governing loss or damage resulting from the inherent defect, quality or vice of the cargo carried". This allows air carriers to exclude their liability in this respect: Art 23(2));

- Arts 23 and 32 – 33 of the Warsaw-Hague-MAP1 Convention (#Australia is not a party nor acceded to this Protocol, which otherwise came into force generally on 15 February 1996);*

- Arts 23 and 32 – 33 of the Warsaw-Hague-MAP2 Convention (#Australia is not a party nor acceded to this Protocol, which otherwise came into force generally on 15 February 1996);*

- Art 23(1) and 32 – 33 of the Warsaw-Hague-MAP4 Convention (Art 23(1) "shall not apply to provisions governing loss or damage resulting from the inherent defect, quality or vice of the cargo carried". This allows air carriers to exclude their liability in this respect"); and

- Arts 26 – 27 of the Montreal Convention 1999 (where Art 18(2)(a) specifically excludes the air carrier's liability in respect of inherent defect, quality or vice of cargo, enabling the contract of carriage to exclude carrier liability in this respect).

The third and fourth options above (marked #) are not part of Australian law, although an Australian (or other) airline transporting freight between two states where one or the other of those options is, in fact, the latest version of the IACLRs in force, would be subject to the provisions in that version.

Note that the other four versions do permit airlines to contract out of liability for "inherent defect, quality or vice of the cargo", and the Montreal Convention 1999 goes further by expressly excluding any airline liability for such inherent defects. So, there is no need to contract out of it, although the Qantas GCC for cargo does so anyway (clause 12.3). Other aspects of the freight carriage liabilities of airlines are discussed in Chapter 6-7.

5. Passengers: Injury or Death Claims

Most passenger injury claims are governed by the special liability rules. Compensation claims by air travellers for injury or death arise almost inevitably out of "commercial" air carriage (see Chapter 2), which is governed, **for Australia**, by the IACLRs and CACLA; and **for NZ**, by the IACLRs and NZCAA, (but NZACA if in domestic air carriage). IACLRs apply only to international air carriage, but in Australia, equivalent provisions in CACLA apply to domestic air carriage claims.

Private air carriage is not subject to any version of the IACLRs – some private domestic air carriage, **in Australia**, is governed by the general law and **in NZ**, by the same local legislation (especially the NZACA) that governs commercial domestic air carriage. Indeed, some boundaries between "commercial" and "private" (see Chapter 2) are a little vague.

What Claims Are Covered by the IACLRs?

IACLRs only cover claims for injury occurring during air carriage. All versions of the IACLRs give passengers suffering death or injury during air carriage independent statutory remedies against airlines, but only for claims falling within the scope of, and when made in accordance with, the applicable version of the IACLRs. Failure to comply with such rules and the procedures they embody, is fatal to the claim.

We have already discussed (in Chapter 2):

- who can make claims (not airline staff etc); and

- against which airlines claims can be made; and

- that claims must be made in certain countries; and

- that claims must be made in "courts" (unless arbitration is agreed).

Other rules restrict claims for compensation, for example the need to comply the precise wording of provisions in the applicable IACLR's.

In broad terms, the IACLR relating to passenger baggage (loss, damage and delay: discussed below) resemble the rules relating to freight (loss, damage and delay) but there are individual differences in the details (see Chapter 6). However, as regards passenger claims, the precise wording of the rules differs according to whether the claims are for

- passenger injury or death;

- baggage loss or damage; or

- delay of passengers or baggage.

Also, although the Montreal Convention 1999 applies very widely, different versions of the IACLRs may apply to air carriage between different countries. (Which version applies is discussed in Chapter 2 – essentially the latest version in force in both the country of departure and the country of ultimate destination.). In the different versions of the IACLRs, airline liabilities differ slightly according to the precise wording and slightly different terms used in each version (see below).

Additionally, passenger claims against airlines are subject to various procedural restrictions found in each version of the IACLRs, such as time limits, notices requirements, claim procedures (see below).

However, other matters of procedure (e.g. how claims are brought, what injuries damages can be awarded for) are governed by the law of the place where the legal action is commenced. So the jurisdiction where legal proceedings are brought may be important, although for most claimants, only one of the jurisdictions specified in the applicable IACLRs will be convenient to pursue the claim (see Chapter 4).

When Is Air Carriage "International" So That IACLRs Apply?

IACLRs apply only to "international" air carriage. The difference between international and non-international (domestic) air carriage, and also how to distinguish between them was more fully discussed in Chapter 2. Essentially, IACLRs apply to air carriage when the parties to the air carriage contract, see it as a "single operation" of air carriage (even if several air carriage contracts are involved):

- with a place of departure and ultimate destination in the same state, provided there is an agreed stopping place in another country; and

- with places of departure and ultimate destination in two different states, both being parties to a convention setting up the IACLRs.

Flights involving a stop in a foreign country are almost always "international" and governed by one or another version of the IACLRs (that is, **for Australia**, CACLA Pts 1A to III; and **for NZ**, NZCAA Pt 9A). The only exception (and it can be almost ignored for present purposes) is if one or both countries had not ratified any version at all of the IACLRs (or renounced any version it was party to). Then, the non-international (domestic) rules apply along with any relevant terms in the contract.

Which Rules Apply to Non-International (Domestic) Carriage?

Domestic flight claims are not always subject to same rules as international flight claims. Almost the same rules apply to international and domestic air passenger claims **in Australia**, (so they are discussed together). However, in respect of air accidents **in NZ**, completely different rules apply to personal injury claims, whether made by NZ residents or non-residents, as there is an accident compensation scheme which includes domestic air passenger personal injury claims.

In summary:

- **for Australia**, the non-international (and domestic) rules in CACLA, Pt IV apply in most cases when the IACLRs do not, (excluded from Pt IV are claims for delay of passengers or baggage, and all claims as to freight: see Chapters 6-7); and

- **for NZ**, when NZCAA Pt 9A (international) does not apply, the following rules do: NZACA for death and personal injury; [NZCAA Pt 9B for passenger *delay* (see below and Chapter 7); NZCaGoA for loss or damage to goods, including baggage and freight) and the general law as regards delay of goods (baggage and freight) (discussed in Chapter 3)].

It is not intended here to discuss the details of NZ accident claims law under NZ general law, notably the NZACA. Specialist advice should be sought to assist with such claims.

When Are Airlines Liable for Passenger Injury or Death?

That the liability of airlines is presumed is the essence of the IACLR liability scheme. This means that if injury occurs in the prescribed manner, wrongdoing by an airline or its staff is presumed and need not be proved by a claimant (although some airline defences do exist).

Where passenger injury or death arises from an accident in the course of any commercial air carriage, airlines are presumed to be liable, based on either:

(a) one of the four main versions of the IACLRs (for international carriage); or

(b) each country's domestic (non-international) rules.

Under all versions of these rules, international and domestic, much of the terminology and many rules are similar, although some differences exist, notably as to compensation limits.

One significant difference is that it is only under the (most recent) Montreal Convention 1999 version of the IACLRs that in the case of passenger death or injury, air carriers must, if required by national law, **make advance payments** "to meet immediate economic needs", without delay and without recognition of liability, to all natural persons entitled to claim compensation [Art 28]. However, neither Australian nor NZ law require this (at the time of writing).

When is airline liability "presumed" and when is it "absolute"?

Exceptionally some airline liability is absolute. Liability of airlines under all IACLRs is usually "presumed" except that under the newest version (that is, based on the Montreal Convention 1999), liability is "absolute" but only for passenger death or bodily injury claims of up to

SDR 113,100: i.e. approx AUD 200,800 and NZD 211,800 (as at end 2014). (By 2016 this figure will likely be updated by 12%-14% under a 5-yearly review provided for in Art 24 of the Montreal Convention 1999.)

But claims for passenger injury or death above that amount are subject to "presumed" airline liability under Art 17. If liability is "absolute", claims are less often opposed by the airlines. If passengers have a claim under the IACLRs, they never have to prove the airline was negligent or at fault, and:

- **presumed liability** means that the airline still may have a defence to the claim, if it can prove no fault or negligence on its part, but
- **absolute liability** means that liability is presumed and there are no airline defences possible.

But in both cases, an airline can also reduce its liability in part, if it can prove that the passengers' negligence or other faulty conduct contributed to their own injuries — that is, there was contributory negligence by the passenger.

How does wording in IACLRs restrict passenger claims?

IACLR liabilities are nonetheless restricted by specific conditions. To be precise, airline liability under the IACLRs, Art 17 (in all versions) is for "death or bodily injury", but only if it is caused by an "accident" and it takes place either on board the aircraft, or, in the course of "any of the operations of embarking or disembarking".

For international air carriage, claims everywhere (including in Australia and NZ) are made under the IACLR, Art 17 (in all versions of the rules).

Non-international (domestic) air carriage claims, are based on essentially the same terminology and concepts, and are made:

- **in Australia**, under s 28 of the *Civil Aviation (Carriers' Liability) Act 1959* (Cth), Pt IV, whereas
- **in NZ**, under NZACA, ss 20,22 (although it refers to "personal" injury, and otherwise quite different terminology is used).

There is often little argument that the claim is within the terminology used, but judicial decisions as to the meaning of these IACLR terms have prevented some claimants from recovering compensation (see below). If there is no right to claim under these rules, then usually no other claim is possible as the "exclusivity" of remedies under the rules, has been interpreted to mean that no claim at all can be brought apart from under the applicable rules.

What is "bodily injury"? Does it include mental anguish?

Slightly different words are used in different versions of the IACLRs and precise meanings have been controversial. In this context, there is no dispute over the meaning of "death", (the only difficulty may be in proving that it occurred during air carriage).

Airlines are also liable for damage sustained in the case of the "bodily injury" of a passenger (although the words "wounding ... or any other bodily injury suffered by a passenger" are used in all the older versions of the IACLRs, Art 17). But, as regards non-international (domestic) air carriage, seemingly more general wording is used: **in Australia**, CACLA, Pt IV, s 28, uses "any bodily injury"; whereas **in NZ**, "personal injury" clearly encompassing mental anguish, is used in the NZACA.

But what exactly is "bodily injury"? In 2002, *King v Bristow Helicopters Ltd*, the House of Lords in the UK, said that bodily injury was a change in part or parts of the body which was sufficiently serious to be capable of being called an "injury". Would this include sickness caused from defective airline food? It is undecided, but probably it would, if effects were severe. However, the words do not include purely emotional upset such as annoyance, distress or mental anguish.

It is still uncertain if compensation for psychological trauma is possible. Can a claim ever be made for mental trauma under the IACLRs and CACLA, Pt IV, where the expression "bodily injury" is used? There are quite a few judicial decisions on this point and the expression "wounding ... or other bodily injury" has been given a wide enough meaning to include mental trauma (nervous shock) **but only if it is linked with some physical injury**. For example, the Federal Court considered that a passenger could recover damages for mental anguish resulting from efforts to evacuate an aircraft with an engine on fire after an emergency landing. Also, both common law and legislation in Australia recognise that as a general rule, mental injuries are compensable in "personal injury" actions, if associated with physical injury, but it is uncertain whether or not an "association" is easier to prove than a "link". (If so, claims concerning domestic flights made by persons other than the passenger e.g. by a passenger's relatives, for their own injuries, may include associated mental injury, as those claims need not be based on CACLA, Pt IV).

However, it is still controversial if a passenger's own mental suffering when not caused by, linked or associated with physical injury, or even the mental suffering of a close relative (e.g. a spouse or parent waiting at an airport for a missing aircraft) witnessing an accident, would be compensated without any closely associated physical injury; indeed some of the Australian state 'civil liability' legislative provisions expressly preclude recovery for pure mental harm if prevented "under any other written or unwritten law" [e.g. s 30(4) *Civil Liability Act* 2002 (NSW)]. Detailed professional advice should be obtained on this difficult issue.

What does "accident" mean? Must it be external to a passenger?

Even the meaning of the term "accident" has been subject to argument. The term "accident" is not defined anywhere in the IACLRs, (although **for NZ** domestic flight injuries, it is defined, for the purposes of the NZACA, in s 25, which is lengthy and complex, but essentially refers to a specific event or series of events involving the application of force or sudden movement external to the body, or twisting of the body; as well as the inhalation, ingestion of solids, liquids, gas, bacteria etc, absorption of chemicals, exposure to temperature, burns etc. This NZACA definition is helpful, but is not determinative for claims under the IACLRs, Art 17, or under CACLA, s 28. Various judicial decisions on this term in the USA and in Europe have helped clarify the meaning to be used in this context.

Essentially, an **"accident" includes most unexpected or unusual events that are external to the passenger.** This could, although decisions are difficult to reconcile in extreme cases, include poor quality cabin air causing a passenger to contract pneumonia, but not the effects of aircraft depressurisation on a passenger's ears (unless proved that it involved an abnormal operation of the aircraft). The aggravation of a pre-existing medical condition by flying is not an "accident", nor is the onset of deep vein thrombosis (DVT), as there is no "accident" (in the sense of an unexpected abnormal event) within the meaning of Art 17. Although a hijacking, terrorist attack or bomb scare would not normally be considered an "accident", an indecent assault by another passenger and turbulent weather conditions have both been regarded as "accidents", but not a bumpy landing. Circumstances of such events are also important and controversy remains except in obvious cases.

An accident can also arise out of the negligent performance of routine operational procedures such as aircraft cleaning, although in a significant UK case in 2010 of *Barclay v British Airways plc*, it was held not to be an accident to fall after slipping on a plastic strip running under the seats covering the seat-fix tracking, which was a standard fitting on the aircraft and was secured to the floor of the aircraft. Likewise, in 2010, in *Brannock v Jetstar Airways Pty Limited*, an 84 year old man tripping on stairs after being given arguably inadequate embarkation instructions was held not to be an accident.

If there is no "accident" within the restricted meaning given to these words in Art 17 of the IACLRs, there is no claim under the IACLRs. Nor would there be any other grounds for a claim for compensation, as common law and statutory-based remedies are not usually available as an alternative, given the very broad interpretation of the "exclusivity" provisions in the IACLR. This extreme interpretation of "exclusivity" should be more controversial than it has been, although it has also been found inapplicable as regards domestic air carriage in Australia.

When can airlines avoid liability for "accidents"?

Some events may be "accidents" but there is no liability as they are not the responsibility of the airline, e.g. when an airline defence of "no negligence" is available, which is not the case if airline liability is "absolute" – that is, when the Montreal Convention 1999 version of the IACLRs applies and claims are for less than 113,100 SDRs. Claims under other versions of the rules are different. For example, baggage falling out of an overhead locker onto a passenger's head during landing may be an "accident", but if the airline has made appropriate announcements warning passengers to take care of such baggage, it may have a defence of "no negligence" (see below). Then it is not necessarily an injury for which the airline is responsible, as such baggage is also in the custody and control of passengers – unlike when a cabin attendant dropped a credit card machine on a passenger's head, which did result in airline liability.

What does "any of the operations of embarking or disembarking" mean?

Airline presumed liability is restricted geographically and temporally. The events causing an injury are only within the IACLRs, Art 17 if they take place "on board the aircraft or in the course of any of the operations of embarking or disembarking" (Art 17). When a passenger is "on board" an aircraft is an uncontroversial question of fact – are you on the aircraft or not – but the words: "in the course of any of the operations of embarking or disembarking", give rise to more uncertainty and different court decisions are not always easy to reconcile.

Slipping while queuing at a check-in counter has been held not to be within the process of embarkation, as embarkation had not begun (although this is arguable as airlines or their agents do sometimes control the check-in" waiting area). But these words may include when passengers queue up to wait for security or baggage checks, prior to boarding. Factors to consider are:

- the extent of the carrier's control over the passenger;

- the activity being performed by the passenger; and

- the location of the passenger when the injury was sustained.

Indeed, falling down an escalator in the airport on the way to the area occupied by Immigration Control, Baggage Claim and Customs or falling in a hallway in transit between two different carriers, have both been held to be outside the process of "disembarking"; although falling as a result of the sudden movement of a step just after actually exiting a small aircraft has been held to be an accident within the scope of "disembarking". Airline control seems to be a critical factor.

If the injury was not caused while actually in the aircraft during air carriage, or while embarking or disembarking, but the airline or airport staff were responsible e.g. negligent, then it would seem logical that civil claims not based on the IACLRs could be made against the entity or person at fault, even if an airline employee, and the "exclusivity" principle in the IACLRs should not preclude a claim being made for compensation.

What Are Compensation Limits For Injury Or Death?

Diverse limits on compensation for presumed/absolute airline liability exist for injury or death claims. Depending on which version of the IACLRs or domestic rules applies, compensation limits range from some AUD30,000 to an unlimited amount. The maximum compensation limits for death and bodily injury claims, are:

1. **Montreal Convention 1999**: 113,100 SDRs (absolute liability) (approx. AUD215,000) (adjusted upwards approx. 5 yearly) and Unlimited compensation (under standard presumed liability rule – but some defences available: see below)

2. **Warsaw-Hague-MAP4 Convention**: 250,000PGF (approx AUD30,000); but for Australian international air carriers, by CACLA, s 11A, 260,000 SDRs (approx. AUD495,000)

3. **Warsaw-Hague Convention**: 250,000PGF; but for Australian international air carriers, by CACLA, s 11A, 260,000 SDRs (approx. AUD495,000)

4. **Warsaw Convention**: 125,000PGF but for Australian international air carriers, by CACLA, s 21A, 260,000 SDRs approx. AUD495,000)

5. **Australian Domestic**: 260,000 SDRs for international air carriers undertaking domestic air carriage (but AUD725,000 for Australian domestic carriers) under CACLA, s 31(1)

6. **NZ Domestic**: payments are in accordance with the NZACA.

Although now of minimal use, the value of the Poincaré Gold Franc (PGF) used in the earlier versions of the IACLRs is based on the price of gold and that price fluctuates considerably, but as a rough guide at the time of writing, 1,000 PGF is approximately AUD120.

When can compensation limits be avoided?

Different grounds exist in different versions of the IACLRs for avoiding the compensation limits. These death and bodily (personal) injury limits can be avoided, so that all actual losses are compensated, if a claimant can prove one of the grounds for avoiding the compensation limits set out in the applicable version of the IACLRs:

1. **Montreal Convention 1999**: that the liability for damage or loss is caused by an act done with intent to cause damage or recklessly or with knowledge that damage would probably result by servants or agents of the airline: Art 22(5)

2. **Warsaw-Hague-MAP4 Convention**: that the liability for damage or loss is caused by an act done with intent to cause damage or recklessly or with knowledge that damage would probably result by servants or agents of the airline (Art 25); or, failure to provide the passenger with a ticket in proper form complying with the IACLRs Art 3(2).

3. **Warsaw-Hague Convention**: that the liability for damage or loss is caused by an act done with intent to cause damage or recklessly or with knowledge that damage would probably result by servants or agents of the airline (Art 25); or, failure to provide the passenger with a ticket in proper form complying with the IACLRs Art 3(2).

4. **Warsaw Convention**: that the liability for damage or loss is caused by his wilful misconduct or by such default on his part as, in accordance with the law of the Court where the case decided, is considered to be equivalent to wilful misconduct (Art 25); or, failure to provide the passenger with a ticket in proper form complying with the IACLRs Art 3(2).

5. **Australian domestic**: no equivalent provision in CACLA.

6. **NZ domestic**: no equivalent in the NZACA.

Awards of damages may also be reduced by a **passenger's contributory negligence** (see below), if a passenger's own negligence is proved to cause the injury. This is allowed under Art 20 of the IACLR based on the Montreal Convention 1999 (and Art 21 of the other versions). The court assesses the full damages, then reduces them by any contributory negligence finding; and later applies the compensation limit.

What kinds of damages may be claimed, interest, costs etc?

Courts will decide what kinds of damages can be awarded. Determination of what kinds of losses can be claimed for (compensable heads of damage e.g. pain and suffering, loss of income earning capacity etc) and the amount of damages, is, as with other matters of procedure, mostly for the law of the court where an action is brought (see below). Unless otherwise provided for and settled by CACLA or NZCAA Pt 9A or 9B (or other legislation e.g. the NZACA) (see below), the usual general law principles apply e.g. as to pure economic loss etc, and consequential damages, such as the cost of hiring replacement items or loss of future profits have been held to be recoverable.

Some legislation exists (**in Australia**, but not expressly in NZ), requiring that specific kinds of payments to a passenger claimant are not to be taken into account (deducted) when assessing damages e.g. death or personal injury insurance or even future premiums now not needing to be paid; superannuation or provident fund payments; acquisition of an interest in property under succession.

Payment of **interest** on damages awards is usual, but is made in accordance with the law of the place where the claim is made. Interest is added after compensation limits apply, although this is only specified in the more recent Montreal Convention 1999, Art 22(6) which allows for interest and costs and expressly states that it is to be paid apart from compensation limits. Otherwise, interest is almost always payable under the general law in the various State and Territory jurisdictions in Australia (but there are exceptions) and in New Zealand.

The payment of the **costs** of the litigation in addition to the liability limit, is also recognized to occur in accordance with the law of the forum (in Art 22 of all the versions of the IACLRs, except the oldest version based on the Warsaw Convention), but the award of costs has sometimes been controversial.

What Airline Defences Exist In Death and Injury Claims?

Specific defences are available to airlines. When a claim for compensation for passenger injury or death occurring during carriage is made, airlines might, as mentioned above, argue that there was no "accident" within the meaning of the convention or that it didn't occur during the air carriage and thus, they are not presumed to be liable under the IACLRs.

However, even if the claim is within the IACLRs and there is "presumed" liability, there are specific defences set out in the IACLRs that are sometimes available to airlines notably a passenger's contributory negligence (see below). Air carriers must prove any such defences to avoid their liabilities.

However, it is less certain if and to what extent IACLR defences are available to airline employees or non-airline agents or subcontractors, if claims are made against them separately. Anyway, claims against such persons are not based on IACLR airline liability, but on general law principles, so those general principles would also allow the usual general law defences, notably contributory negligence (see below).

What if passenger negligence contributes to their own injuries?

A useful airline "defence" is contributory negligence. It may be argued that the injured passenger was wholly or in part responsible for his or her own injuries. This is an airline claim of **contributory negligence** (though it is more like a 'set-off' or 'counter-claim'). It allows an air carrier to reduce in whole or in part, its liability to pay compensation to claimants.

This defence is not available when the liability of the airline is "absolute" for passenger injury or death claims up to 113,100 SDRs (about AUD215,250) under the Montreal Convention 1999 (Arts 17, 20-21), but it does apply to claims exceeding that amount. It also applies to claims made by persons deriving their rights from the passenger (e.g. personal representatives) and even persons other than the passenger seeking compensation for their own losses (e.g. a family member), by reason of the passenger's death. However, slight differences in this "defence" exist between the Montreal Convention 1999 version and the other versions of the IACLRs. Under Art 21 of the three older versions of the IACLRs.

Essentially, this defence allows and airline to be exonerated either wholly or in part from its liability, in accordance with the law of the place where the action is brought, if the injury was caused or contributed to by the "negligence of the injured person". When the claim is made by a person other than the passenger, for example, a relative, for their own injury, there is uncertainty under the older versions, as to whether or not contributory negligence of the passenger has any effect. This may be resolved by local legislation or general law principles.

Significantly, compensation limits (see above) are invoked **after** the apportionment of liability for contributory negligence, in accordance with general law principles.

As to do **domestic** (non-international) airline liabilities, contributory negligence provisions similar to the three older versions of the IACLRs are found (**for Australia**) in Pt IV of CACLA, s 39; and (**for New Zealand**) in Pt 9B of NZCAA, s 91ZB (which of course, applies only to passenger delay claims).

Does negligence of a third party affect airline liability?

Third party negligence may also be a defence. The airline defence that the injury or damage was not caused by the airline, but was "solely due to the negligence or other wrongful act or omission of a third party" is also provided for in Art 21(2)(b) of the latest version of the IACLRs (Montreal Convention 1999). However, under the Montreal Convention 1999, this defence also only applies to "presumed" airline liability for claims in excess of 113,100SDRs (AUD215,250) and not to where there is "absolute" airline liability. (The airline could always seek a contribution from the third party responsible.)

Negligence of a third person is not a defence expressly stated in any other version of the IACLRs (nor in Pt IV of CACLA dealing with non-international or domestic air carrier liabilities), and it could not even be argued that the "accident" resulting in the injury was caused by a third party. Of course, the airline could argue that it was not negligent at all; but if found liable under the applicable versions of the rules, the airline always has separate recourse against such third party for full indemnity or a contribution (see Art 37, Montreal Convention 1999).

When can airlines rely on the "no negligence" defence?

"No negligence" is also an important airline defence to some passenger claims. This defence exists for death and bodily injury under all versions of the IACLRs, **except** for claims within the "absolute" liability death and bodily injury category of up to 113,100 SDRs under the latest Montreal Convention 1999 version of the IACLRs. When available, this defence requires that the airline prove that it and its "servants and agents" (employees) took

"all measures that could reasonably be required" (Montreal Convention 1999, Art 19),

or, for all claims under the three older versions of the IACLRs, (in what seems to be somewhat stricter wording, but in practice it is not), that such person took

"all necessary measures to avoid damage, or, that such measures were impossible to take" (the other versions of the IACLRs, Art 20).

Thus, there is a complete defence to any compensation claim if an airline and its employees were not negligent.

As the burden of proving "no negligence" is on the airline, mere failure to be able to explain the cause of the injury or loss is insufficient to establish this defence. Likewise, merely showing that normal procedures were followed is not enough, provided additional measures were required. However, it may be sufficient to show that it was impossible to take such additional measures (under the three earlier IACLR versions, Art 20). For example, an air carrier is not required to exclude all suspicious characters in order to avoid possible hijackings, although it may be less arguable to suggest that airlines do not need to take measures to avoid natural disasters such as cyclones, especially as they have access to sophisticated meteorological data.

Finally, although rare in recent times, as this occurred when older IACLR versions applied, airlines may waive their rights to this defence as regards passenger injury claims in their contracts of carriage Thus, air carriage contracts should be examined closely to see if this waiver has occurred.

What Formalities And Time Limits Apply to Claims?

Formalities include a two-year limit for claiming. We have already seen that "air carriage" claims made under the IACLRs and CACLA or NZCAA, must be made in "courts" not tribunals (unless legislation in a particular jurisdiction gives a tribunal powers to hear and determine such air carriage liability claims). Furthermore under the IACLRs there are only certain places (countries) where such claims may be made, notably the place of ultimate destination of the air carriage – which for return travel is also the departure place and the likely residence of the claimant – but there are other options (see Chapter 2).

Otherwise under the ICALRs, **no notices are required for passenger injury or death claims** (unlike baggage and freight claims: see Chapter 6), and the general laws of the place where the claim is being made will govern the procedures for the making of the claim in court. Civil court procedures are complex and local court rules may require notices etc, especially for personal injuries claims and professional legal assistance in the relevant jurisdiction, should be obtained to ensure compliance with local procedural requirements.

When does the two-year time limit for taking legal proceedings apply?

Two-year time limit for claims overrides all other laws, except in NZ. A significant change to most local procedures for personal injury and death claims (which usually allow a three-year time limit for making such claims) is that there is a mere two-year time limit for commencing such international and domestic claims under the IACLRs (Art 29) (**in Australia**, CACLA, s 34 for non-international carriage); and **in NZ**, NZCAA, s 91I, but, for non-international carriage in NZ, all accident claims are made under the NZACA which imposes essentially a one-year time limit for making claims (NZACA, s 53).

This two-year limit is absolute and all rights are extinguished when it expires. Local courts cannot suspend or extend the period or revive expired claims.

6. Baggage & Freight: Loss or Damage Claims

Baggage and freight are considered together. Claims for loss, destruction or damage to **registered (checked) baggage** and for **freight** in **international** air carriage are based on "presumed" airline liability, created by Art 17(2) and Art 18 for the Montreal Convention 1999 version (or Art 18 in all other versions of the IACLRs). The damage or loss must be caused by an "event" (or an "occurrence" in older IACLR versions), and that "event" must take place during the period of the carriage by air - that is, while the items are "in the charge of" the airline.

Cabin baggage claim rules are rather different (see below).

In Australia, under the **non-international (domestic)** rules, airlines are also "presumed" liable under s 29, Pt IV of CACLA for destruction, loss or injury to registered baggage (similar to under the IACLRs). Hand (cabin) baggage rules differ slightly (see below). (**Domestic freight claims** are not provided for in CACLA and are subject to general law principles: contract, implied guaranties, negligence etc.)

In NZ domestic air carriage, airlines are presumed liable for loss or damage to "goods" (freight and baggage) under NZCaGoA, s 12(2)(3), "while [they are] responsible for the goods" (s 9(1)). Carry-on (hand or cabin) baggage rules differ.

Although the wording used in the different provisions is not identical, there is some similarity in principles governing the extent of airline liability, airline defences, claim procedures, notices and liability compensation limits involved.

6.1 Cabin Baggage

Are Airlines Liable For Damage To Cabin Baggage?

Cabin, hand or carry-on baggage and personal effects are largely the passenger's responsibility. They are treated quite differently to registered (or checked) baggage and freight, although for international air carriage, some rules in the IACLRs apply to claims for both cabin and registered baggage, for example, the strict two-year time limit for claiming against airlines.

What passenger must prove for IACLR cabin baggage claims?

Basically, general law principles apply to cabin baggage claims. Airline liability is **not** presumed for loss of or damage to cabin baggage and personal items carried by passengers onto an aircraft. Passengers must prove the "fault" (e.g. negligence or other wrongdoing) of the airline or its employees, if they seek to recover compensation from an airline (Montreal Convention 1999, Art 17(2), last sentence). In all the other (older) versions of the IACLRs, no rule is expressed as to the precise nature of airline liability for (unchecked) cabin baggage; but it is not treated as "presumed" (unlike for passengers and registered baggage and freight). Thus it is assumed that passengers must likewise prove fault or wrongdoing of the airline or person responsible.

However, similar procedural requirements e.g. time limits for claims, as well as defences and compensation limits are prescribed for claims in respect of cabin baggage (Montreal Convention 1999, Art 29; all other version of IACLR, Art 24).

Of course, a separate claim alleging fault or wrongdoing under general law principles might also be made against any other passenger or person who damages your cabin baggage if you know their names (or a claim can be made on the claimant's travel insurance policy). If the claim is against an airline employee or subcontractor, assuming they are acting in the course of their duties, they benefit from some of the same IACLR protections as the airline, notably compensation limits (Montreal Convention 1999, Art 43 and see below)

In summary, liabilities of airlines or other persons or entities in respect of cabin baggage can only be based on the general law of the place where the claim is made, notably,

- the common law, that is, the tort of negligence or some other "fault" basis (including for claims against persons other than airlines); or
- breach of a legislative provision, such as the implied consumer guarantees as to reasonable care and skill being exercised or the services provided being reasonably fit for the purpose made known to the air carrier under consumer laws: the ACL; or NZCGA (see Chapter 3); or
- other breaches of the air carriage contract.

However, air carriage contracts (passenger and freight) usually protect the airline from claims by containing liability exclusion or limitation clauses (discussed in Chapter 4). For example, in the Qantas Airways Conditions of Carriage for passengers and baggage, clause 7.5 (last sentence) states:

"You are responsible for your personal items that are in your care and control."

and clause 16.1 states:

"Other than as specified in these Conditions of Carriage or applicable laws, we exclude all liability for any costs, expenses, losses or damages whatsoever that may arise in any way in connection with the carriage."

and specifically as regards international air carriage, clause 16.4 (b) provides:

"Our liability for loss of, damage to, or delay in the carriage of, your Baggage is limited by the applicable Convention as follows:
- Montreal Convention 1999 ... 1,131 SDRs (about AU$1,735 [but AUD2,152 at time of writing]) cumulative for both Checked Baggage and Cabin Baggage ...... **We will only be liable for Cabin Baggage if we were at fault** [emphasis added]
- Conventions other than the Montreal Convention 1999 - ... 5,000 francs (about AU$600) for your Cabin Baggage, unless Article 25 of the Warsaw Convention [removing limits for an airline's wilful misconduct] applies, in which case these limits do not apply"

and as regards **domestic** air carriage in Australia, clause 16.4 (c) provides:

> "Where your travel is wholly within Australia and is not International Carriage, our liability for loss or damage is limited to A$1,600 per Passenger for your Checked Baggage and A$160 per Passenger for your Cabin Baggage."

Those exclusions and limits on compensation that are set out in air carriage contract (which may apply if the exclusion clause is effective: see Chapter 3), relate to some liabilities, but are not necessarily effective to exempt airlines from all liabilities. For example, they may be construed narrowly by a court, or not apply to claims based on implied guarantees which cannot be excluded by the contract (discussed in Chapter 3).

No provision is made in the IACLRs as to **notice** having to be given to the carrier of any loss or damage to cabin baggage, (but Australian legislation does require it for domestic flights: see below). However, the air carriage contract may itself require this – though passengers wouldn't have the whole contract to hand at the time – so the preferable course is to give immediate written notice of complaint to the airline concerned.

What compensation limits exist for cabin baggage?

IACLRs do limit the compensation recoverable in cabin baggage claims, even though they do not create a presumed airline liability. This is also done in the air carriage contract (see above) and provisions in applicable Australian and NZ legislation. Compensation limits set out in the various versions of the IACLRs and domestic rules are:

1. **Montreal Convention 1999**: 1,131SDRs [AUD2,152 at time of writing] (total for checked and cabin baggage (Art 22(2) (subject to 5 yearly review, next in 2015: Art 24)

2. **Warsaw-Hague-MAP4 Convention**: 5,000PGF (AUD600) per passenger (Art 22(3))

3. **Warsaw-Hague Convention**: 5,000PGF or (AUD 600) per passenger (Art 22(3))

4. **Warsaw Convention**: 5,000PGF or (AUD600) per passenger (Art 22(3))

5. **Australian Domestic**: AUD160 per passenger (CACLA, s 31(3)

6. **NZ Domestic**: NZ2,000 per item of cabin baggage (NZCaGoA, s 15(1))

Such limits may not apply. They don't apply if there has been a declared value of goods carried, which has been accepted by the airline at the time of carriage, or, **if the claimant can prove the grounds for avoiding compensation limits** set out in the applicable version of the IACLRs, namely:

1. **Montreal Convention 1999**: that the liability for damage or loss is caused by an act done with intent to cause damage or recklessly or with knowledge that damage would probably result by servants or agents of the airline: Art 22(5)

2. **Warsaw-Hague-MAP4 Convention**: that the liability for damage or loss is caused by an act done with intent to cause damage or recklessly or with knowledge that damage would probably result, by servants or agents of the airline (Art 25); or, failure to provide the passenger with a ticket in proper form complying with the IACLRs Art 3(2).

3. **Warsaw-Hague Convention**: that the liability for damage or loss is caused by an act done with intent to cause damage or recklessly or with knowledge that damage would probably result, by servants or agents of the airline (Art 25); or, failure to provide the passenger with a ticket in proper form complying with the IACLRs Art 3(2).

4. **Warsaw Convention**: that the liability for damage or loss is caused by his wilful misconduct or by such default on his part as, in accordance with the law of the Court hearing the case, is considered to be equivalent to wilful misconduct (Art 25); or, failure to provide the passenger with a ticket in proper form complying with the IACLRs Art 3(2).

5. **Australian domestic**: no equivalent provision in CACLA.

6. **NZ domestic** (NZCaGoA s 15(2)) : that the liability for damage or loss is caused by an act done intentionally by the airline, its servants or agents.

Do domestic "carry-on" baggage rules resemble the IACLRs?

Domestic rules for cabin baggage claims are different. In Australia, to recover compensation for loss or damage to carry-on (unchecked or unregistered) baggage or carry-on personal effects on domestic (non-international) flights, the legislative provisions are complex, bordering on obscure. CACLA, Pt IV, s 29(1) appears to create presumed airline liability:

"the carrier is liable under this Part, and not otherwise ... if the occurrence which causes the destruction, loss or injury takes place during the period of the carriage"

Liability is exclusive (the words "and not otherwise" exclude other general law remedies) for loss or damage to cabin baggage, even if occurrence is the act of another passenger.

However, the presumption of airline liability is qualified by s 29(4) which makes s 29(1) subject to the **presumed contributory negligence** of the passenger; by saying that for:

"the application of section 39 [contributory negligence] ... in respect of baggage other than registered baggage, the carrier shall be deemed to have proved that the damage was caused by the negligence of the passenger, except so far as the passenger proves that he or she was not responsible for the damage".

Thus, if the airline alleges contributory negligence of a passenger under s 39 (as it would almost certainly do), there is a presumption that the passenger is liable for any damage to his or her own cabin baggage, except to the extent that the passenger proves he or she was not negligent. This is odd as taking the provisions together, it appears that passengers do not have to prove that the air carrier was negligent: it is presumed (s 29(1)), but if the air carrier merely alleges that the passenger was contributorily negligent, this is presumed too; and the passengers then has to show that they were not "responsible for the damage" (s 29(4)).

Essentially, it is all about which of the two: the passenger or the airline can satisfy their burden of proof that they did nothing negligent. How is this done?

****

It may be easier for passengers to prove they were not negligent than for the airline to do so as the passenger can testify to what he or she saw and did. However, it will still be quite difficult.

How would they do this? Aside from testifying to having seen damage being done during the period of carriage, a passenger could prove that damage occurred during carriage by showing that the cabin baggage was undamaged (or a missing item was inside a bag) before it was placed in the overhead locker; but this was not the case, when it came out (perhaps passengers should photograph cabin baggage on both occasions); and also that the passenger had done nothing to justify it being considered responsible for the damage (though how this is proved other than by testimony is uncertain).

Therefore, the damage must have been the result of "an occurrence" during carriage.

Compensation limits are AUD1,600 total, for all passenger baggage? but for cabin baggage, it is just AUD 160 (CACLA, s 31(2),(3)) per passenger. This is repeated in the Qantas Airways Conditions of Carriage for passengers and baggage, clause 16(4)(c) referred to above.

All this may be a lot of trouble for AUD 160.

****

In Australia, written **notice of complaint** as to damage, loss or destruction of cabin baggage is required to be given to the airline within 3 days of the carriage ending (CACLA, s 30(2)(c), but if it is "just and equitable by reason of special circumstances" – thus, for a good reason – a court may allow proceedings to be commenced even without the required notice (CACLA, s 30(3)).

Compensation limits are as set out immediately above.

In NZ, liability of domestic airlines for damage to cabin baggage is also fault-based (as with the IACLRs) because the NZCaGoA applies to cabin baggage (s 12(3)). Passengers making claims must prove the airline's "negligence or wilful default" (s 12(4)):

> "A carrier is liable as such for the loss of or damage to any hand baggage occurring during the period in which the passenger is on board the mode of transport or in the course of any of the operations of embarking or disembarking, if the loss or damage is caused wholly or partly by the negligence or wilful default of the carrier."

Notice of the claim for damage or partial loss (not delivery) must be given within 30 days (except if there is airline fraud): NZCaGoA, s 18.

Of course, the airline may escape full or partial liability if it can prove the contributory negligence of the passenger in the usual manner (see above) under NZCaGoA, s 12(5).

However, there is a quite generous maximum compensation limit of NZD2,000 per unit, that is, item of baggage (s 15(1) and s 3(1)(h) which defines an item of baggage as a "unit"). Otherwise, see compensation limits set out above.

6.2 Checked Baggage and Freight

Is There Presumed Airline Liability For Checked Baggage & Freight?

Checked baggage and freight are discussed together as quite similar rules apply to impose airline presumed liability. The term "goods" is used to refer to baggage and freight. The terms "checked" and "registered" baggage mean the same. However, there are other concepts used in the rules that need clarification.

What must passengers prove in international air carriage goods claims?

Checked baggage and freight claims are subject to essentially the same rules. All versions of the IACLRs apply quite similar principles as regards the liability of airlines for loss or damage in the international air carriage of both registered (checked) baggage and freight, but in slightly differently worded provisions (see below).

There are also some exceptions, especially for **domestic carriage**. In **Australia**, the equivalent domestic, non-international air carriage rules in Pt IV of CACLA, s 29, apply only to passenger baggage, **as freight is not encompassed by Pt IV**, and general law principles apply. In **NZ**, the NZCGA (not the NZCAA) applies to all claims for domestic airline baggage as well as freight air carriage (see below).

As regards **international air carriage**, according to the IACLRs, airlines are "presumed" to be liable – that is, negligence or fault does not have to be proved by the claimant – for any damage (physical deterioration), destruction or loss (including loss of economic value, as delay may amount to "loss" after a period of time), to checked (registered) baggage and freight, if caused by:

- an "event" (Montreal Convention 1999, Art 17(2)) or
- an "occurrence" (other IACLR versions, Art 18),

when such goods are left "in the charge of" the airline or its agent.

The main exception to presumed airline liability is if the damage is caused by an "inherent defect or vice" in the goods etc and this is effectively an airline defence to any claim (see below).

The claimant must prove that the damage was caused by an "occurrence" during the carriage by air, which could be evidenced by there being external physical damage to the baggage or freight. It is not enough to say that, for some inexplicable reason, the baggage or goods arrived in an unfit state, if it is otherwise apparently undamaged.

Aside from the few minor wording differences, there is no significance in the fact that in older versions of the IACLRs, baggage and freight are treated together (as occurs for delay liability), but in the Montreal Convention 1999 version baggage and freight are treated separately.

The principles establishing "presumed" air carrier liability under all versions of the IACLRs are found in:

* Arts 17(2) (baggage) and 18 (freight) of the Montreal Convention 1999 – the most widely applicable version of the IACLRs;

* Art 18 (baggage and freight) of the Warsaw Convention – the oldest and now more rarely applicable version;

* Art 18 (baggage and freight) of the Warsaw-Hague Convention – which still has some application; and

* Art 18 (baggage and freight) of the Warsaw-Hague-Montreal No 4 Convention (Warsaw-Hague-MAP4) – which also still has some application but is more significant to international freight carriage.

Fortunately, on closer examination all these minor wording differences are of minimal effect.

When is baggage or freight "in the charge of" the airline?

To be liable for loss or damage, the airline must have control of checked baggage or freight. Despite using somewhat different terminology in the different IACLR versions, being "in the charge" of the airline or having control means much the same.

The Montreal Convention 1999 version (the most modern and widely-used version) of the IACLRs, Art 17(2) imposes presumed airline liability **for checked baggage** during any period "within which the checked baggage was in the charge of the carrier".

At the same time, airline presumed liability **for freight loss or damage** sustained operates for the period "during the carriage by air", under the Montreal Convention 1999, Art 18(1), but by Art 18(3), this is said to comprise "the period during which the cargo is in the charge of the carrier". Decisions on earlier versions of the IACLRs have adopted much the same meaning. So, in effect, the liability is for the same period.

Outside airport extension: certain geographical limits apply to when freight is "in the charge of the carrier" under the Montreal Convention 1999, as it excludes any land or water carriage outside an airport **unless** for loading, delivery or transhipment for the purpose of the carriage: then the "damage is presumed ... to have been the result of an event which took place during the carriage by air" (Art 18(4)). To state this positively: when carriage of freight occurs outside an airport for delivery or transhipment purposes, it is still "in the charge" of the carrier and airline liability is presumed.

This limited extension of airline liability existing for freight is not expressly stated to apply to carriage of checked baggage e.g. when it is delayed baggage and it is delivered outside the airport to the passenger's address, but logic would dictate that the same rules would apply.

Are there other limits to being "in the charge of" the carrier?

Only formally checked-in baggage is in the charge of the airline. It is unlikely that being "in the charge of" the carrier extends to when cabin baggage is put into the custody of airline staff on board an aircraft – it doesn't become "checked", as the baggage is not registered or checked in the normal way.

Nor does being in the charge of the carrier extend to loss or theft of baggage from an airport baggage carousel immediately prior to collection by the passenger, nor to a situation where the passenger hands the baggage, after collection, back to an airline employee to put on a conveyor belt to go upstairs to street level, as the air carriage cannot be revived after it has been completed. That is, the IACLRs and airline presumed liability had already ceased to apply to the baggage and thus, any potential airline liability was a question for the general law: especially, contract, bailment and negligence.

What happens if it is unclear which airline the loss or damage occurs on?

Joint presumed liability is possible under the IACLRs. Baggage and freight may move from one aircraft to another on a long-distance flight and it may not be known on which airline the loss or damage occurs. Thus, presumed liability for destruction, loss and damage applies not only to a contracting carrier, but also, in the case of "successive" carriage, to the first and last carrier (as well as any performing carriers, if it can be proved that the loss or damage occurred on their flight). Also, presumed liability usually applies to any "actual" carrier (that is, performing carrier, not otherwise falling within the definition of a "successive carrier": see above) on whose flight the loss or damage can be proved to have occurred.

What Formalities Apply to International Baggage and Freight Claims?

Notices and other formalities must be complied with. It has already been pointed out that "air carriage" claims made under the IACLRs and CACLA or NZCAA, must be made in "courts" not in tribunals (unless legislation in a particular jurisdiction has given a tribunal power to hear and determine such air carriage liability claims). Furthermore, there are only certain places (countries) where such claims under the IACLRs can be made, notably the place of ultimate destination of the air carriage – which for return travel is also the departure place and the likely residence of the claimant – although there are other options (see Chapter 2).

Apart from the fact that **notices of complaint are required for baggage and freight claims** under the ICALRs (see below) (unlike passenger injury or death claims: see Chapter 5), the general laws of the place where the claim is made will govern the procedures for making a claim in court.

When is a written complaint required?

Written notice of complaint must be given quickly. In international air carriage, receipt of checked baggage or freight without complaint is prima facie evidence (meaning it is accepted unless there is contrary proof) that baggage or freight is in good condition on arrival. In international air carriage, if there is damage to registered baggage or freight, the claimant (person entitled to delivery) **must make written complaint** in respect of any damage: almost immediately. Time limits differ for baggage and freight; more precisely, for claims under:

- **Montreal Convention 1999**, Art 31; (Warsaw –Hague; Warsaw-Hague-MAP4, Art 26): for checked baggage, within 7 days; and for freight, within 14 days;

- **Warsaw Convention,** Art 26 (now rarely applicable): for checked baggage within just 3 days; and for freight, within 7 days.

In the absence of a notice of complaint, no legal action can be taken against the airline **except where there is fraud** (some sort of dishonesty) on the part of the airline.

Who to complain to. Complaints should be made to the airline being claimed against, that is, the airline responsible under the IACLRs. But this can be an airline other than that originally contracted with, so some options are available.

Baggage and freight claims may be made by passengers and by shippers (or their personal representatives) against:

- the first or last air carrier, or,

- if several perform carriage, the "successive" carrier performing the carriage when the damage occurs (Montreal Convention 1999, Art 36).

Extra options exist for freight carriage. Freight carriage claims can be made by either consignors or consignees, as both have rights to delivery (Arts 12-14), and in the case of "successive" carriage, consignors and consignees may also sue the airline on which the damage occurred (if identifiable) for compensation in respect of damage (or delay) (Art 30).

"Actual carriers" may also be claimed against. Passengers (for baggage) and consignors (for freight) may also claim against "actual carriers" (a subcontracting airline which is not a "successive carrier"). This occurs under the extended carrier liability provisions in the Montreal Convention 1999, Art 39 or the Warsaw-Hague-MAP4 Convention, Art XXIII, or, for the other two versions, if the Guadalajara Convention also applies to the carriage (for discussion of these matters, see Chapter 2).

What Formalities Exist For Domestic Baggage and Freight Claims?

More complicated formalities exist for claims concerning domestic air carriage than for international air carriage of goods. Requirements for notice and time limits for baggage and freight are different.

In Australia, all baggage loss or damage claims on domestic air carriage are made under CACLA, Pt IV, which establishes the same "presumed" liability of airlines as the IACLRs (CACLA, s 29). (It does not deal with domestic freight claims.)

Written complaint of any such registered baggage loss or damage suffered domestically must be made by the passenger (or person acting on their behalf), within a maximum of

- 3 days of when the damaged baggage is received, or

- 21 days from when the baggage suffering loss or destruction "should have been placed at the disposal of the passenger" (CACLA, s 30(2)).

For other than registered baggage (e.g. cabin baggage) written complaint must be made within 3 days from when the carriage ended. (CACLA, s 30(2)(c)).

Time limits: a strict two-year time limit exists for commencing any legal proceedings in domestic air carriage baggage claims (CACLA, s 34).

Freight claims in respect of domestic air carriage are not subject to CACLA but governed by contract, consumer law and the general law.

Written complaint requirement: Claims are made in the ordinary way in accordance with general law principles, subject to any requirement for notice of the claim set out in the airline's contract of carriage.). However, notice procedures may differ from one airline's contract of carriage to another. For example, the Qantas Airways Conditions of Carriage for cargo, applies similar rules and notice requirements to both international and domestic air carriage (clause 8.4: receipt without complaint; and clause 13.1.1: time limits for complaints): within 14 days for damage or partial loss and within 120 days for non-delivery

Time limits for the commencement of legal actions are governed by general law principles, which usually impose a six-year time limit. Professional advice should be obtained on this matter in the place where the claim is to be made.

In NZ, claims for loss or damage to **baggage and freight** in domestic carriage, are made under NZCaGoA (not NZCAA). Airline liability (both contracting carrier and actual carrier) is provided for under complicated provisions in s 10. Claims for carriage of hand (cabin) baggage and checked baggage is the same as under a contract for the carriage of goods (s 12(3)) (but made more complex as most of the provisions of the Act, ss 8-13, do not apply to carriage of hand baggage: s 12(2)).

Notice of claims for damage to or partial loss – but not total loss – of hand or checked baggage and for freight must be given (except if there has been airline dishonesty) to the contracting carrier (and any "actual" carrier) within 30 days of the date when the airline's responsibility for the goods has ceased, **unless**

- the airline ought to be aware of the damage or partial loss, or
- the airline consents to or a court grants leave to commence the action (s 18(1),(3)).

Time limits for the commencement of legal proceedings for freight loss, damage or partial loss are governed by NZCaGoA, s 19, which (except if there has been airline fraud), imposes a one-year time limit), **unless**

- the airline consents to a claim out of time, or
- a court grants leave for the action out of time (up to a limit of six-years) provided there has been a mistake of fact or law or any other reasonable cause and the airline has not been materially prejudiced in its defence by the delay.

What Defences Do Airlines Have To Baggage and Freight Claims?

Aside from disputing values of loss or damage, airlines have three main defences. Various airline defences (or counterclaims) are available in international air carriage in respect of claims for loss or damage to checked baggage and freight under the most recent versions of the IACLRs, as compared to those available under the older versions of the IACLRs. Defences also exist for domestic carriage claims.

When is "inherent defect" of baggage or freight a defence?

Airlines avoid liability if they prove there is an inherent defect in the baggage or freight. In claims for lost or damaged checked baggage or freight in international carriage, airline presumed liability is avoided if the loss or damage is the result some inherent defect in the goods. This is an important defence to a claim, but the onus of proof of the defect existing rests with the defendant airline.

This airline defence is only available in respect of **checked baggage** claims under the most recent version of the IACLRs (Montreal Convention 1999, Art 17(2)), whereby the carrier

"is not liable if and to the extent that the damage resulted from the inherent defect, quality or vice of the baggage".

It is not available for baggage claims when other older versions of the IACLRs (e.g. .Warsaw Conventions), apply.

As regards **freight** loss or damage claims, airline liability is avoided under the two latest versions of the IACLRs (Montreal Convention 1999, Art 18(2) and Warsaw-Hague-MAP4 Convention, Art 18(3)), if it is caused by

- an inherent defect or vice, defective packing of the freight, or
- an act of war or armed conflict; or
- an act of a public authority to do with the entry or exit of the freight e.g. going through customs.

No equivalent defence provision is made in older versions of the IACLRs.

However, for claims in respect of **domestic** air carriage of goods, slightly different provisions exist for this "inherent defect" airline defence.

In Australia, legislation does not create this defence, but CACLA, s 34(2) does authorize airlines to contract out of their liabilities as regards "inherent defect, quality or vice of goods carried", which of course, they usually do: see e.g. Qantas Airways Conditions of Carriage of goods, clause 12.3.

In NZ; a similar defence is available to domestic baggage and freight claims under NZCaGoA, s 14.

When is taking "all necessary measures" a defence?

Another important airline defence is that it took "all necessary measures". The defence is, in effect, that there was no airline negligence. This is a defence to both checked baggage and cargo loss or damage claims under all but the latest version of the IACLRs (Art 20 of all older versions of the IACLRs). The airline must prove that it and its servants and agents have taken

- "all necessary measures" to avoid the damage; or,

- that it was impossible for it or them to take such measures.

However, note that this airline defence of "no negligence" is restricted to delay claims under the latest version of the IACLRs (Montreal Convention 1999 version, Art 19).

Negligent pilotage defence now rare. Although a "dead letter" today, a separate variation of the "no negligence" defence in baggage and freight claims, is the airline defence under the oldest (Warsaw Convention) version of the IACLRs, whereby an airline proves that the damage or loss was occasioned by "negligent pilotage" or negligence in the handling of the aircraft or in its navigation, and that in all other respects, the carrier and its agents have taken all necessary measures to avoid the damage (Warsaw Convention version, Art 20(2)). Note that this version still applies to one-way carriage e.g. carriage of freight or baggage between Australia to Indonesia. It would not apply to baggage on return flights from Australia, as Australia would be both the place of departure and destination; so the Montreal Convention 1999 would apply.

When is passenger/consignor contributory negligence a defence?

Contributory negligence is a partial or complete airline defence. As regards both checked baggage and freight claims in international air carriage, airline liability may be reduced wholly or in part by proof of contributory negligence of the passenger, consignor or another person causing the damage or loss. This is an airline defence under the Montreal Convention 1999, Art 20 (and under Art 21 of all the other

IACLR versions in force). It would also be a defence under the general law if persons other than an airline are claimed against.

In **Australia**, for *domestic checked baggage* claims, this defence of contributory negligence is available under CACLA, s 39; and for *domestic freight* claims, under the general law.

In **NZ**, for *domestic checked baggage* claims, this defence of contributory negligence is available under NZCaGoA, s 12(5), but there is no equivalent provision for domestic freight claims.

What Are Compensation Limits for Baggage and Freight Claims?

Compensation limits for baggage and freight are low. Low compensation limits exist for loss of or damage to checked baggage and freight claims in international air carriage under the most recent IACLR version (Montreal Convention 1999, although these are reviewed upwards every five years). Limits are even lower under the older versions of the IACLRs:

1. Montreal Convention 1999 (Arts 22(2), (3) and 24): baggage: 1,131SDRs (approx AUD 2,152) (total for all baggage) and freight: 19 SDRs per kg (AUD 36 per kg)

2. Warsaw-Hague-MAP4 Convention (Art 22(2): baggage: 250PGF (approx AUD30) per kg and freight: 17 SDRs per kg (AUD 32 per kg);

3. Warsaw-Hague Convention (Art 22(2)): both baggage and freight 250 PGF (AUD30) per kg;

4. Warsaw Convention (Art 22(2)): both 25OPGF (AUD30) per kg

5. Australian Domestic: baggage (in total per passenger, AUD1,600; or AUD90 for cabin baggage, set by regulation)

6. NZ Domestic: NZD 2,000 per unit under the NZCaGoA, s 15(1) and s 3(1) defines "units" as baggage items and freight as containers, pallets, packages.

Such limits may not apply if there has been a **declared value** of goods carried, which is accepted by the airline at the time of carriage.

Similarly, such limits may not apply if the claimant can prove one or another of the grounds for avoiding the compensation limits which are set out in the applicable version of the IACLRs, namely:

1. **Montreal Convention 1999**: that the liability for damage or loss is caused by an act done with intent to cause damage or recklessly or with knowledge that damage would probably result by servants or agents of the airline: Art 22(5).
2. **Warsaw-Hague-MAP4 Convention:** that the liability for damage or loss is caused by an act done with intent to cause damage or recklessly or with knowledge that damage would probably result by servants or agents of the airline (Art 25).
3. **Warsaw-Hague Convention**: that the liability for damage or loss is caused by an act done with intent to cause damage or recklessly or with knowledge that damage would probably result by servants or agents of the airline (Art 25); or, the airline failed to provide the passenger with an Air Waybill in proper form complying with the IACLRs Art 9.
4. **Warsaw Convention**: that the liability for damage or loss is caused by his wilful misconduct or by such default on his part as, in accordance with the law of the Court seised of the case, is considered to be equivalent to wilful misconduct (Art 25); or, the airline failed to provide the passenger with an Air Waybill in proper form complying with IACLRs Art 9.
5. **Australian domestic**: no equivalent provision.
6. **NZ domestic** (NZCaGoA s 15(2)): that the liability for damage or loss is caused by an act done intentionally by the airline, its servants or agents.

What kinds of baggage or freight damage may be compensated?

Local laws determine which kinds of damage are compensated. Calculation of the amount of the claim and what kinds of losses can be claimed for (known as compensable heads of damage e.g. consequential loss) and thus, the amount of damages, as with other matters of procedure, is usually determined by the law of the court where an action is brought (see below).

These "air carriage" claims are essentially made under the relevant legislation e.g. CACLA, NZCAA or NZCaGoA, or for breach of an implied contractual guarantee or other term. So what law applies are the usual principles governing damages claims in contract (e.g. as to pure economic losses and consequential damages, such as the cost of hiring replacement items or loss of future profits), that have been held by local courts to be recoverable in breach of contract cases, **unless** otherwise expressly provided for in:

  - CACLA, NZCaGoA or general law principles and other legislation in the various Australian jurisdictions and NZ); or

  - the air carriage contract. For example, Qantas Airways Conditions Of Carriage for Cargo, purport to exclude generally all liabilities except those agreed to; in clause 12.5:

> "Except as may be otherwise provided in any applicable Convention, carrier is not liable to the shipper, consignee or any other person having an interest in the cargo in tort or contract or bailment or otherwise for any, and the consequences of any, delay in collection of cargo or loss of or damage to or deterioration of cargo or mis-delivery or failure to deliver or delay in delivery of cargo for any reason whatsoever including, without limiting the foregoing, the negligence or breach of contract or wilful act or default of the carrier whether or not the same occurs in the course of performance by or on behalf of carrier under this contract or in events which are in the contemplation of carrier and/or shipper or in events which are foreseeable by them or either of them or in events which may constitute a fundamental breach of contract or a breach of a fundamental term."

Of course, such liability exclusion clauses in consumer transactions may be nullified by the court, as they are subject to, **in Australia**, the ACL; and **in NZ**, the NZFTA, NZCGA and NZCaGoA. General principles in respect of liability exclusion clauses have been discussed earlier (Chapter 3).

Can interest and legal costs be recovered?

Recovery of court costs and interest on claims is also possible and awarded in addition to compensation limits. Payment of **interest** on compensation awards is made in accordance with the law of the place where the claim is made. Although interest is specifically provided for only in the more recent version of the IACLRs (Montreal Convention 1999, Art 22(6)), it is almost always payable under the general law principles in the various State and Territory jurisdictions in Australia (but there are exceptions) and in New Zealand.

The payment of the **costs** of litigation in addition to the liability limit, is also recognized to occur in accordance with the law of the court concerned (in Art 22 of all the versions of the IACLRs, except in the oldest version based on the Warsaw Convention), but the requirement that costs be awarded has sometimes been controversial.

Of course, some consumer courts and tribunals do not award legal costs (see Chapter 3).

7. Delay: Passenger, Baggage & Freight Claims

Two different kinds of delay can be claimed for by passengers: pre-flight delay and in-flight delay. Although the common factor in all "delay" is that the arrival time is much later than planned; the remedies available for these different kinds of delay are quite different.

First, **pre-flight delay** can occur and be caused by flight cancellation, cancelling, rescheduling or refused or denied boarding (which may be "for cause" e.g. passenger drunkenness, or, as a result of "overbooking"). All occur before the carriage by air begins. In all those cases, remedies are based on the air carriage contract, consumer protection law and **denied boarding compensation schemes** (where they exist). (See below. Discussion of this also occurred in Chapter 3.)

Second, **in-flight delay** can occur as a result of problems actually arising during air carriage – after carriage begins (e.g. sitting on the runway for hours waiting to depart, en route delays) – and then a remedy must be based on the 'presumed' air carrier liability provisions in the IACLRs or in any equivalent domestic air carriage legislation. If negotiated settlement fails, these kinds of claims must be made in court.

When is Refusal to Carry Allowed and a Refund Available?

Refusals to carry a passenger may be permanent or temporary and refunds are uncertain. A refusal to carry may be definitive and permanent, or it may be temporary (for a particular flight). It can be a refusal to carry passengers, baggage or freight. Airline powers to refuse carriage under the contract of carriage, have already been discussed in Chapter 4, where it was seen that detailed provisions in air carriage contracts usually provide airlines with many grounds – some based on safety and security, others on convenience or commercial reasons – for refusing carriage, especially of passengers and baggage. Under the contract, a refusal to carry on a particular flight (or at all) will not necessarily result in the provision of alternative carriage arrangement (with or without compensation), or even the right to a refund; and some tickets have conditions in the contract of air carriage, to that effect – for example, if passengers arrive late, the ticket may be valueless.

Some conditions in tickets (or AWBs for freight carriage) preclude or limit refunds, and these conditions may be effective, assuming consumers are adequately informed of them at the proper time so that they are part of the contract (discussed in Chapter 4). These ticket (or AWB) conditions may even be contained in the airline "tariffs" which are incorporated into and supposed to be part of the air carriage contract. Although the contract does contain a general provision for refunds, it does recognize that for some fare types (that is, some tickets with certain conditions and restrictions) refunds may be minimal: e.g. see the words

"a refund is payable in accordance with these Conditions of Carriage unless otherwise specified in these Conditions of Carriage .."

which are contained in Cl.13.2 of the Qantas Airways Conditions of Carriage for Passenger and Baggage. Part of Cl.13 reads:

****

13.1 When a Refund is Available

You will be entitled to a refund if we:

- are unable to carry you and you have a confirmed reservation
- delay your flight to the extent that you have to cancel your travel
- make a significant change to the scheduled flight time, which is not acceptable to you and we are unable to book you on an alternative flight acceptable to you
- downgrade you from the class paid for
- fail to stop at a Stopover or the destination specified on your Ticket
- cause you to miss a connecting Qantas flight on which you have a confirmed reservation, or

- cancel your flight

In these circumstances we will provide a refund on request as set out in 13.2

[Note that only missed connections on QF flights are referred to as regards refunds.]

13.2. What Refund is Available?

Where a refund is payable in accordance with these Conditions of Carriage, unless otherwise specified in these Conditions of Carriage the refund will be equal to:

- the fare paid, if no part of the Ticket is used
- alternatively, if part of the Ticket is used, the difference between the fare paid and the fare that would have been payable if booked for the travel taken,

including any taxes and carriers charges, less any applicable fees.

Depending on the fare type, where a Ticket is partly used, the unused part may have little or no refund value.

****

It may be that some of these standard terms and conditions are actually **not** part of the contract at all (for reasons discussed earlier in Chapter 4), or, that they may be misleading, unfair or unconscionable and void in accordance with consumer law (ACL or NZFTA which were discussed in Chapter 3). These are matters as yet to be judicially determined. However, the obscurity and uncertainty that appears on closer examination of many such contractual terms, would substantiate the argument that such terms are not even part of the contract.

7.1 Pre-Carriage Delay of Passengers and Baggage

Pre-flight delays are not subject to the IACLRs. General law and contract terms determine airline liabilities for pre-flight delay. Pre-flight delays can affect the whole flight or a single passenger and can result from flight cancellation, technical issues or denied boarding. They can be the fault of airlines, air traffic control, industry entities or passengers themselves.

If passengers are at fault e.g. arriving too late to board, they have almost no rights to refunds or alternative arrangements (unless they have full fare tickets with changeable dates) – whatever is done to assist them is based on airline good-will.

Minor pre-flight delays, slight changes in scheduled departure or arrival times do occur, but obtaining compensation for them is rare, even if losses are caused, as airline contracts of carriage don't guarantee departure times (see below).

However, more lengthy delays may occur if flights are cancelled as a result of technical or operational problems, or weather or environmental conditions such as pervasive clouds of volcanic ash. Such delays may have serious consequences, such as, missing a connecting flight for which there is no refund. (Travel insurance may not even cover such events.)

Consumer law protections: Guarantees as to performance of a service (such as air carriage) within a reasonable time, are implied into all consumer transactions **in Australia** (by ACL, s 62) and **in NZ** (by NZCGA, s 30, together with the NZCaGoA). These consumer guarantees **apply to all pre-flight delays** in international and domestic air carriage. While all international in-flight delays are governed only by the IACLRs, not all domestic air carriage liabilities are covered by CACLA and NZCAA, so implied consumer guarantees will also **apply to in-flight delays in domestic** freight **in Australia**, and domestic baggage and freight **in NZ**.

(As discussed in Chapter 3, airlines cannot, by terms in their air carriage contracts, reduce their obligations under implied guarantees in consumer transactions, although they can reduce obligations to some extent in non-consumer transactions.)

Compensation schemes: There are also some special compensation schemes in a few countries, notably in the EU (for flights within and from Europe – which are very important considering the large amount of air traffic within and to Europe from Australasia) and are discussed below.

Aside from such consumer protection laws and special compensation schemes, any airline liabilities for pre-flight delay of passengers, baggage and freight derive almost exclusively from the air carriage contract. However, the air carriage contract terms and conditions usually try to exclude any airline liabilities for pre-flight delay.

Can Air Contracts Exclude Liability For Pre-Flight Delays?

Carriage contracts may exclude liabilities for delays in some cases. Any claim relating to passenger, baggage or freight delay will be subject to the terms of the airline carriage contracts. The nature and considerable scope of typical airline powers and the minimal obligations they accept in air carriage contracts as regards pre-flight delays, were discussed in Chapters 3 and 4, as was the possibility that airline acts may

- breach consumer guarantees (e.g. as to carriage within a reasonable time) implied into air carriage contracts;

- use "overbooking" practices that contravene consumer laws as to accepting payment without intending to provide a service; or

-engage in other unfair practices.

Usually airlines purport to exclude or limit all their liabilities, except as may be provided for in the contract or under the IACLRs or other applicable laws e.g. consumer laws or EU regulations (none of which can be contracted out of).

For example, Cl.9.2 of the Qantas Airways GCC provides:

****

Where your flight is delayed or cancelled as a result of an Event Beyond our Control, whether you have checked in or not, we will:

- use reasonable endeavours to rebook you on the next available flight on our services at no additional cost to you

- alternatively, if we are unable to rebook you on services acceptable to you, we will refund the applicable fare.

We will not be responsible for paying any other costs or expenses you may incur as a result of the delay or cancellation, except as otherwise provided in these Conditions of Carriage or required by applicable laws.

****

More specifically as to delays, we see from Cl.9.1 of the Qantas Airways GCC, that "flight times" are excluded from the contracts of carriage. Some other airlines assert that "times shown in timetables, schedules or elsewhere are subject to change at any time". Thus, assuming that as a result of such terms, no flight times are agreed, it is often difficult to establish that a delay has in fact occurred, and, if it has, that the delay can be the basis for a claim for compensation. The Qantas Airways GCC even imposes on passengers, an obligation to verify and be aware of proper flight times, in Cl.9.1, it states:

****

(a) *Schedules Not Guaranteed:* We will use our reasonable endeavours to operate in accordance with our published schedules. However, we do not guarantee the flight times and they do not form part of your contract of carriage with us.

(b) *Flight Changes:* Before we accept your booking, we or our Authorised Agent will tell you the scheduled departure time of your flight and it will be shown on your Ticket [or Itinerary/Receipt]. We may need to change the scheduled departure time of your flight after your Ticket has been issued. If you give us or our Authorised Agent contact information, we or they will use our reasonable endeavours to let you know about any changes. In any event, prior to your flight you should check to ensure your flight times have not changed. You should check the flight departure and arrival information posted at the airport. Except as otherwise provided in the Convention or any applicable laws, we will not be liable to you for any losses that you may incur if you fail to do so.

****

It is still uncertain to what extent such words in contracts of air carriage actually impose any obligations on passenger to take steps to verify flight times and if they do not do this, whether or not such failure to verify will absolve airlines of responsibility, but they will always be used by airlines to deny liability and even found an argument for an *estoppel* in respect of any claims for delay.

Do airlines provide "denied boarding" compensation?

Airline denied boarding schemes are variable. Airlines try to limit their obligations to passengers when denying boarding even when it is their own fault, such as when there is overbooking. For example, Qantas Airways (QF) General Conditions of Carriage (GCC) for passengers and baggage (as with other airlines) states, in the second part of Cl. 10.3 that:

****

"If you are denied boarding on an overbooked scheduled international flight for which you have both a valid Ticket and a confirmed reservation, and you have presented at check-in by the Check-In Deadline and complied with all applicable requirements for travel as set out in these Conditions of Carriage, we will offer you as seat on the next available flight on our services. If this is not acceptable to you, we will provide compensation and any care required by any law which may apply or in accordance with our policy if there is no applicable law. This will depend on the jurisdiction in which the denied boarding occurs.

Our denied boarding compensation policy is available on request"

****

Eligibility for airline voluntary compensation depends on the passenger complying with all contractual requirements – so arrival at a check-in counter one minute late means ineligibility. Compensation and assistance is provided in accordance with applicable laws, if there are any (such as exist in the EU but almost nowhere else) or with airline "policy" (whatever that is or may be at any point of time).

Denied boarding procedures are far from clear. Taking the Qantas Airways example, the airline must solicit volunteers before anyone is denied boarding involuntarily, but it is not specified what sort of compensation such volunteers receive (QF GCC, Cl.10.3). Passengers volunteering would not normally know what compensation to ask for, as there is no contractual term or regulatory provision requiring the airlines to give volunteers or any customers being denied boarding, any form of notice with full information as to the assistance and compensation available to them. This is not the case with persons "bumped" involuntarily, as the airline GCC states that an "airline policy" document is available at their international check-in counters. (Of course, this may not be the case in practice.) Nor is it easily available on airline websites.

Is there an alternative to airline denied board compensation?

Consumer claims may also be made at a later time. The overall effect of rather unclear and unhelpful contractual terms and rather tenuous legislative protections against denied boarding in Australia and NZ, is that it is unlikely that claims for compensation for losses suffered in respect of pre-flight delay will be successful. Furthermore, accepting compensation at the airport will usually involve signing a waiver of any right to make other claims against the airline.

While Australian and NZ consumer laws provide some ex post facto grounds for recovery of damages in tribunals or courts (and even prosecutions), they do not provide assistance or compensation to travelling consumers at the time delays occur (unlike what occurs in the EU) and making a claim subsequently is not easy (see Chapter 3). The Australian Competition and Consumer Commission (ACCC) has taken little interest in airline "overbooking" practices since the 1980s when the (then) Trade Practices Commission required compliance with a code of conduct for denied boarding (travel agent licensing was also introduced), although even that weak voluntary code of conduct seems to have fallen into disuse.

How Does The EU Delay Compensation Scheme Work?

Denied boarding, flight cancellation and delay compensation is mandatory in the EU. The relevant EU regulation requires airlines to pay compensation to passengers in respect of (a) denied boarding; (b) flight cancellation; and (c) long delays. Thus, the scheme covers mainly pre-flight delays of passengers. The rights and benefits accorded by the EU to passengers in the event of denied boarding, flight cancellation and long delays are as is required by the EU *Regulation (EC) No 261/20* (discussed below).

However, some airlines, especially "low-cost" still try to avoid their obligations and challenge claims. Claims should be made as soon as possible and some airlines argue that their contract terms and conditions determine time limits for making claims, although laws applying in the country where the claim is made in court will usually apply, e.g. 6 years in the United Kingdom, but there is uncertainty in other jurisdictions. Airlines have also attempted to avoid liability under the EU regulation when the baggage drop-off and check-in queues they manage are so long that they cause passengers to arrive late at the boarding point, but this has been rejected.

EU regulatory controls apply to all airlines flying in the EU, but there are some exceptions for non-EU airlines (e.g. non-EU airline flights going to the EU are not subject to these EU rules). Airlines carrying passengers within the European Union (EU) will set out in their documentation or carriage contracts, the special rules applying to their flights to and from the EU. This is required by all applicable EU regulations, including those providing compensation for cancellation and delay.

The Qantas Airways GCC for Passenger and Baggage, Cl.20 does this. Note that non-EU airlines provide less protection to passengers than EU airlines in respect of delays, cancellation or denied boarding as only their flights **from** EU airports are covered by the EU regulation.

If the passenger is travelling on an EU "community carrier" (an airline licensed in an EU member state e.g. British Airways, KLM etc), then the EU regulation applies also to flights **to EU airports** even if the flights are from non-EU airports, e.g. Sydney or Auckland. Passengers are thus better protected on EU "community carriers" when flying to or in the EU.

What EU compensation is provided for denied boarding?

Denied boarding in the EU is always compensated and assistance is provided. The EU regulation (EC) No 261/20 provides for compensation and assistance to passengers in respect of any "denied boarding" (which includes more than just being "bumped" from a full flight), as well as for cancellation and long delays: discussed below. (Incidentally, passengers with reduced mobility or accompanied by certified service dogs are to be given priority in all circumstances [EU reg, Art 11(1)]).

Airline obligations are a combination of their responsibilities under the EU regulation and under their air carriage contracts, but the provisions in the EU regulation take precedence over any inconsistent contractual terms. By the EU regulation, no passenger rights can be waived or limited by the contract [EU reg, Art 15], and EU member states must establish procedures for complaints and enforcement [Art 16]. Furthermore, other rights of redress passengers may have e.g. separate claims for consequential damages, are not diminished by compensation or assistance given pursuant to EU regulation:

> ".. no provision of this Regulation may be interpreted as restricting its right to seek compensation from any person, including third parties, in accordance with the law applicable. In particular, this Regulation shall in no way restrict the operating air carrier's right to seek reimbursement from a tour operator or another person with whom the operating air carrier has a contract."[EU reg, Art 13]

Finally, note that for passengers on board "community carriers" (EU licensed airlines), flights departing from EU airports and also from non-EU airports destined for airports in the EU are all subject to these EU rules. However, for passengers on board a non-EU airline, these EU rules concern only delays etc arising out of departures from any EU airport.

How do voluntary and involuntary denied boarding differ?

EU rules differ as regards passengers who voluntarily surrender their rights to be carried and those who do not. Overall, subject to negotiating a better incentive arrangement at the time, the benefits for volunteers may be less than for passengers involuntarily denied boarding (for example, there is no requirement that volunteers receive accommodation and meals etc [under EU reg, Art 9]. Also, any involuntarily 'bumped" passengers have a right to seek further compensation beyond that required to be given by the EU regulation [Art 12], provided they do not sign a waiver to make such claims.

More specifically, certain procedures must be followed.

- **voluntary surrender of reservation: an incentive**

If denied boarding is likely in the EU, a prescribed procedure must be followed. Airlines must first call for volunteers who negotiate their compensation. (Volunteers should ask for a large payment and accommodation etc. if needed, as it is not expressly stated that volunteers will receive any "assistance" e.g. meals, telephone calls etc under Art 9 (see below)). It is merely stated [**EU reg, Art 4(1)**] that:

> "When an operating carrier reasonably expects to deny boarding on a flight, it shall first call for volunteers to surrender their reservations in exchange for benefits under conditions to be agreed between the passenger concerned and the operating air carrier."

Contracts of air carriage can also affect these "benefits".

For example, under the Qantas GCC, passengers voluntarily accepting denied boarding are to be offered "an incentive … [but will] not be entitled to any further payment, refund or compensation" [Cl 10.3]. Volunteers can negotiate unspecified financial compensation at the time [QF GCC, Cl 20 – EC 261/2004], but they do not necessarily know if it is more of an incentive than the "benefit" to be offered for involuntary denied boarding under Art 7 of the EU regulation (below).

Volunteers are also entitled to re-imbursement or re-routing under Art 8 of the EU regulation [EU reg, Art 4(1)]. So this should be offered separate to any "benefit" negotiated.

- **involuntary denial of boarding: compensation**

Passengers involuntarily denied boarding are to be offered immediate financial compensation, as specified in Art 7 of the EU regulation; "assistance" in the form of meals, accommodation where necessary, and if a stay of at least of one night is required, hotel–airport transport and telephone calls as specified in Art 9; as well as re-imbursement or re-rerouting as specified in Art 8.

More specifically, the EU regulation, Art 4, provides:

> "If an insufficient number of volunteers comes forward to allow the remaining passengers with reservations to board the flight, the operating air carrier may then deny boarding to passengers against their will" [Art 4(2)]; and the operator shall immediately provide

- compensation in accordance with Art 7, amounting to:

"(a) EUR 250 for all flights of 1,500 kilometres or less;

(b) EUR 400 for all intra-Community flights of more than 1,500 kilometres, and for all other flights between 1,500 and 3,500 kilo-metres;

(c) EUR 600 for all flights not falling under (a) or (b).

In determining the distance, the basis shall be the last destination at which the denial of boarding or cancellation will delay the passenger's arrival after the scheduled time." (see below for full text Art 7)

- re-imbursement or re-routing under Art 8 (see below); and

- care and assistance under Art 9 (see below for details).

- **voluntary and involuntary denied boarding: re-routing**

Aside from the "incentive" (for volunteers) or "financial compensation" (for non-volunteers), under the EU regulation, both volunteers and involuntarily 'bumped' passengers must be given re-routing or re-imbursement as follows [**EU reg, Art 8**]:

1. Where reference is made to this Article, passengers shall be offered the choice between;

reimbursement within 7 days of the full cost of the ticket at the price at which it was bought, for the part or parts of the journey not made and for the part or parts already made if the flight is no longer serving any purpose in relation to the passenger's original travel plan, together with, when relevant, a return flight to the first point of departure on your ticket, at the earliest opportunity; or

- re-routing, under comparable transport conditions, to the passenger's final destination, at the earliest opportunity; or

- re-routing, under comparable transport conditions, to the passenger's final destination at a later date at the passenger's convenience, subject to availability of seats.

2. Paragraph 1(a) shall also apply to passengers whose flights form part of a package, except for the right to reimbursement where such right arises under Directive 90/314/EEC.

3. When, in the case where a town, city or region is served by several airports, an operating air carrier offers a passenger a flight to an airport alternative to that for which the booking was made, the operating air carrier shall bear the cost of transferring the passenger from that alternative airport either to that for which the booking was made, or to another close-by destination agreed with the passenger.

- **involuntary denied boarding only: assistance**

Although no assistance is required for volunteers by EU regulation Art 4(1,(3) (but it may be negotiated), it is obligatory for airlines to offer meals and accommodation assistance under Art 9, to all passengers involuntarily denied boarding [**EU reg, Art 9**]:

1. Where reference is made to this Article, passengers shall be offered free of charge:

(a) meals and refreshments in a reasonable relation to the waiting time;

(b) hotel accommodation in cases

— if a stay of one or more nights becomes necessary, or

— if a stay additional to that intended by the passenger becomes necessary;

(c) transport between the airport and place of accommodation (hotel or other).

2. In addition, passengers shall be offered free of charge two telephone calls, telex or fax messages, or e-mails.

3. In applying this Article, the operating air carrier shall pay particular attention to the needs of persons with reduced mobility and any persons accompanying them, as well as to the needs of unaccompanied children.

Unaccompanied children and persons with reduced mobility and their companions are entitled to care and assistance "as soon as possible, under EU regulation, Art 11(2).

What compensation etc is provided for flight cancellation in the EU?

In the EU, late cancellation of flights is compensated except in "extraordinary circumstances". Early cancellation – with more than 14 days' notice – is allowed. Airline obligations are determined by the terms of the contract of air carriage (to the extent that they are not overridden by the EU *regulation EC No. 261/2004*), or other applicable consumer protection laws.

Air carriage contracts protect airlines and usually provide that although air carriers will use their best efforts to meet scheduled flight times, flight times mentioned on the ticket are neither guaranteed nor form part of the contract of carriage. Further, the air carrier purports to exclude almost all liability for any loss suffered by the passenger as a result of a delay or cancellation except as stated in the contract. (Contractual provisions and their effect were discussed in Chapter 4.)

The EU regulation only provides compensation and assistance for **late cancellation,** (i.e., 14 days or less before scheduled departure, **and not if a close re-routing is offered** under Art 5(1)(c)) [EU reg, Art 5].

The compensation and assistance that the airline operator must give for late cancellation is on a graduated scale, depending on two factors: (a) the amount of cancellation notice; and (b) the equivalence of re-routing. **EU reg Art 5** provides:

1. In case of cancellation of a flight, the passengers concerned shall:

(a) be offered assistance by the operating air carrier in accordance with Article 8 (*reimbursement or re-routing*); and

(b) be offered assistance by the operating air carrier in accordance with Article 9(1)(a) and 9(2) (*meals and telephone calls*), as well as, in event of re-routing when the reasonably expected time of departure of the new flight is at least the day after the departure as it was planned for the cancelled flight, the assistance specified in Article 9(1)(b) and 9(1)(c) (*hotel accommodation and transfers*); and

(c) have the right to compensation by the operating air carrier in accordance with Article 7 [(see below)], unless:

(i) they are informed of the cancellation at least two weeks before the scheduled time of departure; or

(ii) they are informed of the cancellation between two weeks and seven days before the scheduled time of departure and are offered re-routing, allowing them to depart no more than two hours before the scheduled time of departure and reach their final destination less than four hours after the scheduled time of arrival; or

(iii) they are informed of the cancellation less than seven days before the scheduled time of departure and are offered re-routing, allowing them to depart no more than one hour before the scheduled time of departure and to reach their final destination less than two hours after the scheduled time of arrival.

2. When passengers are informed of the cancellation, an explanation shall be given concerning possible alternative transport.

3. An operating air carrier shall not be obliged to pay compensation in accordance with Article 7, if it can prove that the cancellation is caused by extraordinary circumstances which could not have been avoided even if all reasonable measures had been taken (e.g. cyclones, but not mechanical problems).

4. The burden of proof concerning the questions as to whether and when the passenger has been informed of a cancellation of the flight shall rest with the operating air carrier.

The amount of compensation for late cancellation (as for long delays: see below) is also specified in EU law.

****

Article 7
Right to compensation

1. Where reference is made to this Article, passengers shall receive compensation amounting to:

(a) EUR 250 for all flights of 1 500 kilometres or less;

(b) EUR 400 for all intra-Community flights of more than 1 500 kilometres, and for all other flights between 1 500 and 3 500 kilometres;

(c) EUR 600 for all flights not falling under (a) or (b).

In determining the distance, the basis shall be the last destination at which the denial of boarding or cancellation will delay the passenger's arrival after the scheduled time.

2. When passengers are offered re-routing to their final destination on an alternative flight pursuant to Article 8, the arrival time of which does not exceed the scheduled arrival time of the flight originally booked

(a) by two hours, in respect of all flights of 1 500 kilometres or less; or

(b) by three hours, in respect of all intra-Community flights of more than 1 500 kilometres and for all other flights between 1 500 and 3 500 kilometres; or

(c) by four hours, in respect of all flights not falling under (a) or (b), the operating air carrier may reduce the compensation provided for in paragraph 1 by 50 %.

3. The compensation referred to in paragraph 1 shall be paid in cash, by electronic bank transfer, bank orders or bank cheques or, with the signed agreement of the passenger, in travel vouchers and/or other services.

4. The distances given in paragraphs 1 and 2 shall be measured by the great circle route method.

****

Note that no time limits are specified for making the payment of the compensation and airline carriage contracts sometimes provide that the airline has several weeks to make the payment.

Can airlines avoid compensating in "extraordinary circumstances"?

Airlines can avoid paying cancellation compensation. This occurs if they can prove that the cancellation is caused by

"extraordinary circumstances which could not have been avoided even if all reasonable measures had been taken".

These circumstances could include cancellations due to volcanic ash clouds following an unexpected eruption, but not necessarily, if due to weather phenomena that could have been foreseen by taking reasonable measures. Indeed, airlines have sophisticated meteorological services. Finally, technical problems inherent to the normal operation of aircraft are not extraordinary circumstances allowing avoidance of payments.

What is the EU compensation and assistance for long delays?

In the EU short delays are tolerated, but assistance, compensation and even re-imbursement is provided for long delays. These provisions are unclear in two respects: the right to monetary compensation for long delay is not expressly stated but has been taken to be implied by the court (see below); and it is unclear if the provisions apply only to pre-flight delays of passengers, although this would seem to be the case, because the IACLRs apply to in-flight delays (see Chapter 7.2).

Long-haul flights of more than 3,500km, can depart up to 4 hours late without providing compensation and assistance (but only 2 hours delay is tolerated for short flights). Under EU regulation (EC) 261/2004, Art 6, the airline operator must provide graduated levels of assistance for delay depending on the period of pre-flight delay (measured from scheduled time of departure to arrival time) compared to the length of the flight. A five hour delay entitles the passenger to full re-imbursement, so passengers travel free. **EU reg Art 6** provides:

1. When an operating air carrier reasonably expects a flight to be delayed beyond its scheduled time of departure:

(a) for 2 hours or more in the case of flights of 1,500 kilometres or less; or

(b) for 3 hours or more in the case of all intra-Community flights of more than 1,500 kilometres and of all other flights between 1,500 and 3,500 kilometres; or

(c) for 4 hours or more, in the case of all flights not falling under (a) or (b),

passengers shall be offered by the operating air carrier:

(i) the assistance specified in Article 9(1)(a) and 9(2) (*meals and telephone calls*) [(see above)]; and

(ii) when the reasonably expected time of departure is at least the day after the time of departure previously announced, the assistance specified in Article 9(1)(b) and 9(1)(c) (*hotel accommodation and transfers*); and

(iii) when the delay is at least five hours, the assistance specified in Article 8(1)(a) (*re-imbursement within 7 days and return flight*).

2. In any event, the assistance shall be offered within the time limits set out above with respect to each distance bracket.

Monetary compensation is also to be paid for long delays. Different amounts are payable in accordance with the length of the flight, in the same way as compensation is paid for actual cancellation under EU reg Art 7 (set out above), because they are comparable situations. It does not matter that Art 6 makes no specific mention of compensation for delay (unlike Art 5 dealing with cancellation).

7.2 DELAY IN CARRIAGE: PASSENGERS, BAGGAGE & FREIGHT

Airline liability for in-flight delays in international air carriage is presumed. Airlines are "presumed" liable under the IACLRs "for damage occasioned by delay" of "passengers, baggage and cargo", **but only if it occurs "in the carriage by air"**. This is stated in all versions of the IACLRs, Art 19. It seems that the term "baggage" includes cabin baggage, however described, although this is only expressly stated in the latest version of the IACLRs (Montreal Convention 1999, Art 17(4)) that:

> Unless otherwise specified, in this Convention the term "baggage" means both checked baggage and unchecked baggage.

Delay "in the carriage by air" under the IACLRs does not include where a passenger is denied boarding (discussed above) before carriage begins, although being "bumped" off a connecting flight when in transit would occur after the carriage begins, so it would be "in the carriage by air".

In **domestic** air carriage, **in Australia**, liability for delay is not provided for in the parallel rules governing non-convention (domestic) air carriage under CACLA, Pt IV. Consequently, claims for delay in the course of Australian domestic air carriage can only be made on the same bases as pre-flight delay claims discussed in Chapter 7.1, above.

However, **in NZ, passenger delay is provided for** in the parallel domestic rules and airline liability for it is presumed (NZCAA, Pt 9B, especially s 91Z). Essentially the same rules apply as with international air carriage. But for baggage and airfreight delay, the contract of air carriage and general law principles govern claims in domestic air carriage of goods.

What must be proved in order to bring a delay claim?

Delay in air carriage must cause the damage complained of, for there to be presumed airline liability. The claimant must prove "damage occasioned by delay" (Art 19); that is, there must be damage suffered by the claimant, and this "damage" must be "occasioned" by the delay during air carriage. (Incidentally, **in NZ**, NZCCA, s 91Z makes a carrier liable "for damage caused by delay", but the wording difference seems to be irrelevant.)

But what is "damage" in this context? It is not defined in any version of the IACLRs nor qualified in any way, so it can be given its widest natural meaning. Different kinds of damage may be caused by:

- delay of passengers e.g. missed connections, reservations, meetings, tourism activities – many of which have been paid for and are not refundable; or
- delay of baggage, e.g. the cost of buying replacement clothes for a meeting or event such as a wedding, as well as any inconvenience. Similar kinds of damage can result from the delay of baggage and air freight sent by a traveller. (Commercial air freight delays e.g. equipment sent, may also result in damage.)

What amounts to in-flight delay?

Delay must be for an unreasonable period of time. What amounts to "delay" in the carriage of passengers and the delivery of baggage, may differ from what would amount to "delay" in the delivery of freight. Often a short delay of passengers and baggage may be significant and thus unreasonable, when it would be insignificant for freight; unless the contract makes specific provision in respect of delivery times.

As "delay" is not defined in the IACLRs, normal principles apply to determine its meaning, but essentially, carriage should take place within a reasonable time, having regard to all the circumstances of the case.

This test echoes the guarantee to perform a service within a reasonable time, which is implied into consumer transactions **in Australia**, by ACL, s 62 which would apply to delay in the domestic air carriage of baggage and freight in Australia (as they are not covered by CACLA Pt IV), and **in NZ**, by NZCGA, s 30 and NZCaGoA, which apply to delay in the domestic carriage of baggage and freight (as they are not covered by NZCAA Pt 9B).

(For international air carriage, implied guarantees to perform air carriage within a reasonable time apply only to pre-flight delays as the former are governed exclusively by the IACLRs: see above).

Although airlines cannot contract out of their IACLR liabilities nor their obligations to consumers in domestic air carriage (under, **for NZ**, NZCAA, Pt 9B and NZCGA, and **for Australia**, the ACL: see Chapter 3), contractual commitments may still play a role where the applicable rules are silent e.g. airlines, in contracts of air carriage, normally exclude any duty to abide by an established timetable.

For example, the Virgin Australia Conditions of Carriage, Cl 11 and Qantas Airways Conditions of Contract[6] on air tickets provide in Cl 9 that:

****

We will use our reasonable endeavours to operate in accordance with our published schedules. However, we do not guarantee the flight times and they do not form part of your contract of carriage with us. ... Before we accept your booking, we or our Authorised Agent will tell you the scheduled departure time of your flight and it will be shown on your Ticket. We may need to change the scheduled departure time of your flight after your Ticket has been issued. If you give us or our Authorised Agent contact information, we or they will use our reasonable endeavours to let you know about any changes. In any event, prior to your flight you should check to ensure your flight times have not changed. You should check the flight departure and arrival information posted at the airport. Except as otherwise provided in the Convention or any applicable laws, we will not be liable to you for any losses that you may incur if you fail to do so. ...

We will not be responsible for paying any other costs or expenses you may incur as a result of the delay or cancellation, except as otherwise provided in these Conditions of Carriage or required by applicable laws.

****

Who can claim for in-flight delay and from which airlines?

Passengers, consignees and a few others may claim against airlines for in-flight delay. Passengers who are delayed and persons entitled to delivery of delayed baggage or freight (shippers or anyone so entitled as specified in the contract of carriage), and their personal representatives, may make delay claims under the IACLRs. Also, other persons awaiting the arrival of a passenger or delivery of goods, may claim if they have suffered a provable loss as a result of the delay.

Several airlines may be claimed against. Usually, contracting air carriers and any airlines performing carriage on which delay occurs, are liable for any delay damage that occurs and claims can be made against them. The "contracting carrier": the airline named on the ticket; is the most obvious airline to make delay claims against under IACLR liability provisions.

However, the situation is a little more complicated if delay occurs on an airline which is a sub-contracting carrier. Then, the airlines that can be claimed against in different circumstances are:

- **"successive carriers"**: subcontracting airlines who are contemplated by the parties, may be claimed against under all versions of the IACLRs, for:

(a) passenger delay, if performing the carriage when the delay occurs;

(b) baggage delay if they are airlines that are the first, last or the performing carrier, when the delay occurs;

(c) freight delay claim can be made against: the first carrier (by the consignor), the last carrier (by the consignee) and the performing carrier when the delay occurs (by both).

- **"actual carriers"**: subcontractors who are performing carriers when the delay occurs (but who are not a "successive carrier": see Chapter 2.1), may also be claimed against, either:

(a) when the Montreal Convention 1999 applies (as it includes Guadalajara Convention principles: see Chapter 2); or

(b) when one of the other IACLR versions apply and the states between which the air carriage occurred are both also parties to the Guadalajara Convention (see Chapter 2).

What does "in the carriage by air" mean?

Only a limited period is covered by the expression: "in the carriage by air". Delay on international flights, must occur "in the carriage by air" of passengers, baggage or cargo (IACLRs, Art 19), although this period does not expressly include disembarkation and transfers; so appears to be more limited than for.

- claims for passenger injury, where "carriage by air" expressly extends to the process of embarkation or disembarkation for passengers (see Chapter 5);

- claims for denied boarding which occurs before embarkation (see Chapter 7.1)

- claims for baggage and cargo damage or loss, which expressly extend to all occasions when goods are "in the charge of" a carrier and in transhipment, e.g. if in airport storage (see Chapter 6).

However, it would seem that delays, e.g. in providing facilities for disembarkation should be counted as a delay in the carriage by air.

Can "in-flight" denied boarding be claimed for as delay?

Denying a passenger boarding after a stopover is "in the carriage by air" and within the application of IACLRs, Art 19. Any pre-flight denied boarding ("bumping" often arising from "overbooking") occurring before air carriage begins, would be outside the ambit of the IACLRs.

Domestic in-flight delays are different. **In Australia,** domestic in-flight denied boarding, like other domestic in-flight delay, is outside the non-international or domestic rules (CACLA, Pt IV, ss 28–29), but still subject to the air carriage contract applicable in each case, and all those terms implied by relevant legislation e.g. consumer guarantees governing the acceptance of payment despite knowing that there is an inability to provide it and requiring that the service, that air carriage be supplied within a reasonable time (except for cargo) etc (see Chapter 3).

In NZ, domestic air carriage delay liability, including "in-flight" denied boarding, is similar to airline liability under the IACLRs. The airline is presumed "liable for delay in the carriage of passengers" as in international liability of airlines for passenger delay, **except** that there are express exclusions of delay liability as regards any carriage by aircraft used solely for military purposes and for single flights departing and returning to the same place, as in a sightseeing flight (in NZCAA, s 91W).

When can international airlines avoid liability for delay?

If "all necessary measures" were taken or there was contributory negligence, airline liability may be avoided. The most recent version of the IACLRs, based on the Montreal Convention 1999, qualifies the presumed air carrier liability for delay, in a proviso to Art 19, so that the presumption of liability for delay can be overturned if the airline

> "proves that it and its servants took all measures that could reasonably be required to avoid the damage or that it was impossible for it or them to take such measures"

This seems slightly easier for airlines to prove than the stricter "all necessary measures" defence set out in Art 20 of the other versions of the IACLRs which applies to all claims (discussed in Chapter 5).

Under the most recent and all other versions of the IACLRs, there is also an airline defence to delay (and other) claims, if the damage was caused or contributed to by the negligence of the passenger or injured person (see Chapter 5: "contributory negligence". However, it is difficult to see how such a defence might arise as regards delay unless that passenger's behaviour caused a flight diversion.

Can domestic airlines avoid liability for passenger delay?

If "all necessary measures" were taken, there was contributory negligence or other good reason, airline liability is avoided. First, there is no airline liability for delay in domestic air carriage **in Australia**, except under the contract of carriage and under general law and general law defences are also available. **In NZ**, in a domestic passenger delay claim, an equivalent defence to that in Art 20 of all IACLRs (not the latest version) is provided if "all necessary measures" were taken (NZCAA, s 91ZA: see above and Chapter 5); and in respect of the contributory negligence of the passenger (NZCAA, s 91ZB: see Chapter 5).

Other good reasons for avoiding liability exist in NZ. In NZCAA, s 91Z(2), it is provided that despite presumed airline liability for passenger delay, that liability is avoided:

"if the carrier proves that the delay—

(a) arose by reason of—

(i) meteorological conditions; or

(ii) compliance with instructions, advice, or information given by an air traffic control service; or

(iii) obedience to orders or directions given by a lawful authority; or

(b) was made necessary by *force majeure*; or

(c) was necessary for the purpose of saving or attempting to save life."

These "good reason" defences to passenger delay claims on NZ domestic flights are in addition to the international ones.

How much compensation can be recovered for delay?

Losses cause by delay must be proved to the limits prescribed. Compensation for delay occasioned in international air carriage (like claims for passenger injury and loss or damage to baggage and freight: discussed above), are subject to maximum IACLR limits (unless avoided). Damages awards for delay are rarely high, as only losses arising as a natural consequence of a delay are compensable, unless special circumstances are communicated to and accepted by the carrier (and this would be rare).

Diverse compensation limits exist as regards presumed airline liability for delay (as with injury or death claims), ranging from some AUD32 per kg for freight to almost AUD9,000 for passenger delay, depending upon which version of the IACLRs or the domestic rules apply to the carriage. The maximum compensation limits under the various rules are:

1. Montreal Convention 1999:

    (a) passenger delay: 4,694SDRs (approx AUD8,920) – some defences are available: see below).

    (b) baggage delay: 1,131SDRs (approx AUD 2,150) (total for all baggage)

    (c) freight delay: 19 SDRs (AUD36) per kg

2. Warsaw-Hague-MAP4 Convention (Art 22(2):

    (a) passenger delay: 250,000 PGF (in total for injury, death and delay)

    (b) baggage delay: 250PGF (approx AUD30) per kg

    (c) freight delay: 17 SDRs (AUD32) per kg

3. Warsaw-Hague Convention (Art 22(1)-(2)):

    (a) passenger delay: 250,000 PGF (in total for injury, death and delay)

    (b) both baggage and cargo: 250 PGF (AUD30) per kg

4. Warsaw Convention (Art 22(1)-(2)):

    (a) passenger delay: 125,000 PGF (in total for injury, death and delay)

    (b) both baggage and cargo delay: 25O PGF (AUD30) per kg

5. Australian Domestic: no provisions exist for delay claims

6. NZ Domestic: NZCAA s 91ZC and NZCaGoA, s 15(1)

(a) passenger delay: maximum of 10 times the sum paid for the air carriage

(b) goods delay NZD 2,000 per unit under the NZCaGoA, s 15(1) and s 3(1) defines units as baggage items and freight as containers, pallets, packages.

The now virtually obsolete Poincaré Gold Francs (PGF) value is based on the price of gold and the price of gold fluctuates considerably, but as a rough guide at the time of writing, 1,000 PGF is approximately AUD120.

Can airlines make discretionary payments for delay?

Airlines sometimes make advance payments to passengers when delays occur. There is usually no mention of such payments in air carriage contracts, but when baggage delays occur informal requests may be made to the airline for compensation within the prescribed limits (see above) in order to purchase necessities, for which receipts must be kept.

8. Surface Damage or Injury Claims

Claims can be made for injury to persons or damage to property on the surface subject to legislation and the common law. Aircraft, especially small aircraft, helicopters and drones do sometimes crash, for example while carrying out crop dusting, surveying, photography or leisure activities. Fortunately large aircraft crashes are rare – as when Pan Am flight 103 crashed into the village of Lockerbie, Scotland on 23 December 1988 – but in either case, persons on the surface can be injured or property damaged. It's just worse with large aircraft. Usually, aircraft operators or pilots are liable for such injuries under legislation or the common law, but this has nothing to do with those laws and international conventions governing carriage by air, discussed in Chapters 5 – 7.

Other circumstances can arise when injury or damage is occasioned to persons or property on the surface as a result of activities incidental to aircraft operations. These mainly occur in the context of aircraft flight and airport operations and involve noise and vibrations, which are discussed below in Chapter 8.3 and in Chapter 9. Liability for other injuries or nuisance at or near airports are mentioned in Chapter 10.

What Laws Apply?

Offences exist and legislative provisions govern liability for aircraft causing damage on the surface on the earth. Prosecutable offences exist in relation to unauthorised dropping of things or people from an aircraft in flight – exceptions exist for authorised parachute jumps and agricultural operations, as well as for the dropping ballast from hot-air balloons or jettisoning fuel or cargo in an emergency when there is no danger to persons or property on the surface.

Also, civil liability may result in compensation for injury.

Uniform rules for airline liability for surface damage were established by the 1952 Rome Convention but it was never ratified by NZ and it no longer applies in Australia. However, it does apply in almost 50 other countries, and as the uniform rules may apply to Australian or NZ aircraft or persons in those foreign countries, a brief discussion of the relevant rules occurs at the end of this chapter.

In Australia, surface damage liability is governed by the *Damage by Aircraft Act 1999* (Cth) (DBAA), complemented by equivalent State enactments, which relate only to intrastate flights (at which the Commonwealth legislation does not apply for constitutional reasons, as with CACLA). There is also some scope for the operation of the common law, most importantly, the torts of trespass and negligence.

In NZ, some equivalent legislative provisions establish strict liability of aircraft owners (NZCAA, s 97) and common law remedies for surface damage are also available.

8.1 ARE AIRLINES LIABLE FOR SURFACE DAMAGE?

Airlines are strictly liable for any surface damage they cause. In respect of surface damage to persons and property, both Australia and New Zealand have legislative provisions establishing strict liability of civil aircraft operators for damage caused on the surface, except in specified circumstances.

In Australia, this is done through the DBAA, which has wide application to foreign and Australian registered aircraft, including Commonwealth aircraft but not to Defence Force aircraft, although the DBAA also applies to "the Crown in each of its capacities" (ss 8-9 DBAA). The DBAA applies to acts, omissions, matters and things within Australian territory and to each external Territory by such aircraft operating in Australia. (As the DBBA is Commonwealth law, its application is subject to minor constitutional limitations which are overcome by the existence of complementary state legislation: see below).

In NZ, the provisions of the NZCAA, s 97(3)-(8) are similar to those in Australia, but there is no express exception for Defence Force aircraft.

What Is The Effect Of The Australian Legislation?

Strict liability of aircraft operators for surface damage is created in legislation. In Australia, if injury is caused by aircraft in flight or anything or anyone falling from them, the DBAA and complementary State enactments are the primary basis for the strict liability of aircraft operators and aircraft owners (unless the owner had no active control and another person had the right to exclusive control of the aircraft, under a lease or other agreement). This is not an exclusive remedy, in that it does not exclude alternative claims based on common law in appropriate cases. (In this sense, it is unlike the remedies available against air carriers under CACLA for loss and injury during air carriage.)

Strict liability applies to all aircraft (which would include helicopters and hot-air balloons) except "model aircraft" (s 4, DBAA) and would seem to apply to drones, as they are usually more than toys, but this has not yet been judicially decided nor subjected to regulatory modification.

Aircraft operators and owners are liable if, as set out in DBAA, s 10(1):

[A] person or property on, in or under land or water suffers personal injury, loss of life, material loss, damage or destruction caused by:

(a) an impact with an aircraft that is in flight, or that was in flight immediately before the impact happened; or

(b) an impact with part of an aircraft damaged or destroyed while in flight; or

(c) an impact with a person, animal or thing that dropped or fell from an aircraft in flight; or

(d) something a result of an impact of a kind mentioned in paragraph (a), (b) or (c).

Compensation for any such injury, loss, damage or destruction is recoverable in an action, without proof of intention, negligence or other cause of action, in the same way as if the injury or damage had been caused by wilful act, negligence or default (s 11 DBAA).

What does the aircraft have to do for there to be liability?

Liability relates to aircraft "in flight". The term "in flight" can cause difficulties and can include being on the ground; certainly if it crashes. It is defined as being from when power is applied for take-off until the landing run ends (s 5, DBAA). This is slightly narrower than in the complementary NSW, Victorian, Tasmanian and WA legislation which refer to aircraft "in flight, taking off or landing" which may, but probably do not extend this period.

When is damage or injury caused by an impact?

Liability exists only if damage is caused by an impact or "something that is a result of an impact". This wording extends liability somewhat. It could also include a fire started by an aircraft crash or, for example, to being electrocuted by a fallen power line, caused by, but occurring elsewhere than at the place of impact of the aircraft.

Incidentally, in the abovementioned case, the High Court held that contributory negligence of the claimant was not a defence to reduce the liability of the operator or owner, although the DBAA was then amended and s 11A now specifically allows for an airline defence of contributory negligence by the claimant. Others may be partly responsible for damage suffered and an aircraft owner may be indemnified by other persons such as aircraft operators (and a lessee, charterer or hirer in certain cases).

Assuming some personal injury or material damage can be established (see below), it could perhaps be argued that even noise and vibrations coming from aircraft, which are usually able to be measured physically, may amount to an "impact with ... a thing that fell or dropped from an aircraft" or the "result of [the] impact" (DBAA, s 10(1)-c),(d)). This would be an alternative to making claims on common law grounds, e.g. in trespass or nuisance, for noise or vibration damage, (which are sometimes excluded by legislation in all Australian States except Queensland, if the noise or vibrations are not excessive (see below).

What sort of injury or damage must occur to justify liability?

There must be some physical or material injury suffered before a claim can be made. Mental injury or nervous shock injury is only compensated if the claimant also suffers personal injury, or, if property owned by the person claiming suffers material loss or damage (DBAA, s 10(1A)). For example, a person who suffers psychological trauma by seeing their home destroyed by an aircraft crashing into it, would likely obtain compensation for the mental injury as well as the physical damage.

What is the effect of complementary laws in the States?

In all Australian States, legislative provisions complement the DBAA to ensure similar strict liability applies to aircraft on intrastate flights. For flights having no interstate or territorial character, the relevant state legislation applies (as federal law does not).

The liability created is for material loss or damage caused to any person or property on land or water by a person or article falling from an aircraft in flight, taking off or landing. In such cases, unless the loss or damage was caused or contributed to by the person suffering it, damages are recoverable without proof of negligence, intention or any other cause of action, in the same manner as if the loss or damage had been caused by the wilful act or neglect or default of the aircraft owner.

There are some slight wording differences in the various State enactments (aside from the reference to "in flight" mentioned above), but a notable difference in the South Australian legislation is the exclusion of liability for fire-fighting, standard crop-dusting etc activities under the legislative provisions.

Mental injury or nervous shock would also be compensated according to the law of the State in which the claim is made, but normally only if the person suffers personal injury or property owned by the person suffers material loss or damage (as with the Commonwealth legislation mentioned above). This area of the law is gradually evolving to accept mental stress as a personal injury even without any associated physical injury.

What Is The Scope And Effect Of The NZ Legislation?

NZ strict liability provisions for surface damage apply only to property claims. Briefer provision is made in the NZCAA, s 97(3)-(8) for strict liability of aircraft owners or operators and by s 97(3), the recovery of damages from the owner of an aircraft for:

> "material damage or loss ... caused to property on land or water by an aircraft in flight, taking off, landing, or alighting, or by any person or article in or falling from any such aircraft ... [is] without proof of negligence or intention or other cause of action, as if the damage was caused by his or her fault ..."

Thus fault is presumed and by s 97(8):

> "fault means negligence, breach of statutory duty, or other act or omission which gives rise to a liability in tort;. or would give rise to a defence of contributory negligence."

Only claims for property damage are included under the NZCAA as claims for personal injury, including mental injury, are compensable only under the NZACA accident compensation scheme (see Chapter 5).

The term "aircraft" is broadly defined in s 2(1) and would include all sorts of aircraft, even drones and apparently, even model aircraft.

Owners are the persons liable under the NZCAA and it is only if the aircraft has been hired out for more than 28 days without a crewmember, that the hirer assumes these liabilities (s 97(7)).

On the other hand, if the surface damage is caused by a person descending from the aircraft by parachute, that person assumes the liabilities of the owner, unless the descent was required to avoid injury or death (s 97(6)). Provision is also made for the indemnification of the aircraft owner if some other person is otherwise liable to pay damages and if the fault of the injured party contributed to the damage (s 97(4),(5)).

8.2 What Common Law Remedies Exist?

Aside from the legislation creating strict airline liability for surface damage, common law remedies may also be available. Surface damage to persons or property in Australia or New Zealand may occur, for example, in circumstance where the cause of the injury is not within the terms of any legislation. Then, common law remedies, which would include claims for breach of contract or for the recovery of damages for wrongful acts, such as in tort for e.g. negligence, nuisance or trespass (see below and Chapter 3). These remedies may also be sought as alternatives to claims under the DBAA and NZCAA, s 97 (see Chapter 8.1).

In Australia, it may be that the injury results from operations of an aircraft which is not "in flight" (within the definition in DBAA, s 5), or if there is a specific exclusion of the application of that legislation, such as in the DBBA, s 9(2) in respect of Defence Force aircraft. **In NZ**, there may also be exclusions of the statutory strict liability e.g. as regards a parachute descent made to avoid injury or death as in the NZCAA, s 97(6).

It is especially when legislative provisions do not apply or establish a remedy, that an alternative claim may be made, for example, that a general duty of care is owed to members of the public for careless acts causing damage. This would even apply to the Defence Forces. although such a duty may well be nullified by 'public policy' immunity in war-time, but not in peace-time. **In Australia and in NZ**, most remedies will be found in the common law: contract or tort (especially negligence and perhaps in consumer protection principles), but the remedy will depend on the facts of individual cases.

The circumstances in which any such events may give rise to a claim are too numerous to discuss here, and other books deal in detail with common law and consumer remedies (for the basics, see Chapter 3). Suffice it to say that, in this context, loss or damage on the surface may result from the falling of an object from an aircraft, or even the crashing of an aircraft on the surface; from operations at an aerodrome (which could also implicate other aviation industry entities, such as air traffic controllers: mentioned above); or from the flight of an aircraft above the property of the party injured, if excessive vibrations or noise resulted, although airline liability for "mere flight" is usually excluded by legislation (see below).

What liabilities exist in contract and consumer protection?

Contracts and consumer laws may determine liabilities. There may sometimes be a contractual relationship between the person suffering injury or loss and the aircraft operator, such as in the case of aerial photography, aerial spraying and crop-dusting; or there might be an employment contract between the injured person on the ground and the entity causing the injury, such as the air operator. Then the contract is the first document to consider, as it may expressly provide for, limit or exclude liabilities in such circumstances, or, it may provide for alternative means of dispute resolution e.g. arbitration etc.. There may also be terms (guarantees) implied in contracts, as to the quality of the services provided e.g. under the ACL or NZCGA or in employment legislation, that apply.

Where the contract is a consumer transaction, questions as to misleading or unconscionable conduct and unfair contract terms (ACL, ss 23-27, NZFTA ss 26A,46I,46L) may also provide grounds for a claim or affect or prohibit the enforceability of liability exemption clauses in contracts. The issues are too diverse to discuss here, although aspects of these sorts of claims were dealt with in Chapters 3 and 4.

What liability exists in tort: negligence, trespass or nuisance?

Common law remedies for wrongdoing can be pursued to obtain compensation for injury or loss. Here, the most important remedies are negligence, trespass and nuisance.

Negligence claims

Some surface damage claims may be based on negligence. These grounds derive from the traditional principle set out in *Donoghue v Stevenson* [1832] AC 562, establishing a general duty of care, which if breached, founds a cause of action for damages. Various liabilities to provide compensation may be based on the negligence of an aircraft operator in causing physical or economic damage as a result of an aircraft coming into collision with the surface (or even injuries caused by what is sometimes referred to as "mere overflight": see below).

Alternatively, specific statutory duties which are enforceable as civil actions, may be created by provisions in applicable aviation legislation, such as the *Civil Aviation Act 1988* (Cth), s 20A or the NZCAA, ss 43A-44, which prohibit the reckless operation of aircraft in a manner that might endanger life or property. Likewise, the dropping of articles or other things from an aircraft in flight is an offence (except for authorised parachute jumps, agricultural and other approved operations, dropping ballast in the form of fine sand or water, or, in an emergency, the jettisoning of liquid fuel or even cargo over ground or water where there is no hazard to persons or property: see **in Australia**, under the *Civil Aviation Regulations 1988* (Cth), reg 150; or **in NZ**, e.g. *Civil Aviation Rules Part 91 (General Operating and Flight Rules)*, r.91.235; the *Civil Aviation Rules Part 101 (Parasails, Balloons etc)*, r.101.15).

Conviction of an offence and the imposition of penalties would not preclude a person pursuing a civil action for damages for negligence (or perhaps even for breach of statutory duty in some cases) for any injury or loss suffered as a result of such action.

Establishing that a general or other duty of care existed may not be difficult, even if the air operator did not know of the precise details of the land or property that may be damaged.

Proving that a breach of such a duty (general or statutory) occurred e.g. that a particular item fell from a particular aircraft, and also that the kind of injury suffered was not too remote (i.e., that the kind of injury was reasonably foreseeable), may present serious problems of proof in individual cases, such as where the damage complained of was fright caused to animals and the stampeding of a landowner's herds of cattle or horses, or perhaps the death of and failure to breed mink on a mink farm.

Finally, recovery of damages for the tort of negligence requires that the complainant be occasioned actual damage, which could include physical and emotional trauma, as well as property damage or loss. The usual principles of the law of negligence and breach of statutory duty will apply.

Trespass to land

Trespass to land, including airspace, may found a claim for damages even if there is no injury. A person with an interest in land also has a property interest in the airspace above that land, extending upwards to what would be a reasonable height in the circumstances.

When an aircraft enters into the airspace above land or comes in contact with the surface of the land without permission of the proprietor, it may be actionable in trespass (whether there was any physical damage or not), especially if the low altitude of flight was unreasonable in all the circumstances (see legislative exclusions below). In *Baron Bernstein of Leigh v Skyviews & General Ltd*, Griffiths J said that a landowner has property rights in superjacent airspace "to such height as is necessary for the ordinary use and enjoyment of his land and the structures upon it, and ... above that height he has no greater rights in the air space than any other member of the public". Of course, if there was no actual damage, then compensation is likely to be nominal.

Nuisance claims

Claims can be made to obtain compensation for injury based on the tort of nuisance. An action seeking damages for private nuisance will involve two neighbouring occupiers with competing property interests. This will not normally be the case when an aircraft is in flight as the operator is not the occupier of that part of the airspace above the injured person's property. It requires that some "injury" (not necessarily physical or material) be occasioned and what must be proved is an unreasonable interference by the occupier of one of the premises with a neighbouring occupier's beneficial use and enjoyment of their premises. It does not require actual impact of any kind with the surface or person there.

Nuisance might be occasioned by noise and vibrations etc from the take-off, landing or flight of aircraft over neighbouring premises, such as an airport, but ordinary flight over any other premises in permitted flight lanes or airspace would not normally be sufficient to give rise to a claim for nuisance in these circumstances.

When does legislation exclude claims for "mere flight"?

Legislation provides immunities against claims in trespass and nuisance for "mere flight". Assuming compliance with all applicable aviation legislation (e.g. **in NZ**, NZ Civil Aviation Rules, Part 91) or regulations (e.g. **in Australia**, Civil Aviation Safety Regulations 1998 (Cth) and Air Navigation Regulations 1947 (Cth)); and that the height of the aircraft flight above the ground is reasonable having regard to wind, weather and all the circumstances, five Australian States (not Q'ld or the Territories) and NZ have enacted statutory immunities to exclude air operator liability in trespass and in nuisance, for what is often described as "mere flight" and its ordinary incidents.

"Mere flight" would normally not include low flight or the dropping of articles from aircraft or aircraft coming into contact with the surface (and so does not exclude liabilities and claims in Australia, under the DBAA and State equivalents; or **in NZ**, under NZCAA, s 97 (see above).

Noise and vibrations emanating from aircraft and causing damage will in some cases benefit from a separate immunity (see Chapter 9) and would anyway not normally fall within the scope of the legislative provisions, such as the DBAA, dealing with articles or persons falling from aircraft (see above), although they may be within the "ordinary incidents" of most flights, assuming that relevant regulations and noise certifications are complied with. The same would apply to emissions of smoke or gas and fuel spillage (see below).

Can Claims Arise From Emissions, Noise or Vibrations?

Claims may sometimes be made for damage resulting from aircraft engine emissions, noise and vibrations. Noise and vibrations from aircraft and at airports is a big topic and possible claims in respect of those matters are discussed in more detail in Chapter 9. In particular, breaches of rules or standards relating to engine emissions and fuel spillage may provide the grounds for claims in some cases.

What rules govern aircraft engine emissions, fuel spillage?

Aircraft emissions and fuel spillage are regulated. Most rules that apply to these events reflect ICAO standards and recommended practices. **In Australia**, Commonwealth regulations govern both aircraft engine emissions and the control or prevention of spillage or release of fuel from aircraft in flight. They are found in the *Air Navigation (Aircraft Engine Emissions) Regulations 1995* (Cth) and *Air Navigation (Fuel Spillage) Regulations 1999* (Cth). **In NZ**, these matters are encompassed in the NZ *Civil Aviation Rules*, Parts 21 and 91 (engine emissions) and Pts 119, 125 and 135 (fuel spillage), with holders of Air Operator's Certificates being required to have a fuel policy governing such matters.

Breach of regulations or standards by aircraft operators may give rise to prosecution, or in appropriate cases, found a civil claim for compensation based on the breach of a statutory duty (as an independent cause of action). This can be a hurdle, as for such a duty to exist, the court would have to accept that it was Parliament's intention that the regulations create a private right of action for a particular class of persons who may suffer injury from its breach, even if it is difficult to identify the particular class of persons who were to benefit, under such regulations.

Alternatively, a legal action for damages in negligence may also be possible if injury or loss was occasioned. Other grounds for legal action are problematic, as except in extreme cases, there is immunity from most claims in trespass or nuisance (but not negligence) in the Australian States (except in Qld and the Territories), and in NZ (see above). Finally, unless it can be shown that some impact with the surface occurred, a claimant could not rely on the DBAA or NZCAA, s 97 (see Chapter 8.1).

What happens if fuel spillage rules are breached: Australia?

'Fuel Spillage' regulations set up a fuel spillage control scheme. It involves strict liability offences (offences with no mental element e.g. intent or negligence need be proved: *Air Navigation (Fuel Spillage) Regulations 1999* (Cth), s 6(1)), for unauthorised fuel release during flight. Releasing fuel as a result of an honest and reasonable mistake is a defence to a prosecution: reg 6(2),(3). The scheme applies to aircraft operators (other than non-corporations flying only intrastate flights), who should have their own fuel inspection system.

The Secretary of the Department may also carry out inspections as a preventative measure and on giving five days' written notice (following consultation), any Commonwealth jurisdiction aircraft may be inspected to find out if its fuel system might release fuel during flight. If this is likely, a "grounding notice" will be served on the operator, and it is not withdrawn until proper maintenance has been carried out.

Exceptionally, permission for fuel release during flight can be given by air traffic controllers or CASA, especially in emergency situations. As to civil claims, the jettisoning of fuel etc that makes contact with the surface, clearly falls within the strict liability provisions of the DBAA (discussed above). However, even if injury or loss can be proved, establishing common law or other grounds for a claim may be difficult.

What Rules Govern Surface Damage Claims in Foreign Places?

Foreign laws govern injury and damage in foreign places. When overseas, travellers from Australia and New Zealand, as well as Australian and NZ registered aircraft are subject to foreign laws. Those laws will apply if they are injured or injure someone there. Foreign surface damage laws are similar in many countries, and are discussed here briefly.

If you're in a foreign country, it is the law of that place that applies to persons injured there by something falling from an aircraft or aircraft in flight, whatever their nationality. In almost 50 countries, the uniform rules of the 1952 Rome Convention are in force and apply to foreign aircraft whose state of registration is a contracting party to that Convention – which Australia and NZ are not – but in some of these states, local laws will also give these uniform rules general application to all occurrences of aircraft surface damage in that state, whether caused by foreign aircraft or not, and whether they are from signatory states or non-signatory states to that Convention.

What "uniform rules" apply in foreign countries?

Aircraft operators in many foreign countries are presumed to be liable for surface injury. Essentially, any person who suffers damage on the earth's surface, shall, upon proof that the damage was caused by foreign aircraft in flight, or by any person or thing falling from it, be entitled to compensation from the aircraft operator or person lawfully using the aircraft (or other person maintaining control of the navigation of it). So the air operator is strictly liable to compensate those injured. Compensation is to be in accordance with limits which apply under the convention to all claims for a surface damage incident (see below).

In many countries where the 1952 Rome Convention is in force, local law will resemble the rules of the Convention. So even if the 1952 Rome Convention rules do not apply for one reason or another, then similar general law principles in force in that country will apply.

Thus, the situation under the 1952 Rome Convention rules or equivalent local laws, is the following. First, claims made under the convention are exclusive of any other remedies (except where there is a deliberate act or omission, with intent to cause damage) (Art 9). Second, there is no strict liability if damage suffered is not a direct consequence of the incident or if it results from the normal passage of aircraft through airspace in conformity with existing air traffic regulations. (The "mere flight" immunity is discussed above). Nor does it apply when the damage is caused by military, police or customs aircraft (Art 26) or where liability is regulated by contractual relations between the person suffering damage and the operator e.g. employment; aerial spraying etc (Art 25). (This is similar to the rules in Australia and NZ.)

As "in flight" is widely defined in the 195 Rome Convention, Art 1(2) (and includes lighter-than-air craft), 'end-of-runway' incidents or crashes occurring on take-off or landing are usually included.

What airline defences exist?

Air operator defences under the 1952 Rome Convention include contributory negligence and act of a state authority. Where the uniform rules (under the convention) or a domestic law version of those rules applies, it is a complete or partial defence to a claim (even if made by the personal representative or a survivor of a deceased person), that the entity otherwise liable proves that the damage was caused or contributed to by the negligence of the person who suffered it (or even that person's employee or agent acting within the scope of their authority at the material time) (Art 6(1),(2)).

It is also a complete aircraft operator defence to liability if the surface damage complained of is a direct consequence of armed conflict or civil disturbance: Art 5. Similarly, it is a complete defence if the airline operator who is otherwise liable has been deprived of the use of the aircraft by a public authority, for example, where an aircraft has been requisitioned, for a time, by a government agency (such as if a state of emergency occurs). Aircraft operators that are state authorities may also be able to claim state immunity from civil legal action e.g. if the harm caused was the direct and necessary consequence of an activity the performance of which was required by legislation.

How is compensation assessed under the Convention?

A fund is created under the 1952 Rome Convention to compensate all claimants. The uniform rules use arrangements similar to the traditional "shipping collision" procedure to assess air operator liability for surface damage by providing for a fund which is the full amount available to settle all claims arising from the incident, and setting a scale of aircraft operator liability limits according to the weight of the aircraft (Art 11(1)). If claims exceed the fund, proportional distribution of payments is made (Art 14).

A maximum liability of 500,000 Poincaré gold francs per person is set for any claim for loss of life or personal injury. However, no limit exists for property damage claims (Art 11(2)).

When do compensation limits not apply?

Liability limits may be inapplicable if there are wrongful acts or an intent to cause damage. In such case, there is unlimited liability of the aircraft operator. The limits don't apply if the aircraft operator wrongly made use of the aircraft without the consent of the person entitled to use it; or if the injury which occurred was caused with intent to cause damage, by the deliberate act or omission of the operator (or its employees or agents acting in the course of their employment or scope of their authority) (Art 12). Thus, a pilot who jettisons fuel knowing that it will cause damage on the ground, but with only the intent to save the aircraft, would avoid unlimited liability because of a lack of intent to cause damage on the ground.

What formalities, claim notices are needed?

Various claim formalities must be met by complainants. Notice of claims must be given to the aircraft operator within 6 months of the incident and all legal actions commenced within 2 years (although courts may suspend the period for up to one more year, after which, all rights to claim are extinguished (Art 21).

Civil actions to recover damages based on the Rome Convention 1952 can only be brought in the country where the damage occurred (and if it is party to the convention), except where a different jurisdiction is agreed upon by the parties or the claim is submitted to arbitration (Art 20(1)).

All actions arising from the same incident should be consolidated and the defendant given notice of all interested parties; (Art 20(2),(3)). Court judgments made under the Convention may be enforced in other contracting states under the ordinary law of the place where they are sought to be enforced, although enforcement may be refused on grounds of public policy. Otherwise, normal complicated procedures for enforcing judgments in a foreign country need to be followed.

9. Aircraft, Airport Noise & Vibrations

Air travel has an environmental impact and compensation claims may be made by those affected. Various measures, more in the area of public law (regulatory controls) than private law (compensation claims), have been introduced to deal with the environmental impact of aircraft operations. So there is less scope for private claims for compensation by persons affected by aircraft and airport noise, than for administrative relief. Aside from requirements for noise certificates for aircraft (see below), regulations affect airport activities, curfews, sound insulation programs for buildings near major airports, compensation schemes for depreciation of property values, administrative remedies (including planning objections and appeals), and meet the problem of noise from aircraft, especially at major airports.

If *unreasonable* noise and vibration occur and cause injury or loss, the law of torts, especially negligence and nuisance – which can involve reliance on regulatory duties and standards – remains the main basis for obtaining compensation or injunctive relief (court orders that the activity cease) for noise-related activities of aircraft operators and airports.

Noise from aircraft operations is considered separately here, to noise from airport activities.

9.1 - WHAT NOISE CONTROLS APPLY TO AIRCRAFT?

Aircraft operational noise control is subject to a complex international regulatory regime. Local laws throughout the world implement internationally accepted standards that are set out in Annex 16 to the Chicago Convention, most importantly, noise certification.

In Australia, the *Air Navigation (Aircraft Noise) Regulations 1984* (Cth) (ANANR), deals with aircraft noise emissions but many other regulations, including certification rules in the Civil Aviation Safety Regulations (CASR), relate to aircraft noise. **In NZ**, the aircraft certification process and operating rules in the Civil Aviation Rules (NZ) (CARNZ), Pts 21 and 91 implement the international aircraft noise standards.

What are noise certificates?

Noise certificates are issued to prove conformity of aircraft with internationally accepted standards. A current noise certificate must be obtained by virtually all aircraft before they engage in air navigation. Although, exceptionally, the Secretary of the Department may permit certain limited classes of aircraft to engage in air navigation without the certificate e.g. when aircraft (other than supersonic aircraft) are being tested; when older aircraft participate in air shows; and for aircraft of historical significance or when aircraft are to be used "solely for a purpose that is in the public interest". Flying without a valid noise certificate may be an offence and result in prosecution. It may also found a civil claim for damages in appropriate cases. On the other hand compliance with noise certification makes civil claims for noise compensation very difficult to establish.

Manufacturers usually attest to an aircraft's compliance with noise standards. A noise certificate is deemed to have issued if the manufacturer has included in the aircraft's Flight Manual a statement that, unless revoked, the aircraft conforms with the relevant standard, or, complies with a law relating to control of aircraft noise in a contracting state to the Chicago Convention. Otherwise, owners or operators of aircraft must apply for a noise certificate (or permission to fly without a noise certificate, if a subsonic jet or supersonic aircraft). Applications are made to the Secretary of the Department (who delegates this power, **in Australia**, to authorised officers, CASA and Air Services Australia; or, **in NZ**, the power is delegated to CAANZ).

Noise monitoring also exists. In Australia, for example, inspectors have powers (under the ANANR, reg 14):

- to require (on production of their identity cards) the operator of aircraft to make an aircraft available for inspection at a reasonable time, and

- to inspect aircraft and carry out tests (in flight or otherwise) necessary to measure the noise emitted by an aircraft to ascertain if an aircraft conforms with relevant standards.

Where an aircraft ceases to conform to standards, a notice may be served on the operator (and owner if a different person) expressing an intention to revoke the noise certificate within the prescribed period. Thereafter, if the aircraft does not comply with the reasonable requirements of an inspector, without reasonable excuse, the noise certificate may be revoked. These decisions may be challenged by administrative review, although it would normally be only the aircraft operator who would be entitled to seek such a review.

Thus, the possibility of civil actions for damages based on compliance with aircraft noise standards, is quite limited: for example when it involves challenging the granting of a noise certificate by the responsible public authority (see Chapters 11 and 14 for claims against public authorities). It is similarly difficult, in view of the sophistication of maintenance systems for major commercial air carriers, to prove an aircraft's non-compliance with noise certificates; or to prove that it breached any conditions related to noise certificates.

Of course, any civil actions for nuisance or trespass arising out of the noise of aircraft engaged in ordinary flight and the normal incidents of flight are also precluded by a statutory immunity in NZ and most of Australia: at least in five States, but not in Queensland and the Territories. Claims for compensation may more easily be made if there is abnormal activity resulting in excessive noise, for example if the frequency of flights, commercial or test flights, has increased noticeably or unusually. A question might then arise as to the extent of the statutory immunity e.g. would the scheduling of say, twenty flight each day over someone's property be protected from civil action by the immunity? This has not been judicially decided.

9.2 - WHAT NOISE CONTROLS APPLY TO AIRPORTS?

Airports are required to manage any noise associated with their operations. Some airport noise in inevitable. Airports are much regulated and noise control is just a small part of this. Noise can arise from the flight (take-off and landing) of aircraft at airports, as well as from other activities, such as maintenance, testing etc. Airport-operator companies and others performing functions at airports may be liable in civil suits, for injuries or losses occasioned to other persons, not only from noise occurring in the course of the construction, development and management of airports, but also in the course of ordinary airport operations. However, it is only noise from the operation of an airport that concerns us here.

In Australia, noise and other pollution controls at and around airports are complicated and derive from not only regulations governing the establishment and the operation of aerodromes and airports, notably in their Master Plans and Environmental Strategies and the requirements of Pt 6 – Environmental Management, of the *Airports Act 1996* (Cth) (AA), the *Airports (Environment Protection) Regulations 1997* (Cth) (AEPR), but also from a series of enactments establishing curfews at major airports (see below), which are sometimes complemented by sound insulation programs for buildings near major airports.

In NZ, aircraft and airport noise is not subject to specific and detailed legislative control, but the NZCAA, s 97(1) grants an immunity from civil actions being brought "in respect of the noise or vibration caused by aircraft or aircraft engines on an aerodrome", in accordance and in compliance with the regulations made under ss 28,29 or 30.

What is the effect of airport curfews?

Curfews restrict airport use and breach of curfews may give rise to claims for compensation. In Australia, curfews are imposed by legislation and regulation at several airports: Sydney (Kingsford Smith) Airport, Adelaide Airport, Essendon Airport (Melbourne) and Gold Coast (Coolangatta) Airport. Curfews also have an impact on other airport operational procedures, including the slot allocation scheme Sydney Airport relevant airports' user-charges policies and their Environment

Strategies (required as a part of each airport's final Master Plan (see below)).

Broadly similar curfew schemes are in force at these four airports. The curfews operate between 11 pm and 6 am (local time), during which time, take-offs and landings are restricted to primarily smaller aircraft such as the Bae-146 and DC-9. The least restrictive appears to be Gold Coast Airport which additionally authorises 24 domestic passenger jet movements each year outside curfews, for which permits are granted. However, the relevant provisions are complex and designed to suit different airport needs as their circumstances differ markedly, e.g. Essendon is close to two other airports without curfews – Tullamarine and Moorabbin, whereas Sydney Airport is Australia's major international airport. On the other hand, Gold Coast Airport is a major domestic tourism airport. Summaries of curfews can be viewed on the relevant airport websites.

If curfews are not complied with, there would seem to be no reason why civil claims for compensation and injunctions could not be sought against the airport concerned, subject to a complainant's claim meeting the usual requirements for civil claims based on nuisance, negligence or breach of statutory duty (see below).

Can Airport Master Plans & Environmental Strategies Justify Claims?

Noise standards are specified in each airport's Master Plan. In Australia, the Master Plan (MP) for an airport and any Major Development Plans (MDPs) for any airport development must, amongst many other things, annex an approved Environment Strategy for the airport under the *Airports Act 1996* (Cth) (AA), ss 71(2),71(3)) This document is to deal with a range of environment issues: pollution (air, water, soil and noise), as well as heritage issues. It must also make arrangements for the impact of aircraft noise (see below).

The MP and MDP must contain procedures for dealing with noise problems at airports, and (by s 71(2)(d)), must contain:
1. an Australian Noise Exposure Forecast (ANEF) for surrounding areas having regard to the Australian Standard AS2021 ("Acoustics – Aircraft Noise

Intrusion – Building Siting and Construction") and also indicate flight paths at the airport; and

2. plans developed after consultation with air operators and local government for managing aircraft noise intrusion in areas above ANEF standards.

ANEF standards are quite technical and often reviewed. The Resource Planning and Development Commission, has said]:

> The "meaning" of ANEF contours on the ground can be hard to grasp and may seem unrealistic in the light of current aircraft movement numbers ... As noted in a [Department of Infrastructure, Transport, Regional Development and Local Government (as it then was)] publication, [*Guidance Material for Selecting and Providing Aircraft Noise Information* (18 June 2008)] ... "Experience has shown these contours, which are based on logarithmically averaged 'annual average day' aircraft noise energy, do not portray noise in a way that the non-expert can readily relate to".

The technical aspects of ANEF standards primarily affect development outside airports and in surrounding areas, and, aside from noise standards imposed on aircraft, are relevant to public and other challenges to airport MPs, MDPs and curfews (see above).

Excessive noise at airports is subject to standards imposed on potentially polluting airport activities, under the AA, Pt 6, together with the AEPR which, in conjunction with national environment protection measures made under the *National Environment Protection Council Act 1994* (Cth), s 14, are designed by reg 1.02,

    a. to establish a Commonwealth system of regulation of, and accountability for, activities at airports that generate, or have potential to generate:

        pollution; or

        excessive noise; and

    b. to promote improving environmental management practices for activities carried out at airport sites.

These regulations and practices involve development of Environment Strategies for airports, with detailed environmental standards to regulate potentially pollutant activities and monitor and remedy breaches (AA, ss 132-13). All are implemented through the AEPR.

Which airports are affected by Environment Strategies?

Major airports have their own noise standards. In this context, airport noise is a common reason why local residents use local administrative and planning appeal options to oppose the approval of airport development. Many smaller airports in Australia are regulated only by applicable State or Territory environment laws, but in practice, some follow AA requirements.

A system of environment management regulation found in the AA, Pt 6, applies at the 13 "core regulated airports" (as specified in the AA, s 7), and at 7 smaller airports (specified in the AEPR, reg 3.01).

The 13 core-regulated airports in Australia are:

(a) Sydney (Kingsford-Smith) Airport;

(b) Sydney West Airport;

(c) Melbourne (Tullamarine) Airport;

(d) Brisbane Airport;

(e) Perth Airport;

(f) Adelaide Airport;

(g) Gold Coast Airport;

(h) Hobart International Airport;

(i) Launceston Airport;

(j) Alice Springs Airport;

(k) Canberra Airport;

(l) Darwin International Airport;

(m) Townsville Airport; and

(n) any airport specified in the regulations, if the site is a Commonwealth place.

The additional 7 airports that have their own environment controls are:

- Archerfield,

- Bankstown,

- Camden,
- Essendon,
- Jandakot,
- Moorabbin, and
- Parafield.

What does an Environment Strategy involve?

Airport Environment Strategies require compliance with various rules. The above twenty leased Federal airports are those airports subject to land-use and MP controls (AA, Pt 5), requiring Environment Strategies and compliance with the detailed provisions of AEPR, Pts 4 – 8.

Environmental duties of "operators" of "undertakings" at an airport are prescribed (see below) in Pt 4, local environmental standards at airports are set out in Pt 5 and provisions for monitoring, reporting, enforcement and offence requirements are in Pts 6-8.

How are Environment Strategies approved?

Public input and review of an Environment Strategy is possible, making individual compensation claims more difficult. The process for developing and obtaining approval of a draft Environment Strategy, involves wide government, industry and public consultation, full transparency and disclosure (as is the case for Master Plans). The closer these standards are followed, the less likely it is that resulting losses or injuries can be claimed for.

The AA requires draft and final Environment Strategies to contain specified matters, including provision for noise generation, (as set out in *Airports Regulations 1997* (Cth), regs 5.02A, 5.02B). Other environmental issues are dealt with in the AEPR.

To obtain approval, a draft Environment Strategy is to be annexed to the Master Plan so that it can be passed on to the Minister for the relevant Government Department for comment or requests for further information. Otherwise, the Minister must either approve (with or without conditions) or refuse the draft Environment Strategy when approving the airport Master Plan. Review of this decision may be sought in the AAT (under AA, s 242) by a person whose interests are affected more than as a mere member of the public. Having this special interest is often not easy to establish.

Are duties owed by those performing activities at airports?

Statutory duties are imposed on airport service providers and others. The existence of statutory duties does not necessarily mean that civil claims for damages can be brought for the breach of such duties as public policy may negative the existence of any duty that can found a civil claim for compensation (see Chapter 11).

Persons or businesses that are "operators of an undertaking at an airport" – which includes any authorised activity (but not the airport management companies and airport lessee companies, their sub-lessees and licensees) – are under specific statutory obligations to avoid pollution, preserve the habitat and prevent offensive noise.

Precise obligations are clarified in the regulations. The AA, s 132(1), (3) and (3A) authorises the regulations to make standards, adopt standards approved by the Standards Association of Australia, and impose requirements in relation to prevention or the minimisation of:

1. environmental (air, water and soil) pollution generated at airport sites;
2. impacts on biota and habitats;
3. interference with sites of heritage value and significance to Aboriginal or Torres Strait Islander people;
4. emission of noise generated at airport site other than by aircraft in flight; or
5. disposal or storage of waste at airport sites.

Generation of noise is expressly included, (but noise from aircraft "in flight" is expressly excluded: see item 4 above, which is fairly typical throughout the AA and Regulations).

However, it is less certain if civil claims for compensation based on AEPR or other regulatory breaches would succeed as such regulations do not always give rise to a duty of care (statutory duty) owed to persons suffering injury as a result of their breach (see Chapter 11). It may be that a regulatory breach only amounts to an offence. Contravening regulations is indeed a strict liability offence, although less serious breaches result merely in the issue of infringement notices. More significant breaches may be serious offences, for example under the AA, ss 131B-131D, which deals with conduct directly or indirectly resulting in environmental pollution.

What specific duties require the control of noise at airports?

There is a duty to take all reasonably practicable measures to avoid noise at airports. Aside from a general duty to take all reasonable and practicable measures to prevent or minimize pollution (AEPR, reg 4.01(2)) and to preserve the habitat, there is a duty to take all reasonable and practicable measures to prevent the generation of offensive noise by any undertaking or to minimise it, if prevention is not reasonable or practicable (AEPR, 4.06(1), 4.06(2)). Thus, claims for compensation may be made provided the noise generated is "offensive".

To determine what is "offensive", specific and scientifically verifiable standards exist (in the Guidelines, *Airports (Environment Protection) Regulations 1997* (Cth), Sch 4). They are based on criteria such as "best practice", current state of technical knowledge and benefits and detriments of practicable preventative measures. Also, to satisfy this duty, any machinery used must be properly maintained and operated as well as fitted with recommended noise-control equipment (see AEPR, reg 4.08, 4.09).

However, exceptional cases exist. If climatic, topographic or other such conditions at a particular airport make it unreasonable or inappropriate to apply usual standards for contamination or noise (AEPR, Schs 1 – 4), the airport-lessee company may obtain ministerial approval for the determination of a different local standard.

Also, authorisations to undertake specific projects, valid for periods up to three years, may be obtained from Airport Environment Officers after meeting advertising, notice and consultation procedures. Compulsory annual progress reports are required.

Obviously, if approved standards are adhered to, obtaining compensation for noise pollution would be less likely.

10. Airport Liabilities: Personal Claims

Liabilities for injuries suffered by persons at airports are mostly based on general law principles. Airports and businesses operating at airports engage in commercial and operational (air transport-related) activities, but very few are subject to specific liability rules. Airports are usually developed and managed by private corporations, though, **in Australia**, the operators of the 21 major airports leased from the Commonwealth Government, are subject to additional liability rules under the *Airports Act 1996* (Cth) (AA).

Many commercial and other activities are undertaken at airports and numerous regulatory measures affect airports and activities there. Some prescribe responsibilities for airport operational activities – which are closely and comprehensively regulated for aviation safety and security – and others for airport construction and development: Airport Master Plans, Major Development Plans and Environmental Strategies (which are required for the 21 most regulated airports in Australia) affect both operational and other activities (as discussed in Chapter 9, at least as regards issues related to aircraft and airport noise and vibrations).

What Are The Liabilities of Ordinary Businesses At Airports?

General law principles govern liabilities of airport shops and similar businesses. Commercial facilities such as shops, gambling places, bars and restaurants, especially at larger airports, are separately operated by sub-lessees, subcontractors and licensees of the airport-operator company (or the airport-management company, where one exists).

The airport operator company sometimes has a duty to monitor and direct the activities of sub-lessees etc e.g. in respect of environmental and noise matters (see Chapter 9) and failure to do so may enable claims to be made against the airport operator itself, if losses are suffered as a result.

Otherwise, at any Australian airport (subject to the AA), the activities of private enterprises and any legal liabilities they have to airport users and travellers are quite similar to those in any shopping complex, if a person:

- is injured from defective premises: occupiers' liability and negligence laws etc.; or

- suffers loss or unfair treatment in consumer transactions: consumer protection laws (Chapter 3).

As Commonwealth law applying to such airports overrides conflicting State and Territory laws (Constitution, s.109.), many relevant laws at airports are federal laws, though some State or Territory laws apply, e.g. as to liability of occupiers of premises.

Thus, air travellers are in the same position as any other persons in any commercial premises anywhere, so little else needs to be said here about the liabilities of persons or businesses performing these kinds of commercial activities at airports.

What Are The Liabilities Of Air Transport-Related Businesses?

General law principles apply in many air transport-related situations as well as special airport laws. Except when special liability rules apply (e.g. those as to liability of airlines and their subcontractors for injuries in the course of air carriage itself), general law principles govern most liabilities of air transport-related businesses at airports. Occasionally, some other specialized rules will apply e.g. to air traffic control operations.

Various air transport-related activities are performed by airport-based divisions of private enterprises engaged directly in the air transport industry e.g. airlines, maintenance organizations, freight forwarders, ground handlers of passengers or baggage, air traffic control, as well as the aerodrome (as distinct from airport) operations. Some of their activities are closely regulated as regards safety and security e.g. aerodrome markings, lighting etc, air traffic control, aircraft maintenance and baggage handling.

Indeed, some air transport functions and air transport-related activities at airports are governed by specific sets of detailed regulations – they may even establish statutory duties, (which can sometimes be the basis for civil claims for compensation: see Chapter 11), or the regulations may be important evidence of standards to be met e.g. for air traffic controllers, and aircraft maintenance organisations (see below). However, general law principles usually also apply and enable claims under the common law (especially in tort e.g. negligence and for breach of contract) as well as under consumer protection laws (see Chapter 3).

When are claims against airlines not subject to special rules?

General law remedies are only excluded if claims are made against airlines in respect of "air carriage" loss or injury. Otherwise, general law principles apply. Only claims for "in-flight" passenger death, injury and delay, or for baggage and freight loss, damage and delay, are governed **exclusively** by special rules: international air carrier liability rules (IACLRs) based on international conventions; and by equivalent principles in the "domestic" rules (DACLRs) based on legislation: in Australia, CACLA; and in NZ, NZCAA, NZACA and NZCaGoA (see Chapters 5-7 for detailed discussions).

How do you know if general law liabilities are apply? First, ascertain if the activity complained of is subject to the exclusive IACLR or DACLR remedies – essentially the injury or loss must occur during or in the course of the air carriage. If that is the case and those rules are the basis for the claim, then no claims can be made against airlines or their airline subcontractors based on any other laws. However, the special rules do not apply to claims against **non-airline subcontractors**. Note that exclusivity of remedies under the IACLRs is controversial and also note that slightly less strict exclusivity exists under the DACLRs: **in Australia**, the provisions of CACLA Pt IV allow exclusive remedies only in respect of personal injuries claims (s 36); whereas **in NZ**, exclusive remedies exist under the NZCAA Pt 9B (for passenger delay), NZACA (for passenger injury) and NZCaGoA (for baggage and freight injury, loss and delay). (Discussed in earlier chapters.)

In cases where the IACLR or DACLR remedies do **not** apply, loss or damage resulting from the commercial sales or other non-carriage activities of airlines and other commercial operations at the airport, can be considered to be subject to the same liability rules as for any other business (notably consumer protection laws and common law: see Chapter 3); or any public authority carrying out its functions (see Chapter 11 for special rules affecting public authorities).

What special duties apply to airport-operator activities?

Airport-operator (airport lessee and management) companies are subject to certain additional duties because of their functions. In Australia, because of airport operators' particular status under the AA, and the fact that they manage (what are in most cases) leased Federal airports, airport operators have – in addition to the normally-applicable general law duties relating to their activities – particular duties to perform, under the AA, including a duty to monitor other undertakings' performance of airport activities they are engaged in, at least in relation to the environment and noise (see above and Chapter 9) as well as the construction and development of airports and airport premises (as set out in the AA and various regulations).

Immunities from claims. Sometimes the AA grants certain airport officers immunity from civil claims in respect of their functions e.g. under the *Airports (Building Control) Regulations 1996* (Cth). However, such an immunity may be lost if the airport operator does not use the leased airport in accordance with the terms and conditions of the lease from the Commonwealth (AA, s 31(1)).

Incidentally, if claims concern vehicle operations, note that different regulations apply to the movement of vehicles on the public, "landside" of airports to those on the secure "airside".

What is the significance of aerodrome certification?

Aerodromes are subject to special rules and most are certified by the aviation authority. Certification involves an approval process and compliance with high standards of safety. This can be important in cases where persons are injured and safety standards apply.

When is certification required? Aerodromes to be used by commercial aircraft with 30 or more passenger seats or carrying a load of 3,400 kg or more must be certified under procedures and standards set out in laws (**in Australia**, in Part 139 of the CASR and **in NZ**, in Part 139 of NZCAR.) Even more detailed and precise standards are set out in subsidiary rules known as the Manual of Standards and related Advisory Circulars. These rules run to many hundreds of pages in length, especially **in Australia**, where aerodrome licensing by CASA encompasses 4 categories of aerodromes operating at different levels within a range of safety requirements and controls.

These aerodrome licensing levels are:

- *certified aerodromes* that are open for public use by large (over 30 seats and over 3,400 kg load) aircraft, with appropriately trained staff and a Safety Management System;

- *registered aerodromes* that are open for public use, but must have at least a non-precision (lowest level of instrument) approach runway, and required safety staff and annual safety inspections;

- unlicensed, but *safety-vetted aerodromes* that may be used by medium (10-30 seats) aircraft in regular public transport or charter operations; and

- *other unlicensed aerodromes* e.g. private aerodromes that may be occasionally used by medium (10-30 seats) and small (1-9 seats) aircraft: they need to be adequate for the purpose with a warning system for pilots as to aerodrome conditions.

If a claim is to be made in respect of aerodrome defect, regard must be had to the very detailed regulatory measures setting safety standards for such aerodromes. In a civil claim for compensation based on negligence, the regulations may indicate how much care should be taken; or, in some cases, they may even create a separate statutory duty owed by the airport operator to passengers and others, breach of which is not only an offence but may itself found a civil claim for compensation, when injury or loss is caused (see discussion of statutory duties in Chapter 11).

In the unlikely event that the aerodrome is certified, but erroneously and it should not have been, there may even be the possibility of a claim being made against the licensing authority (CASA in Australia or the CAANZ in NZ) if approval of certification was incorrect or regular surveillance and testing was inadequate (see Chapters 12 and 14). However, there may also be immunities and proving such technical claims can be quite difficult.

Which Air Transport Activities Result In Civil Liabilities?

Air transport-related services at airports are usually not provided by the airport operator company. A part of what airports do is to provide a framework for the supply of services some of which are essential to air transport. Provision of most services is usually subcontracted to independent entities. Airport services or functions specifically related to air-transport include the provision of:

- passenger terminal facilities including parking;

- office and other space for government authorities such as aviation security services (and at international airports, border security, immigration and customs);

- office space another facilities for airlines;

- hangars and aircraft parking space (these may be leased or owned by other entities e.g. airlines); as well as

- runways for aircraft take-off and landing;

- Air Traffic Services (ATS) (including air traffic control (ATC) and meteorological information); and a fire-fighting and rescue service;

- maintenance facilities; and

- passenger, baggage and cargo ground handling facilities.

Apart from the provision of passenger terminal facilities for which an airport operator may be liable to travellers in the same way as any other occupier of premises would be liable to anyone coming onto the premises (e.g. if someone slips on a wet floor), the more significant air transport-related functions of airports are the last four of the above: the provision of runways, air traffic services, aircraft maintenance and ground-handling. At major airports (e.g. leased Federal airports in Australia), most of these functions are contracted out to specialist organisations – thus, few of the airport-operator's activities impact directly on air travellers – except at small airports, where some of these operations may be performed by the airport-operator itself.

Safe and secure runways. Often, provision of safe runways and certain security arrangements for aerodromes and facilities (as distinct from passenger security checks: discussed in Chapter 2.3) may well be the only air transport-related activities of airport-operator companies at major airports, and as mentioned, these are subject to strict regulatory controls. Detailed rules govern the nature, use and maintenance of aerodromes – all under the surveillance of CASA, **in Australia**, and the CAANZ, **in NZ**: (these are discussed below.) The security of the aerodrome and facilities is also regulated. If the safety or security of such facilities is inadequate, it could result in or contribute to injury or loss to travellers or other service suppliers (these are discussed below).

Air traffic services and aircraft maintenance. When airport functions are contracted out, some of the subcontracting entities are also subject to special regulatory controls and duties, notably:

- operation of air traffic services (ATS) (including air traffic control and the training and supervision of air traffic controllers) by Air Services Australia (AA)PP or Airways New Zealand (discussed in Chapter 12); and

- provision of maintenance services for aircraft (including training and supervision of aviation mechanics) (discussed in Chapter 13).

Ground handling (of passengers, baggage and freight) is not similarly regulated, although those activities must comply with security and other rules in force at airports e.g. airside restrictions on vehicles etc.

If any of the above activities are not performed to the required standards imposed either under the common law or in numerous regulatory measures, by the entity responsible for them, they may be liable to those persons suffering injury, loss or damage as a result, especially for claims based on general law principles e.g. negligence.

What obligations exist as to aerodromes and related services?

Safety and security features of aerodromes and at airports are based on international standards. The general obligations of countries to provide aerodromes and related services derive from the Chicago Convention 1944, and the more specific safety and technical requirements derive mainly from the binding Standards and Recommended Practices (SARPs) set out in the 19 separate Annexes to the Chicago Convention. These international law requirements are closely reflected in and often expanded on in the national legislative and regulatory measures for their implementation, both the international requirements and very detailed Australian and NZ regulations and guidelines govern not only airport and aerodrome establishment, operations and management, but also the provision of air traffic services. Perhaps more incidental airport operational activities, such as facilitation matters, customs, quarantine and immigration controls, are in Annex 9. These are not the responsibility of airport operators (and were discussed in Chapter 2).

Aerodrome safety. In the Chicago Convention, Annex 14, there are detailed standards governing the design, marking and operation of aerodromes, movement of aircraft at airports, as well as aircraft noise.

Aviation security requirements at airports. These requirements derive from the Chicago Convention, Annex 17 and several other international conventions, implemented **in Australia**, by the *Aviation Transport Security Act 2004* (Cth) and regulations made under it; and **in NZ**, by the NZCAA, Pt 8.

Air traffic services. The Chicago Convention also requires that each country (contracting state) who is bound by it, provides so far as practicable, air traffic services (ATS) in its territory (Art 28(a)): that is, airport radio services, meteorological services and other navigational aids to facilitate international air navigation, in accordance with the standards and practices recommended or established from time to time, pursuant to the Chicago Convention. Relevant regulations are uniform internationally and derive from the Chicago Convention, Annexes 11 and 12 respectively (see below).

Air traffic control (ATC) and related air traffic services at airports, as well as search and rescue are almost exclusively the responsibility of public corporations, **in Australia**, of Air Services Australia (AA) subject to the CASRs; and **in NZ**, by Airways New Zealand (AirwaysNZ) subject to the NZCARs. These entities may be liable in the event of inadequate provision of services.

If private enterprises, government departments, statutory authorities or public corporations who perform these activities cause injury or loss, they may be independently liable for negligence or breach of statutory duty (subject to special rules relating to civil actions against public authorities and immunities: see Chapter 11).

Airport operators may also be independently liable for choosing or using less than competent subcontractors, though this may be difficult to prove. Further, the special duties of airport-operator companies to supervise the environmental and noise obligations of entities carrying out undertakings at the airport (see above), may also give rise to airport-operator liability.

What are airport operators' duties as to runways and external security?

Airport-operator companies owe precise safety and security duties based on technical standards. Compliance with existing standards does not preclude a claim that higher standards should be adhered to but such claims would be more difficult to prove. Airport-operators are usually only responsible for runway condition, lighting and marking, traffic flow and external security of the aerodrome (as well as visitor and passenger parking and airport use generally). In small airports, they may have wider responsibilities e.g. in respect of ground handling, or even air traffic control.

Aerodromes technical and safety standards. The Chicago Convention requires that each state undertakes to make airports and facilities available in its own territory, "so far as it may find practicable". This means that internationally, there is considerable diversity of airports and related services despite detailed standards and recommended practices being set out in the Chicago Convention, Annex 14, which is complemented by several Supplements and by various design, planning and services manuals, as well as guidance and procedures documents. Additionally, there is each country's national legislation and several sets of regulations that apply.

Consequently, **in Australia** and **in NZ** there is a vast array of international and national regulation establishing standards, for example, as to runway construction, operation, lighting and marking, airside traffic management and related matters.

If an injury was caused by a breach of such regulations, it:

- may provide evidence that the airport operator was negligent and found a common law claim for damages; or

- may give rise to a claim for compensation based on breach of statutory duty.

Statutory duties are sometimes hard to establish. (The court would need to be convinced that it was the intention of the legislature for the regulations to create such a civil right of action: see Chapter 11. Furthermore, the claimant would have to be in the class of persons intended to be protected – which may be easy to prove as air passengers injured as a result of a runway defect would be precisely the class of persons intended to be protected.)

Whether the claimant alleges negligence or breach of statutory duty, another hurdle arises if the claim is made against a **public authority** (see Chapter 11). For example, a claim for an injury suffered when there has been a failure to provide an adequate aerodrome (e.g. it has not been properly maintained in accordance with the regulations), might fail if the airport operator can show that "no duty" is owed for 'public policy' reasons e.g. limited resources. In road accident case where a defect in a road was to blame, it has been held that there is no duty, even if the authority was aware of the defect. Of course, the parallel between a road accident and an aircraft accident on a runway is controversial, given the level of surveillance and responsibilities of airport operators for aerodrome management and the severity of consequences of an accident.

Aerodrome security requirements. Airport-operators may also be subject to a general duty of care, in addition to their specific statutory duties to maintain a transport security systems and external security arrangements at airports. (Transport Security Programs (TSPs) and the functions of other airport security personnel are discussed elsewhere.)

In view of all of the detailed legislative and regulatory provisions affecting airport security, certain regulations may, in appropriate cases, create a statutory duty of care owed to persons using the airport or aerodrome (e.g. if there is non-compliance with the airport's TSP as to controlling access to secure areas of the airport). Alternatively, the security requirements may at least establish standards, breach of which is proof of negligence (a general duty of care would naturally arise from the "neighbour principle" in *Donoghue v Stevenson* [1932] AC 562 or even from the occupation of premises in appropriate cases).

Complications may however arise from the fact that most detailed security standards and procedures – unlike safety standards – are confidential or subject to security classification.

Also, where the security activity is carried out by a public authority in pursuance of statutory powers, policy considerations may preclude the existence of such a duty of care, needed for a claim in negligence (that is, the failure to provide adequate security was a policy or planning decision, as distinct from a purely operational one).

What security liabilities exist for other entities?

Police and border control force activities at airports may cause loss or injury to travellers and be subject to compensation claims. Police, security forces (responsible for screening passengers), immigration, customs or health personnel carry out various functions at airports, some of which directly affect passenger privacy (see Chapter 2.3). They may also be liable for improperly exercising their own specific powers and duties as set out in the legislation governing their activities. Otherwise, normal legal principles apply.

As such entities are often public authorities, they and their employees may be immune from civil claims (see Chapter 11).

11. Public Authorities: Duties & Immunities

Claims made against public bodies or statutory authorities for compensation may be restricted. The option to claim against a public body or statutory authority is important because they perform many roles in air travel and their actions may have partly caused the injury or loss suffered. However, there are restrictions; complex issues are involved and relevant legal principles are vague.

If government departments, public bodies or statutory corporations improperly exercise or neglect to exercise their legislative powers and cause loss or injury as a result, for example, in failing to ensure adequate safety or security standards are met for aircraft or at airports, claims for compensation against them are possible. However, aside from a factual argument that the activity did not cause the injury or that the required standard of care had been met, claims may be precluded for technical reasons, notably because either:

- an immunity from civil claims exists (statutory or otherwise); or

- the legislation does not create a duty of care upon which a civil claim can be based.

Many air travel and aviation-related activities at airports and elsewhere are performed either by employees of a government department, public authority or agency including policing, border control e.g. screening, quarantine, customs and immigration functions (see Chapter 2.3); or by independent statutory corporations, such as Air Services Australia (AA) and Airways New Zealand, who are engaged in air traffic control functions etc., and by CASA or CAANZ who exercise a vast range of aviation safety-related responsibilities.

Civil liabilities of government agencies or statutory bodies – who obviously act through their appointed officers, employees or subcontractors – for their acts or omissions, depends partly on the terms of the legislation giving them their powers, and partly on general law principles (tort, administrative law and consumer protection law).

It is even difficult to predict when liabilities exist as there are differing judicial interpretations of when there is public immunity and when policy factors negative the existence of duties of care. At least, liability of public authorities has been somewhat clarified by legislation. For example, **in Australia**, relatively uniform civil liability legislation – the provisions of which are themselves sometimes ambiguous – seeks to specify and limit the circumstances in which a government department, public authority or person having a power, authority or duty under legislation, will actually owe a duty of care to persons who may suffer injury or loss from the exercise of such powers and also when it is breached (see below).

Additionally, it is provided that where the legislation excludes or limits the civil liability of a person for a tort, it "also operates to exclude or limit the vicarious [employer's] liability of another person for that tort" (uniform legislation, s 3C). So entities to whom such persons are responsible e.g. employers, benefit from the same exclusions and limits that the uniform civil liability legislation provides for their employees.

Who can a claim be brought against?

Legislation usually also indicates precisely who claims can be made against. Any claim for compensation to be made against public entities must be for an injury or loss resulting from an act of (or failure to act by) the entity (or its employee or subcontractor) in pursuance of its powers under legislation or regulation.

The legislation will normally identify the "person" responsible: e.g. the Minister, the Secretary of the relevant Department, the Director of the authority concerned, who exercises power under enactments, and that is the person against whom any claim is made. Usually, legislation also expressly binds the Crown (as Commonwealth and States) and any statutory bodies concerned, which laws, in the contexts of aviation safety, ATS and airports, the following: the *Civil Aviation Act 1988* (Cth) (CAA), s 5, the *Air Services Act 1995* (Cth) (ASA), s 4 and the *Airports Act 1996* (Cth), s 8, respectively. In cases where claims are to be made against police or security services, it may be that the claim is made against the Attorney-General, or less often, the Government e.g. of New Zealand or of the Commonwealth of Australia, a State or Territory. Complications may arise from the federal system in Australia. Legal actions based on federal laws usually name as defendant, the Commonwealth of Australia, individual ministers or departments of government, and are brought in the original jurisdiction of the High Court, or in the Supreme Court of a State or Territory (or any other court of competent jurisdiction) where the claim arose.

Public and statutory authorities can also usually sue and be sued in their own names e.g. **in Australia**, CASA under the CAA, s 5(2). The same may be said **in NZ,** about the New Zealand Government, government departments, individual ministers, Secretaries, statutory authorities and their Directors. This is subject to any express provision in an applicable legislative enactment. On these matters, in each case, professional assistance is essential.

When Do Immunities From Compensation Claims Exist?

When do statutory immunities exist?

Legislation may give immunity from civil claims to the entity responsible for injury. The first thing to consider is if the legislation concerned expressly grants an immunity to the authority or its officers when performing their functions under the legislation; although it is not always easy to locate such provisions. For example, there are thousands of pages of aviation safety and security regulations and it is impossible to consider them all here.

However, even when immunities from civil suit are created, they must be looked at closely to discover if they have limits. For example, **in Australia**, air accident investigators have immunity under the *Transport Safety Investigation Act 2003* (Cth), s 64:

> "A person is not subject to any liability, action, claim or demand for anything done or omitted to be done in good faith in connection with the exercise of powers under this Act."

It is important to consider the precise scope of the immunity and when no immunity exists. So if it can be proved that the activity complained of was not done "in good faith", then the immunity would be lifted. This **bad faith exception** is not uncommon in immunity provisions. The only problem is that if this occurs, the "vicarious liability" (responsibility of the employer) of the statutory authority for its employee may be denied on the ground that the employee acting in bad faith was not acting in the course of his or her employment. For example, taking a bribe is different to being officious and unreasonable. The claim may then only be successful against the employee and not against the authority (unless it can be shown that the authority took inadequate care in hiring or giving responsibilities to the employee: this is more difficult to prove).

Thus, express statutory immunities can be limited and the precise wording of the relevant provision is critical. For example, the CAA, s 28BE(1) places a broad duty of care upon the holder of an Air Operators' Certificate (AOC) for commercial air service operations to:

> "... at all times take all reasonable steps to ensure that every activity covered by the AOC, and everything done in connection with such an activity, is done with a reasonable degree of care and diligence."

However, s 28BE(4) then states that

> "[n]o action lies, for damages or compensation, in respect of a contravention of this section",

... but s 28BE(5) then states that:

> "[t]his section does not affect any duty imposed by, or under, any other law of the Commonwealth, or of a State or Territory, or under the common law".

What these provisions mean has not be judicially determined, but to make sense of them when read together, it is most likely that the immunity would be interpreted to apply only to claims for breach of statutory duty based on s 28BE(4) and no immunity exists as regards claims based on common law negligence or other legislation.

Is there also a common law immunity of public authorities?

A common law "public interest" immunity may exist even if a statutory immunity does not. There are activities of public authorities that either: attract such a public interest "immunity" so that the activity is not open to judicial oversight; or, give rise to a "no-duty" situation, where the court takes into account policy factors e.g. budgetary constraints to decide that no duty of care is owed (see below). These "immunity" and "no-duty" situations overlap and there is some uncertainty as to the boundaries between the two.

Although no general (common law) immunity of the Crown and public or statutory authorities now exists in Australia, an immunity based on 'public policy' (public interest) can still preclude civil claims. An example of this occurred when the police force's public interest immunity was found to exist, but was not available to an officer involved in a shooting because he did not act in accordance with training and instructions. Likewise, there are immunities for military activities during war-time; although this public policy immunity does not exist in peace-time.

At the same time, it has been argued that when CASA safety inspectors investigate breaches of safety regulations, no duty of care (at common law) is owed to a person who is alleged to have breached the regulations However, it is quite another thing to say that there would be 'no duty' (common law or statutory) if a failure to investigate or careless investigation of a breach of safety rules results in a claim for compensation by a third party, such as a passenger, injured as a result of the carelessness.

When Do Public Authorities Owe A Duty of Care?

Policy factors will limit when legislation creates a statutory duty of care and also when a common law duty is owed. Aviation and airport safety, security and regulation usually set standards to be met by public bodies in performing their functions (which may include supervision of its subcontractors and licensees).

Assuming there is no express statutory immunity from claims, both common law duties (where regulations are evidence of the standard or care to be shown) and actual statutory duties of care, (where the regulations create the duty and also set the standards to be met), may exist and be breached when entities perform obligations, powers or discretions prescribed by statute. However, there are two broad qualifications:

- a duty of care, common law or statutory, is less likely to be found to exist when there is a power or discretion to act, and the authority decides not act or only act to a limited extent for 'public policy' reasons e.g. a restricted budget, (see below); and

- a statutory duty which is enforceable in a civil claim for damages made by a private individual, is created only in certain specified requirements are met (discussed in detail below).

(Specific duties relating to air traffic services, certification and maintenance are discussed below: Chapters 12,13 and 14.)

When will an enforceable common law duty of care exist?

Common law duties of care may be owed by a public authority, but less often if it has only a discretion to act. There is no reason why a common law duty of care might not found a legal action or claim for compensation in accordance with the ordinary principles of law relating to negligence and relevant regulatory provisions will set out or provide evidence the standard of care to be met by the authority. Assuming there is no express immunity from claims (discussed above), such duties will be owed to a broad class of persons directly or reasonably likely to be affected by the exercise of the public authority's functions.

Where the authority has **an obligation or duty** to perform a prescribed function, then the existence of a common law duty of care to members of the public is almost certain.

If a **power or discretion** to act is given – the term "may" is often used in respect of a power to act – its exercise can be the basis for a duty of care allowing a private right of action, but this will essentially depend upon whether the decision to act or to act in the particular way that caused the injury, involves a "policy" ("planning") decision, rather than an "operational" decision. If the public authority exercises a power or discretion, taking inadequate precautions as a result of a "policy" decision, it will rarely give rise to a duty of care founding a private right of action against the authority But what is a "policy" decision? In general terms, imposing a limited level of safety inspection e.g. because resources are limited, may be a "policy" decision not giving rise to a duty of care, even if this causes or contributes to air accidents; while decisions made by air traffic controllers (e.g. to restrict information given to pilots), will normally be "operational" and will give rise to a duty of care (unless the real reason for the lack of information provided is e.g. staff reductions based on a policy decision).

Even if a policy decision has been made to provide a particular type and standard of service, the provision of that service in a faulty or inadequate manner, for example, carelessness in giving the planned level of Air Traffic Control instructions, or providing meteorological information (fire-fighting and rescue services are excluded) will more likely render the authority liable to compensate claimants for any resultant loss or injury (not only to aircraft but also to passengers and shippers).

On the other hand, failure to act at all, when a discretion or power to act is given, rarely gives rise to a duty of care that can found a claim by a private individual, (unless there has been fraud, bad faith, improper purpose, a failure to accord natural justice or unreasonableness involved in making the decision not to act).

However, claimants need to take care before making claims as there is still much uncertainty as to whether a public authority will owe an enforceable duty of care to a claimant suffering injury as a result of the authority's acts or failure to act in any given situation.

In Australia, the civil liabilities of public authorities are clarified by the uniform civil liability legislation which states:

> "... the fact that a public or other authority exercises or decides to exercise a function does not of itself indicate that the authority is under a duty to exercise the function or that the function should be exercised in particular circumstances or in a particular way." (e.g. s 46, *Civil Liability Act 2002* (NSW))

Further, the legislation (e.g. *Civil Liability Act 2002* (NSW), s 42) sets out the kinds of factors or circumstances to consider when deciding if a public authority owes a duty of care (see below). In brief, these factors are:

- functions to be exercised,

- financial resources of the authority and their allocation;

- compliance with general procedures and standards.

Similar circumstances are taken into account under the common law when the legislation does not apply.

More particularly as regards air operators, airport and air traffic controllers etc, the fact that these entities carry out functions at airports is one of the relevant factors to consider in deciding if the authority owes any duty of care to a particular class of persons (and of course the injured claimant must belong to that class).

Finally, if there is a "special statutory power" not normally exercised without legislative authority e.g. policing of safety matters, another factor to consider is the circumstances in which it is breached – was the act or omission causing the injury so unreasonable that no public authority would consider it to be a reasonable exercise of its functions (**in Australia**, see e.g. s 43A(3), *Civil Liability Act 2002* (NSW)). **In NZ**, the duty of care, in cases of such "special" powers, is easier to establish

When will a statutory duty of care arise from legislation?

A statutory duty is independent of any common law duty of care (discussed above) but it is less often available for making claims. Assuming there are no express immunities preventing claims (see above), a statutory duty or power to perform certain functions may imply the existence of an enforceable statutory duty of care owed to persons who are directly affected. However, there are limits.

When there is an express obligation or a public authority to perform a particular function, it is more likely that a private individual can enforce the statutory duty to obtain compensation for any injury caused by failure to perform it or performing it improperly.

However, when the authority exercises discretionary statutory powers (where a discretion to act is given), it is less likely that there will be a duty of care enforceable by a private person for compensation. As with common law duties of public authorities, "policy" factors (e.g. limited budgets) may negate the existence of such a statutory duty of care (see below). Also, when Ministerial approval is required for the exercise of a discretion, it is presumed that public authorities will **not** owe statutory duties giving rise to civil claims, **unless** such actionable duties are expressed to exist or arise by necessary implication.

Similarly, as with common law duties, when a discretion to act is given to a government department or public authority **failure to act at all** is unlikely to give rise to a private right to claim and reasonable foreseeability of injury is not enough, **unless** the making of the decision involves fraud, bad faith, improper purpose, failure to accord natural justice or unreasonableness. However, courts are reluctant to find bad faith etc or misfeasance in public office without there being clear proof, even when safety is involved – and example might be that investigations have been carried out under the *Civil Aviation Act 1988* (Cth), but it is alleged that they are inadequate.

Additionally, other legislation affects the availability of compensation claims based on breach of statutory duty by a public authority. For example, **in Australia**, it is more difficult to conclude there is an actionable statutory duty, as the uniform civil liability legislation imposes a strict test as to when a breach of any statutory duty will actually occur:

> "…an act or omission of the authority does not constitute a breach of statutory duty unless the act or omission was in the circumstances so unreasonable that no authority having the functions of the authority in question could properly consider the act or omission to be a reasonable exercise of its functions." (e.g. *Civil Liability Act 2002* (NSW), s 43(2)).

This, what could be called, **no reasonable authority test** stated in the legislation makes it even more difficult to prove that action taken by the authority was inadequate. Note that this particular provision is not uniform throughout Australia and some uncertainty exists as to the extent of its application; further complicating such duties.

What factors influence decisions that a statutory duty exists?

Various considerations help determine if there is a legislative intention for a statutory duty to exist. To decide if legislation creates a duty of care, it is important is to identify the intention of the legislature (or what the court considers to be its intention). Unless a civil right of action is expressly created by the legislation (which is unusual), it will be uncertain when a legislative provision creates such a private right to claim damages (statutory duty) though it may still set standards of care that need to be met).

It is only after these various factors are considered by the court that it can decide whether or not this legislative intention exists for a power given in the legislation to a public or statutory authority, also creates a statutory duty which is enforceable by a private individual in a civil claim for compensation.

In Australia, the uniform civil liability legislation expressly requires consideration of the functions to be exercised by the public authority; reference to the broad range of its activities, overall financial and other resources available to the authority to perform these functions and comply with general procedures and standards for the exercise of its functions. (These are basically the same factors required to be considered at common law, as **in NZ**.)

Aviation safety regulation, which includes aircraft certification and maintenance, air carriage, airport and air traffic control all involve strict safety regulation. Although no clear judicial decisions relate to such aviation safety regulation, actionable statutory duties of care are often found in safety regulations, especially as regards claims for personal injuries resulting from any breach. However, not keeping equipment functioning in good order, even if required by regulation, will not necessarily be a breach of a statutory duty.

Other contextual factors are traditionally taken into account in searching for the intention of the legislature.

- First, that an offence or penal sanction is provided for a breach sometimes suggests that there is no duty giving rise to civil claims, but this is not conclusive, although the existence of an alternative remedy, for example, arbitration, judicial review or appeal, may imply that the legislature did not intend to create a private civil right to claim compensation, For example, the Federal Court rejected the existence of a statutory duty of care in the CAA in two cases where the holders of CASA licences sued CASA for damages resulting from the cancellation of their licences, alleging that inadequate care was taken by CASA in carrying out its investigations.

- Second, whose benefit the legislation was enacted for is a factor and was considered by the court in in both those cases. For there to be a right to claim, the legislation must be for the benefit of defined class of persons of which the plaintiff is one and not be for the benefit of the community as a whole. It could be argued that many potential statutory duties in aviation legislation (**in Australia**, the CAA, CASRs; or **in NZ**, the NZCAA or NZCARs) do not give rise to a private right to claim because of the vagueness of the class of beneficiaries and older decisions indicate that air traffic regulations do not necessarily confer a private right of action for breach. However, courts have not decided **if air passengers are a defined class**, but in appropriate cases they could be, despite the fact that there is a large number of persons who would benefit from the duty.

- Third, the injury the subject of the claim, must also be of a kind that the legislation seeks to prevent (e.g. physical injury but not pure economic loss). Safety regulations are intended to protect persons against risks that may occur when the legislative provision is breached, and in appropriate cases, that will encompass personal injury, property damage and may even some economic loss.

Finally, even if a statutory duty is found to exist, it must be proved that the duty was breached: that is, the requisite amount of care was not taken. This may not be easy to establish. **In Australia**, civil liability legislation applying in most of Australia, specifies that breach of a statutory duty will only occur if the act or omission amounting to the breach, **was so unreasonable that no public authority could consider it to be a reasonable exercise of its functions.**

12. Air Traffic Services Liabilities

Air traffic services, including air traffic control, are the responsibility of public entities but may be subject to compensation claims. It is not uncommon for air traffic services errors to contribute to aircraft accidents and resulting passenger injuries (see below). It is for this reason that it is considered separately and it is useful to clarify what activities are involved.

Air Traffic Services (ATS) comprises: Air Traffic Control (ATC), Aeronautical Information Services (AIS), Aeronautical Telecommunication and Radio Navigation Services as well as Aerodrome Rescue and Fire Fighting Services at airports. They are administered, in Australia, by Airservices Australia (AA) and, in NZ, by Airways New Zealand (AirwaysNZ), which are both public corporations operating on a commercial basis, although AA co-operates with (and subcontracts to) some private entities in actually providing ATS.

(Immunities and limits to claims against public authorities and statutory bodies are discussed in Chapter 11.)

What ATS Activities May Incur Liabilities?

It is mainly air traffic control (ATC) activities that give rise to liability claims. In determining the existence of duties of care and liabilities, the statutory functions of an authority are an important factor (as discussed in Chapter 11). For example, **in Australia**, AA's relevant ATC functions are:

(a) to facilitate the safe and efficient conduct of aircraft flights;

(b) to facilitate the safe movement of aircraft on the manoeuvring areas of aerodromes;

(c) to facilitate and maintain a safe, orderly, expeditious flow of air traffic;

(d) to provide advice and information that is necessary for the safe and efficient conduct of flights; and

(e) to notify appropriate organisations about aircraft known or believed to be, in need of search and rescue aid, and to assist those organisations.

In Australia, ATC services are performed, by AA and private entities in cooperation with AA pursuant to contractual arrangements (although fire-fighting, aerodrome rescue and other search and rescue services are independent).

In NZ, ATC services are performed by AirwaysNZ.

Such public bodies and subcontracted private entities perform specific duties and exercise powers to carry out international civil aviation obligations owed under the Chicago Convention 1944 and national legislation. If loss or injury arises from performance of the authorities' aviation or other duties and functions, whether by an officer, employee or a subcontracting entity, then, (subject to the factors to consider in determining the duties and liabilities of public authorities and any immunities) the entity concerned may be liable for claims based on breach of statutory duty or negligence (breach of common law duty of care) for injuries caused by acts or omissions performed either directly or vicariously (through employee etc).

Do ATC providers owe no duties or benefit from immunities?

"No duty" situations and immunities are the same for actual ATC providers as for public authorities generally. These were discussed in detail in Chapter 11. Essentially, where there is a statutory duty or obligation to perform a particular service, the existence of an actionable duty of care (right to claim compensation) is quite common. Such duties may arise expressly or by necessary implication from the legislation; but if not, the common law presumes that no actionable statutory duty is owed by public authorities or their subcontractors, when performance of their activities either requires Ministerial approval, or, it involves the exercise of a power or discretion and public "policy" reasons justify providing a limited or inadequate service.

No ATC immunities from civil claims. No immunity appear to exist for ATS providers and the general (common law) immunity of public or statutory authorities no longer exists **in Australia**, and **in NZ**.

Although there appear to be no express legislative immunities specifically as regards the performance of these ATC functions, **in Australia**, the *Air Services Act 1995* (Cth), s 77(2)(d) provides that regulations made pursuant to that section may make provision for "conferring immunity on AA and its employees from liability arising out of the exercise of powers under the regulations". But none do so. (Even if the regulations did create immunities, given the precise terms of the legislative authority, it is unlikely that any such immunity given to AA and its employees would extend to any subcontracting private corporations and their employees, which have contracted with AA to perform ATC services.)

A specific exception, **in Australia**, is that there is immunity from some claims for the providers of Aerodrome Rescue and Fire Fighting Services (ARFFS) at the 21 leased federal airports, as they are exempted from compliance with all of the general duties not to generate pollution under the AEPR, regs 4.01 – 4.02, for example, when engaging in fire training activities.

No-duty situations for ATS services. Where ATC or the level of ATS provided at any particular airport involves the exercise of discretionary powers found in legislation, the existence of a duty of care allowing a private right of action is sometimes controversial. It essentially depends on whether decisions, within the scope of legislative powers, are clearly made at a "policy" ("planning") level – rarely giving rise to a private right of action against the person or body invested with the power or discretion, – as distinct from an operational level. Staff reductions based on a policy decision involving resources etc may be one of the actual causes of the accident and then no actionable duty will likely exist.

However, most decisions of air traffic controllers that cause or contribute to air accidents will normally be "operational" and give rise to a duty of care. That duty is owed to all person on board the aircraft. It doesn't matter that air traffic controllers do not know the specific passengers on board a flight, the passengers are still entitled to rely on controllers doing their job properly.

Failure to provide the prescribed ATS or any ATS at all, may give rise to a private right of action, but only in unusual cases, as foreseeability of harm is not enough. A court will only find an actionable duty of care to exist, if in deciding not to provide the ATS, there has been fraud, bad faith, improper purpose, failure to accord natural justice or unreasonableness involved in the making of the decision not to act. Except for unreasonableness, courts will be reluctant to make such findings, especially if misfeasance in public office is alleged.

If a particular type and level of ATC service is to be provided, but that service is provided in a faulty or inadequate manner, for example, there is carelessness in giving ATC instructions or meteorological information (fire-fighting and rescue services are excluded), the relevant authority will more likely have breached its duty of care and someone such as a passenger or aircraft operator, suffering loss or injury as a result, will be able to make a claim for compensation: The ATS officers' duty is to take reasonable care and to give all such instructions and advice as may be necessary to promote the safety of aircraft within their area of responsibility.

Negligence of ATC and pilots may be concurrent. Mid-air collisions, as in *Skywards Pty Ltd (in Liquidation) v Commonwealth* (1985) 57 ALR 657, and "near misses" are typical cases of ATS negligence, for example, in not following proper procedures, such as failing

- to ensure adequate aircraft separation,
- to provide a warning to a pilot of the risk of wake turbulence during take-off or landing, the presence of other aircraft, obstructions such as work on a runway, or the likely presence of birds which might be ingested into jet engines.

There are also judicial decisions in the USA requiring Air Traffic Controllers to give pilots adequate warning, for example, of any deterioration in weather conditions or visibility. Failure to provided available information would seem to be actionable but how much weather information available to controllers may be the result of a "policy" decision.

There is also a concurrent liability of pilots to avoid danger, irrespective of ATS information or an ATC clearance. A pilot must always take adequate care and cannot rely on a clearance to land as a complete defence to allegations of negligence. A finding that the pilot was negligent does not preclude a finding of concurrent negligence on the part of the provider of ATC services, even in smaller airports where only minimal facilities are available.

13. Manufacturer and Maintenance Liabilities

Manufacturers and repairers are often strictly liable for product-related injuries but claiming against them may mean suing in other countries. Air traveller claims for compensation against product manufacturers or suppliers are less common but should not be neglected. They involve defective products including aircraft parts and that is the context discussed here. Other claims relating to ordinary products are governed by general law principles, especially consumer laws, some of which are referred to here, but are not focussed on in this chapter.

Aircraft and parts are manufactured by private corporations, mostly in the USA and Europe, but also in Australia where strict manufacturers' liability principles apply. Aircraft are assembled from component parts which are often manufactured in separate countries and by different corporate entities. This applies as much to small electronic parts such as altimeters and navigational equipment, as it does to carpets and cabin seats and aircraft engines and fuselages. Some assembly, and especially maintenance and repairs do occur in Australia, though airlines often use maintenance facilities in foreign countries – often where consumer protection laws are weak. Also, many aircraft parts are certified by local aviation authorities, but claiming compensation from them for errors in certification is not easy (see Chapter 14).

However, proving that a component is defective and that the defect caused the injury complained of, will often depend on an accident investigation report arriving at this conclusion.

To what extent are aircraft manufacturers liable for product defects?

Manufacturers, assemblers, repairers etc are often strictly liable for product defects, but will naturally deny all responsibility. Assuming it can be proved that a defect exists, it is fortunate for claimants suffering injury as a result of a defective or unsafe product, that many large aircraft and components have tended to be manufactured or assembled in the European Union member states, or in the United States where local laws make manufacturers, assemblers etc strictly liable of for defective products. Similar laws also apply **in Australia** although this area of the law is less developed **in NZ**. Elsewhere, manufacturers' liability laws may well provide little assistance to claimants.

Strict liability – which means liability in the absence of fault, so that neither negligence nor fault need be proved by the claimant – derives from the common law and from statutory provisions, but **strict products liability** of manufacturers under the common law derived from the law of negligence; which governs liability of most manufacturers, assemblers etc of parts and equipment used in aviation, for loss and injuries to users, resulting from defects in their products. Common law has now been overlaid by legislation.

In Australia, aircraft and component parts are within the scope of "goods" as defined in the ACL, s 2. The ACL, ss 138-150, imposes on manufacturers, suppliers and importers of goods that cause product-safety related injury, loss or damage, a statutory liability to pay compensation for that injury, loss or damage. Claims for compensation made by air travellers in respect of injury or loss resulting from a defective product or a "safety defect" in goods, under the ACL, are usually consumer claims which are made in consumer courts or tribunals, provided they come within the monetary limits of the tribunal or consumer court concerned (see Chapter 3 where these matters were discussed in detail).

In NZ, almost all personal injury claims are made under accident compensation legislation (NZACA, see Chapter 3), so only in rare cases, for accidents outside the scope of that scheme, could any claim for personal injury be made against a product manufacturer. This does not exclude the possibility of a claim being made in a foreign court. Claims in respect of loss or damage to property would rarely be made under common law in NZ, (especially the tort of negligence), as to the extent that the claim involves contract law and the supply of consumer goods, they would be made exclusively under the NZFTA, NZCGA and NZ *Sale of Goods Act 1908* (NZ) (NZSOGA).

When does aircraft maintenance give rise to liabilities?

Maintenance of aircraft parts is performed by airlines, their subsidiaries or private maintenance organizations. Aircraft maintenance – other than "line maintenance" (cleaning, refuelling) – will usually be in the hands of private corporations which may be completely independent of airlines and aircraft manufacturers. Otherwise, they may be an air carrier's subsidiary companies, joint ventures, entities owned by foreign air carriers or fully government-owned corporations, and their relationships with airlines, including indemnity arrangements will be subject to complex contractual arrangements. So claims in respect of defective maintenance may be quite complicated, but that should not deter consumers.

Few air carriers rely solely on aircraft maintenance by their own employees, even in their own countries, and it may be that the defective repair or maintenance organisation which is responsible for a particular incident, occurred in a country which had little to do with the injured claimant or with the airline on which any injury or loss occurred. Naturally, claiming from these overseas entities is quite difficult and complicated issues may arise as to which country's law applies to such claims. Otherwise, normal general law principles of negligence and manufacturers' (repairers') liabilities (e.g. under the ACL in Australia), also apply to claims against maintenance organisations.

How can defects in aircraft products be proved?

Problems of proof in such cases may be significant, although formal accident reports will be of assistance. It is usually only in the course of aircraft and maintenance inspections – the responsibility of the civil aviation authorities e.g. CASA in Australia and CAANZ in NZ – or aircraft crash or accident investigations performed by other agencies, that defects in certification, equipment or maintenance are uncovered.

Failure to discover such defects in aviation products at an early stage may also give rise to claims. The possibility of claims against surveillance or investigatory agencies in respect of their errors also exists, subject to specific immunities from suit and broader restrictions on claims that may be pursued by private individuals (as are discussed in Chapter 11) based on duties owed by CASA and CAANZ and any other public authority or their authorised delegates engaged in these activities (see Chapter 14).

Maintenance inspections and surveillance are largely in the hands of accredited specialists employed by the maintenance and training organizations concerned and if they can be proved to have acted negligently, they would not benefit from immunities form claims that public authorities may benefit from (see Chapter 11).

In Australia, air accident investigations, are undertaken by the Air Transport Safety Bureau (ATSB), which itself benefits from a substantial immunity from civil claims, by s 64 of the *Transport Safety Investigation Act 2003* (Cth), which states:

> "[a] person is not subject to any liability, action, claim or demand for anything done or omitted to be done in good faith in connection with the exercise of powers under this Act." (see discussion of immunities and the "bad faith exception" in Chapter 11)

In NZ, the Transport Accident Investigation Commission (TAIC), performs investigations under the *Transport Accident Investigation Commission Act 1990* (NZ), but TAIC does not benefit from any express statutory immunity in respect of its duties. Of course, public interest restrictions on actionable duties may limit claims against this agency.

14. Certification and Accreditation Liabilities

Authorities certifying aircraft components etc and authorising or accrediting their delegates to carry out their various responsibilities may also be liable for breach of duty to take care in carrying out their functions. Legal responsibility to provide compensation for an injury or loss caused by aircraft or occurring in flight to a passenger or other person could lie, at least in part, with entities which certified equipment or authorised the activity concerned or licensed the persons performing it. Certification and giving approvals and licences is usually undertaken by public authorities who benefit from certain immunities from claims and limits on the duties of care they owe which are enforceable by individuals (see Chapter 11). There may be private organisations which also engage in licensing or accreditation, for example, the International Air Transport Association (IATA) which accredits travel agents although there would be no question of immunity from claims or 'no-duty' situations in respect of their activities. Accreditation proceeds through sophisticated and very strict competence and financial responsibility criteria, in view of which, it is unlikely that any negligence or breach of duty could be established although it is theoretically possible. ATAS (AFTA) accreditation of travel agents in Australia would be in a similar position (see Chapter 2), except that it may be that their accreditation process is less strict and a breach of duty may be more easily established.

Pilots, air operators, parts manufacturers, aircraft engineers, maintenance and training organisations and even aeronautical authorities (**in Australia**, CASA and **in NZ**, the CAANZ and Airways NZ) have statutory obligations to perform functions in relation to aviation safety, as well as to prevent aircraft from flying unless all of the necessary safety certifications, maintenance and approvals, are complied with. These matters are subject to very detailed regulations and subsidiary rules too vast to discuss here (found mainly, **in Australia**, in the CASRs and **in NZ**, in the NZ CARs).

Often, these authorities delegate the performance of training, certification, licensing and surveillance functions to accredited or authorised intermediate agencies (delegates) who are engaged in training, maintenance and surveillance. These organisations are themselves subject to accreditation, but they are not public authorities. Thus, they do not normally benefit from the express statutory immunities or "no-duty" situations that CASA or CAANZ may have. Thus, compensation claims could be more easily made against these delegates for injuries their inadequate or defective licensing may have caused. Either they may be strictly liable e.g. under the ACL or the complainant may be able to prove that their actions were negligent (see below).

There are also possible common law duties and statutory duties owed by the public authorities responsible for accrediting, approving or certifying organisations that perform functions authorised by legislation or regulations – although they may benefit from immunities or owe no enforceable duties to persons potentially suffering injury (as discussed in Chapter 11). Otherwise, claims alleging negligence or breach of statutory duty in granting approvals etc would be subject to the usual legal requirements.

What are the difficulties in claiming for approval errors?

Problems of proof are significant as are policy issues limit duties of care. Issues as to proof – notably proving that there was an error in the certification or approval process and that the error caused the injury or loss suffered by a claimant – and those uncertainties involved in pursuing a private civil claim against a major corporation or institution (public or private with all their resources) even if it does carelessly or improperly grant a licence, approval, authority or certification, means that seeking compensation from these entities is difficult for complainants. Even with assistance as regards proof from an aircraft accident investigation report in respect of the injury or loss, making a claim would be expensive

As with aircraft and parts design, production, and maintenance, the certification, granting of approvals, authorities and personnel licensing involve serious safety issues and could have dangerous consequences. Thus, they would more likely be considered to be an "operational" rather than a "planning or policy" function. Thus a court would more likely find that a duty of care exists even if the authority is exercising a statutory discretion or power to perform the activity subject to the complaint.

On the other hand, it is likely that the extent of surveillance, oversight, safety monitoring carried out would likely be based on "planning" and "policy" decisions, as a function of available resources and thus less likely to give rise to duties of care enforceable by private individuals (see Chapter 11). A similar argument may be made about regulatory surveillance of training and maintenance where self-reporting of defects and regulatory breaches is allowed.

15. Conclusions

Various activities may give rise to claims in respect of air travel; some are more easily pursued than others. They range from disputes with travel agents, tour operators and airlines over marketing, sales and the provision of air travel services, to incidents at the airport involving police, immigration customs and security controls or even injuries occurring when on commercial or other premises at the airport before departure, during transit or on arrival. Otherwise, claims can arise in respect of injury loss, damage and delay occurring during air carriage itself, for which airlines are strictly liable to passengers and others pursuant to special liability rules. There can even be claims relating to objects falling from aircraft or aircraft coming in contact with or injuring persons or property on the ground, or by the noise that aircraft make during flight or at airports.

A wide range of persons or entities may be responsible and claims can usually be made against them. The obvious ones are airlines, travel agents, airport management, policing and security services, but there may also be claims against the manufacturers and maintainers of parts and components, or against those responsible for ensuring the safety of aviation and the competence of all persons performing duties in the air travel industry.

But claims need to be resolved and if negotiation with those responsible is not successful, then, unless travel or accident compensation schemes apply, consumer remedies in inexpensive consumer courts and tribunals may be available, as discussed in Chapter 3; and only as a last resort should expensive court action be envisaged, given that in many cases, relatively small amounts of compensation is being sought.

The limited availability of adequate, inexpensive and relatively simple dispute resolution mechanisms for many kinds of claims, especially the all too common claims for delay or injury to air passengers and loss or damage to their baggage, is a matter deserving urgent legislative action, seemingly best undertaken in the consumer protection context.

www.ingramcontent.com/pod-product-compliance
Lightning Source LLC
Chambersburg PA
CBHW070558300426
44113CB00010B/1302